THE CHILD'S BILL OF RIGHTS

A Beginner's Guide to Parenting

A primer for parents of children from birth through
six years old

By
John A. Scott, Sr., Ph.D.

Note for Librarians: A cataloguing record for this book is available from Library and Archives
Canada at www.collectionscanada.ca/amicus/index-e.html

ISBN 1-4251-0001-5

Printed in Victoria, BC, Canada. Printed on paper with minimum 30% recycled fibre.

Trafford's print shop runs on "green energy" from solar, wind and other environmentally-friendly power sources.

TRAFFORD
PUBLISHING™

Offices in Canada, USA, Ireland and UK

Book sales for North America and international:

Trafford Publishing, 6E–2333 Government St.,

Victoria, BC V8T 4P4 CANADA

phone 250 383 6864 (toll-free 1 888 232 4444)

fax 250 383 6804; email to orders@trafford.com

Book sales in Europe:

Trafford Publishing (UK) Limited, 9 Park End Street, 2nd Floor

Oxford, UK OX1 1HH UNITED KINGDOM

phone +44 (0)1865 722 113 (local rate 0845 230 9601)

facsimile +44 (0)1865 722 868; info.uk@trafford.com

Order online at:

trafford.com/06-1758

10 9 8 7 6 5 4 3

DEDICATED TO

Sherrye Hunt,
one of God's little ones,
who, in her 51 years never quite
reached the five year old level;
And to the
Arlington, Tennessee Developmental Center's Staff,
who serves devotedly and lovingly
as foster parents to her and hundreds
of her mentally retarded companions.

PREFACE

While this book is intended as a guide for parents of young children during their formative, pre-school years, it will also be helpful for parents of older children.

Use of the book will be enhanced if the reader will meet with and share in discussions with other parents. This can be an informal Koffee Klatch type of meeting or a class with a leader, perhaps at church or school. Questions at the end of each chapter encourage a helpful discussion with other participants. And, having thirteen chapters makes it suitable for a 13 week (1 quarter) period.

Of course, private reading or study enables the parents to focus on the most needed subject in their own family and at their own pace.

You are the bows from which your children
As living arrows are sent forth.
Kahlil Gibran

INTRODUCTION

Based on our constitutional "Bill of Rights" it has become popular these days for various sub-groups to assert their own individual "rights." It's time that children were recognized as having their "inalienable" rights as well. As a group, the children have been virtually ignored, yet they have the potential to make or break this country. The fulfillment of their rights is actually the determining factor in the future of this nation and our civilization.

Yes, children have inalienable rights, and we must recognize them and do something about it. They have been overlooked long enough. Since they can't take their own action we must do so in their behalf.

Evidence that the material of this book is up to date appeared in the newspaper just today (June 6, 2006). One report stated that "the use of potent anti-psychotic drugs to treat children and adolescents for problems like aggression and mood swings increased more than five-fold from 1993 to 2002."

Another interesting article quotes the Center for American Progress as reporting that people recently polled are greatly concerned that the country has lost its moral compass. The survey asked Americans to name the most serious moral crisis in America today. "Atop the list, 28 percent cited 'kids not raised with the right values.' Next came corruption in government and business, followed by greed and materialism, people too focused on themselves, and too much sex and violence in the media."

Another item in the same paper reports that Elizabeth Vargas, who had been an anchor on ABC evening news, was voluntarily leaving to have her baby. It seems some feminists objected, saying she must have been fired. Surely she wouldn't quit such a job of her own volition for a baby. This demonstrates the conflict in the atmosphere all around us of home values versus career values. Presumably, she made a politically unwise decision in putting her baby first.

Well, today's news is just a sample of what's going on currently in our culture. Facts, figures, and reports like this take place on most any day in our time. All of this is a vivid commentary on what I'm talking about in this book. So, today's news gives you a brief glimpse into the subject matter of the next thirteen chapters. Some of the facts and figures to which I refer sound discouraging, and they are. But to recognize the problem is to see the solution. Be optimistic. I am. There's power in this message. It has been applied successfully before with great success. The world and the course of history was changed 2000 years ago by one man. The same message will continue to improve it in our future —one generation at a time.

I must give credit to my partner, my wife, Jo, who has helped me with this project (and many other similar ones) for 61 years. I have been fortunate to be married to a wonderful woman who also is an English teacher. She has, with patience, critiqued, edited, suggested, and proofed, as only a public school teacher can do. But before that, she was the mother of our children. Having learned motherhood from her mother, she shared this with our two boys and a girl. And after that as a grandmother, she passed on her mothering skills with the grandchildren. This has been a wonderful blessing to all of us. And now we share this experience with you, our readers. It is rather like the old days when the aging grandmothers and aunts, widows and spinsters, all living in near neighborhoods in an agrarian environment, shared in the rearing of children of the later generation with wisdom, not from books so much, as from years of shared experiences with the older women in their community.

A literary composition, at any level, does not see successful fruition except there be a proof reader. These noble people often do their work behind the scenes with little praise. Well, I must acknowledge the highly skilled proofing of Ms. Betty Bates. She is a truly professional educator with a more than average broad experience in working with children. She has not only taught English at several levels, but has supervised others in this work. Furthermore, she has worked with children in extra curricular activities and the Sunday School and church contexts as well. She knows English and she knows children. What more could I ask for?

Dr. Waymon Henson, Professor of Family Life and Counseling at Abilene Christian University, has evaluated the manuscript and offered helpful suggestions.

Also, I thank Ms Alice Wheatley, who has graciously supported the production of this book and made suggestions for its improvement.

TABLE OF CONTENTS

CHAPTER 1

LITTLE CHILDREN HAVE RIGHTS TOO

CHILDREN MAKE UP THE KINGDOM OF GOD

Visualize taking your children with a group of your friends and their children to a picnic-like atmosphere where Jesus is teaching and ministering. You are surprised and enthralled to hear Him say: "Permit little children to come to me. Don't discourage them. For they make up the Kingdom of Heaven." (Matt. 19:14 -NIV) Jesus was very concerned about children and issued severe condemnation to those who lay a stumbling block in their way. (Matt. 18:1-6)

"Stumbling blocks" were what Jesus was concerned about. And in our society today there are many. Too frequently (and unknowingly), we parents lay more stumbling blocks in the way of our children than anyone outside the home; more than children's peers, poor environment, bad schools or teachers. This is tragic. How is this? Many homes fail to provide the kind of foundation that prepares a strong, mature character in their own children. Worse than a failure to provide for them materially is to neglect or abuse them at home. Sometimes this is due to ignorance; sometimes it is due to carelessness and sometimes due to broken homes and severely disturbed parents.

Your own children are your hope for the future. Most parents, when they look on their newborn for the first time, think of the future. "Who does she look like?" "What will he become?" "What kind of home will we make together?" Where the child is welcome, the dreams of the future are filled with optimism and great expectations. At this point day dreams can be idyllic. And these dreams, within certain bounds, can be realized if the parents are willing to make them so. That's what this book is about.

DISCOURAGEMENT AND STUMBLING BLOCKS TO SMALL CHILDREN

Jesus would be just as concerned about modern "stumbling blocks" as he was in His day. I have listed seven modern obstacles, but there are more.

1) TV

Although we are reluctant to do so, we must face the fact that audiences have been effectively desensitized to the depiction of fear, sex and violence (on TV as well as by some music) over the years. The principle is similar to one who becomes "hooked" on an addictive drug. Like a toxin, it begins to take more and more to get the expected affect as time goes on, and the body gets conditioned to the drug effects. Kids cannot distinguish between fiction and exaggerated examples of "reality" violence as interpreted by movie producers. Child specialists state clearly that the child's brain cannot filter out as much violence as is seen on TV.

2) TV ADS

Victoria's Secret and Carl Junior ads and others have been described as soft porn, as was the famous Janet Jackson side show at the 2004 Super Sunday game.

3) MOVIES

Film critics were discussing the movie, "Scream 3," and as they discussed the evolution of horror movies over the years, the observation was made that since the "old days" it takes more planning, better writing, and greater and more impressive special effects to create the kind of "fear" that one expects in so-called "horror" films.

4) SPORTS

Recently it was reported that in the last 5 years violence in sports is up 5%. And many kids say, "It's no longer fun." In Massachusetts a father beat another father to death in an argument over a kids' hockey game. Since then one hundred and seventy five cities have signed up for parents to go through conditioning before their kids can play sports at school.

5) CHILD CARE OUTSIDE THE HOME

Dr. Rima Shore of Columbia University grieves that 80% of infants today have care outside the home within the first year of life. In 2001 the National Institute of Child Health and Human Development announced the results of the most thorough study to date on the time that toddlers spend in day care outside the home. A summary of the findings is quite clear in stating the more time toddlers spend in child care (away from mother), the more likely they are to display behavior problems in kindergarten, regardless of who cared for the children (besides mother),

6) PARENTAL NEGLECT AS ABUSE

E. Kent Hays of the Menninger clinic states very pointedly, "Parental neglect is the primary force promoting the evolution of today's disturbed children."

7) OTHER ENVIRONMENTAL INFLUENCES

Other environmental influences are so-called concerts featuring raunchy, drugged up performers with decadent music, provocative dancing and sensual dress. If these sources of decadent influence are not influencing your children directly, they are influencing the children who play with your children.

All of these influences listed above combined make up a general social attitude or demeanor that Michael Medved, author and lecturer, states is worse than just the consequences of drugs, adolescent pregnancy, juvenile crime, and that is an overall "plague of pessimism." They propel these kids into an epidemic worse than AIDS or gang violence, as bad as those ills are, and that is that tens of millions of our youth are infected with clinical depression. It is depression, which slows down the learning process, quenches ambition, interrupts high school and college education, and so often results in an actual suicide or an on-going living suicide of life.

In fact, mere children are coming to have one of the highest suicide rates of any one age group. And the second highest cause of death among adolescents is suicide. This indicates a severe deficit in their earlier childhood rearing. Newborns and infants do not start out in life with a desire to commit suicide. The compulsion to do this in most all cases comes as a result of the immediate environment.

PLEASE NOTE THAT THIS PLAGUE, PREVALENT AMONG PRE-ADOLESCENTS AND ADOLESCENTS, DID NOT HAPPEN OVERNIGHT.

In nearly all cases it started in the pre-school years with the early formation of poor attitudes, bad habits, and personality deficits. And while these outside influences such as TV, movies, peer pressure and other sources of destruction I have enumerated influence our children, it is up to the parents to control their child's exposure to these influences.

Fifty years ago some social workers believed that criminal and delinquent behavior was due primarily to deprivation caused by being reared in poverty.

Bill Cosby has challenged this presupposition by addressing challenges primarily to members of the black community, telling them to quit blaming misbehavior, drugs, teenage pregnancies, poor grades, and school drop-outs on the fact that they were poor. Cosby's challenge is given in no uncertain terms, saying they could and should rise above poverty and become people of integrity. Sound, psychological evidence corroborates Cosby's charge.

If a child grows up in a stable, healthy, home environment, it would take an awful lot of these outside influences to change that person. For children who are "raised" in an unstable home with few guidelines and poor examples –a lack of respect for the child's rights, if you please--these destructive influences will shape their behavior. Hundreds of scenes of violence each week will **callous** their sensitivity. This is what's happening all around us now. Children in this generation **do not have the same amount of companionship with their parents** that children had in previous generations.

NEGLECT IN MODERN SOCIETY

I don't intend to be unfair in charging modern parents with "neglect." However, in today's society the kind of neglect I'm talking about is rampant, and socially-politically acceptable. Well-meaning parents are so caught up with the busy-ness of living their lives in the fast lane that they do, in fact, "neglect" giving their children the basic needs necessary to prepare them for satisfying, mature lives. The starting place of responsibility for child growth is mom and dad who gave them birth. This is where the subject of The Child's Bill of Rights comes in. The environment the parents set up for their newborn infant is the primary determining factor in the outcome of that child.

OUR SOCIETY HAS BECOME ARTIFICIAL

The artificiality of our modern society is {another} stumbling block to our homes. The trouble is that in the last two generations the artificialities of cultural progress (?) have changed the home atmosphere so radically that the natural maternal and paternal instincts have become confused. Today's children and youth face obstacles and philosophies of life never before faced within the home and immediate environment. Modern parents are confronted with the reality of change, of urbanization, crowding, cybernetworks, TV violence, brutal movies, degrading music, decadence of morality instruction, latch-key kids, and a general moral decline of society. Such conditions cause interpersonal relationships to be neglected and result in such conditions as we see depicted daily in the media.

Too many households in America today are represented in Television's "Supernanny," who faces uncontrolled children each week; or Lynette's wild boys in "Desperate Housewives," or frustrated parents on Dr. Phil. Or perhaps you have seen such desperate, frantic, out-of-control children among your circle of friends or acquaintances, or at nursery school. Incidentally, more children are expelled from nursery school each year than adolescents are from high school.

And of course these violent little kids, flailing their arms in the air and on their parents, screaming and cursing epithets at adults, represent just one side of the coin. The flip side, not as ostentatious, is the super quiet child. That's the one in the corner, who already by three, is alone, not participating at all. That's the potential "loner," like school killers or Zachery on "Desperate Housewives," whose pain and frustrations are locked deeply within, waiting like the time bomb to explode in some way.

CONSEQUENCES IN ADOLESCENCE OF THESE EARLY STUMBLING BLOCKS

What's going on anyway? When pre-school children are acting this aggressively daily, cortisol, a bio-chemical, is produced in the body, which in due time permanently affects the thinking processes of that child, and this hostility becomes deeply embedded, then produces unnatural behavior in the years to come.

Consider the adolescents who participate in riots. You see them in the news in the eerie shimmering light of flames as a building burns shouting, "Burn, baby burn." Such children are among the 1,000 children a day who go to courts, detention centers, reform schools, and mental institutions. Or you could sit with me and a distraught mother in a hospital waiting room while the doctor ostensibly "removes a growth" from a 13 year old girl's stomach. The doctors called it "abortion." Those children who don't show up in statistics mentioned above will show up in the class room with various forms of uncontrolled misbehavior, all of which brings the test score averages down, and causes the teachers in the lower grades to be faulted for poor teaching.

Admittedly, this is not an encouraging picture. But these are facts attested to by research surveys, polls of doctors and health care workers, educators, court records, and law enforcement personnel.

THE PURPOSE OF THIS BOOK

As a parent or would be parent, you want to insure against such uncontrolled children's behavior. Furthermore, you want to avoid suffering the consequences in later years of such wild pre-school behavior. It is known from experience that when the small child's natural, in-born needs are adequately met, "normal," acceptable behavior will result. I'm in no position to give you a warranty, but I assure you confidently that adequate prevention, such as is given in this book, will give you the foundation your children require and deserve. Also, you will find here the details on "how to rear a wholesome child."

Parents, who in the child's formative years meet their basic needs, as I am maintaining, will brace and fortify their children against the influences of the environmental ills I have listed above.

My point is that in our efforts to adapt to "modern living" in any age, our instincts alone are not a sufficient guide to effective child rearing.

What am I saying? You parents should use your intuition. Feel confident, and show confidence to your children. But, also, use your head and get guidance where you can find it. Get the best education in child psychology you can get under your circumstances. In my opinion, the greatest career- -profession if you please – a mother and father can have is to specialize in rearing children. There is no more challenging career, no more important avocation, and nothing else can be done, which would have a greater impact on the world, society, and the church than parents who are dedicated to this.

NEED FOR PARENTAL GUIDANCE

So here we are. Why have another book on child-rearing anyway? That's what this is. Isn't (or shouldn't) child-rearing be a natural procedure? Don't we have paternal and maternal instincts that, like a light, should guide us through the shadowy turmoil and societal fog of the early childhood period? "Yes," like the animal world, we have basic instincts to stabilize us and direct us sufficiently to bring an infant to maturity. And "No," our artificial society creates obstacles and pitfalls which form a confusing roadblock to such natural functioning.

THE EXTREME SENSITIVITY OF "LITTLE CHILDREN"

I'm concerned with "stumbling blocks" of the first six years of the child's life, and how to prevent them. And here's why. In the first five or six years of life, a child learns more and absorbs more permanent impressions than it does in any succeeding six year period of its life. And in the second five or six year period it learns more than it does in any succeeding six year period after that. By the time a child is 12 years old, attitudes and impressions on these subjects should be well rooted:

- The child's feelings about him/herself and his/her relationship with others are fixed.

- Their attitude toward authority becomes determined.

- The child's standards of moral-ethical behavior are mostly set.

- The influence of religion (or lack of it) will have taken place.

- Respect for the rights of others has been learned.

- The ability to exercise self-control and self-discipline should be understood.

- The ability to postpone gratification of desires should be established.

- How one relates to the opposite sex has already been observed and absorbed.

- The foundation to maturity should have been laid.

- The ability to communicate should have been learned.

- And, of course, during this period the inclination to read and learn should be acquired.

Upon observing a list such as this, do you wonder that a pre-school child can –and should-absorb such a wide variety of attitudes and impressions, even in a rudimentary way? Doesn't such an ambitious list overload the brain of a small child? Not at all!

Dr. Craig Ramey, a cognitive neuroscientist at the University of Alabama emphasizes that since 1990 our knowledge has doubled about how babies' brains develop. From birth until age 2, about 90 % of the brain's architecture will be laid down. With the use of brain imaging technology, it has been demonstrated that by the age of 3 a child's brain is twice as active as that of an adult's as it experiences the outside world through the senses. Such studies also show that during this period more than 100 billion brain cells develop a network of complex connections among them. These connections, (called "synapses") however, are multiplied as a result of appropriate, positive, and frequent interactions with parents and other caregivers. The skills and attitudes of a life time have their foundation laid at this early age because of the neurological connections among these cells.

INTERPERSONAL RELATIONSHIPS NEGLECTED

Too often these early, stimulating relationships of parents with their babies are neglected. How? Parents get busy and simply do not spend enough time with the newborn and infant. Older children are distracted with too much time with TV, they have too much spending money, they are bored, and this contributes to the neglect of interpersonal relationships.

The admonition from the Bible fits entirely with the above information: "Train up a child in the way he should go and even when he is old he will not depart from it." (Proverbs 22:6 RSV)

Well then, why do so many children fail to achieve these fundamentals to a mature life in the preschool years as they should? It's because the child's basic needs, which strengthen and fortify them, are not met in the first six years of life, and because of external influences, which subvert that child's development.

MOTHERHOOD AS A PROFESSION

If a woman sees this role as a "profession" during her child bearing years and enters it with interest and devotion that she would have for a job outside the home, it will be satisfying and gratifying as a profession. Obviously, it's work. So is the job at the bank or school or anywhere else. As a matter of fact, Ann Crittenden (in two books, The Price of Motherhood and If You've Raised Kids You Can Do Anything) takes the position that the same traits that it takes to manage children are the same traits it takes to manage people in the business world. If a woman has been a successful mother, she should be able to put this information on a resume. For example, some of those traits common to both business and child-rearing are: "The ability to bring out the best in others, giving them the freedom to grow and make their own mistakes while providing enough structure and feedback to keep them from stumbling too badly, etc."

If, however, a mother begrudges motherhood as "drudgery," or hates being at home with a child, then the children may as well be with a child-care substitute. It has to do with her attitude as she approaches child rearing.

THE NEED FOR MOTHER

I have already emphasized that the more time young children spend away from their mothers the more likely they are to display problems in kindergarten. This is one of the reasons I advocate, before having children, making a decision to budget and get along on the husband's income during the child bearing years.

Of course there are exceptions! There are women with part time jobs, those who take a different shift from their husband, and those who have other work arrangements adjusted so they can be with a new born most of the time.

I'm just emphasizing the value of a parent (mother or father) being at home when the children are there – constantly before they start to school, and then in the afternoon hours after they return from school. I do not consider both parents working outside the home and neglecting the children just to live in an up-scale neighborhood, or to have more conveniences or "to keep up with the Joneses," as justifiable.

THE ROLE OF PARENTS

So, after thousands of years of parents rearing their children, we still have to have guidance, such as I advocate in this guide book, to be the most effective parents for our children under our circumstances in our time.

A present day dilemma is that many parents, who have sat in the waiting rooms of courts, psychological clinics, hospitals, and prisons, awaiting the outcome of a crisis, are left to ponder, "Where did we go wrong? We were good parents. We loved them and did not abuse them. We *sent* them to Sunday School", etc. In their remorse and guilt, these parents conclude that they have **done** something **to** their child. But they can't figure out "What?" And they are sincere.

A big part of the answer is this: According to a reliable study of 1000 parents and caregivers, 54 percent said they had little or no time to spend in physical activities with their children. And 94 percent said they see a "relationship between the amount of meaningful time that adults spend with children and the way kids deal with such major issues as substance abuse and discipline." A Harvard psychiatrist who helped oversee the study said approximately 3.5 million households—representing 7 million youngsters—spend an hour or less a week in some type of physical activity with their children, like taking a walk or playing catch.

When all is said and done, it is the parents who teach the children swear words and crude talk by their example. It is the parents who fail to teach the children respect for authority and who permit them to sit glued to the TV an average of 27 hours per week (in the inner city it is 11 hours a day).

On the positive side, the parents set the child up for education, relationship with peers, communication, morality training, self-image, respect for authority, structure, self-control, etc. And that's what this book is about.

POST SCRIPT: A TRAGIC EXAMPLE

A few years ago 16 year old Cheryl Pierson said, in her defense in court, that when she was eleven, her father began abusing her sexually, progressing until he was having sexual intercourse with her as often as three times a day. He even had sex with her in the car when she was on the way to the hospital to visit her sick mother. She said, "It was awful. I felt hopeless." Her resentment and rage came to a head one day when she and a classmate, Sean Pica, were sitting in homeroom in Newfield High School in Selden, NY, discussing an article in a local paper about an abused wife who hired someone to murder her husband.

Cheryl wondered about who would do such a thing, and Sean, also 16 years old, said he would for a price. He carried through three months later, shooting Cheryl's father, James Pierson, five times with a .22 caliber rifle. Due to the provocative circumstances, proved, Cheryl was sentenced to six months in jail and five years' probation. Pica was sentenced to eight to 24 years in prison. The lives of these two teenagers were, thus, forever besmirched by entangled circumstances which got out of control.

The above example took place in the 1980's. But don't situations like this remind you of similar tragedies current in our newspapers today?

QUESTIONS FOR STUDY AND/OR DISCUSSION

1. What has been your response to media reports on school shootings?

2. What do you think are some causes of these tragedies?

3. Have you personally observed examples of child delinquency?

4. What are some changes in home atmosphere that you have observed over time?

5. What's your opinion of media influence on our society today?

6. In your experience have you or your friends been in the dilemma of when or whether to work outside the home?

7. What do you hope to gain from a study of this book?

CHAPTER 2

FEATHERING THE NEST:

THE JOY AND SATISFACTION OF PARENTHOOD

PREPARATION FOR PARENTHOOD

Nora Ephron, in the novel *Heartburn*, wrote that having a baby is like tossing a hand grenade into a marriage. And newspaper columnist Kathleen Kelleher commented that "A tiny all-powerful emperor," the infant's needs for everything, takes precedence in the lives of the parents from showers to sex. "Remaining lovers through the consuming, marathon days of child rearing is, to put it mildly, a challenge."

WHY A "CHILD'S BILL OF RIGHTS?"

Many groups these days (such as "women's," "patient's," "gay," and others) are asserting they have rights that must be recognized. But no group has the potential to make or break the country as do children, and they can't speak for themselves. The fulfillment of their rights is actually the determining factor in the future of this nation and our civilization. Yes, they have inalienable rights, and we must recognize them and do something about it. They have been ignored and taken for granted long enough. Since they can't take their own action, we must take it in their behalf.

There is no need to assemble on the capitol mall or march in lines and carry placards. Just start with yourself and do something about seeing that the "rights" are spread to all would-be parents in your circle. The next generation will be different.

I confess that I did not originate the title of this book. I first heard the title in about 1953 when a beloved and highly respected child psychiatrist, O. Spurgeon English, MD, used it as the title of a lecture he gave to a class at the

Philadelphia Divinity School. I am deeply indebted to him for his knowledge and experience, and for early inspiration and guidance in this field. Dr. English died October 3, 1993, at the age of 92 after many years of profound influence on children's rights,   One does not need an authority like Dr. English to impress us with the need for starting the study of healthy children with a study of their parents. Stockbreeders and farmers can give elaborate testimony on the importance of careful mate selection prior to breeding. In fact, more careful thought is usually given to livestock breeding than is given by a would-be husband and would-be wife to the offspring they would produce after marriage.

THE MEANING OF PARENTHOOD

Do you realize how closely children observe their parents? When a group of children were asked what love meant, a 7 year old boy named Danny replied, "Love is when my mommy makes coffee for my daddy, and she takes a sip before giving it to him to make sure the taste is OK."

Due to so many adolescent pregnancies and marriages falling out of favor in the last two decades, about a third of American children are born out of wedlock. And recent census figures indicate that there is a decline in the percentage of traditional households which have two parents with children in them.

Facts, figures and scientific surveys indicate that children from single parent homes, like those born to adolescent single girls, suffer many disadvantages in our society. Many well-meaning women have rationalized that they can have children singly or with a lesbian partner and provide for them adequately and emotionally for their future well-being. This experiment of the last several years is proving to be a failure. This is sad for the women and tragic for the children. A beloved teacher of English one time said, "You *raise* hogs, but you *rear* children." Get the point?

TO BE PARENTS OR NOT TO BE PARENTS

Some years ago a young unmarried couple came to me for pre-marital counseling because they had reached an impasse in their plans for marriage. He was certain he wanted children. She was certain she did not want children. Although they had discussed many aspects of their relationship, they correctly felt they should come to some sort of agreement on this before having the ceremony.

Too often couples do not talk about serious subjects like this before marriage. Since they aren't ready at the moment to get pregnant, the subject isn't usually discussed. They assume they'll see eye to eye on that in due time. When "due time" comes, they may have a serious difference of opinion as to when to have children or whether to have them at all. Issues of education, jobs, finances, financial commitments, living conditions, health, even in-law concerns influence the feelings of the couple.

This couple postponed the marriage, but family and friends propelled the plans for a wedding. They remained together a few years, not happy, but finally divorced – childless. It was a painful experience for all concerned.

CHILDREN SHOULD BE PLANNED

There should be some basic agreement on whether to have children and approximately "when," and under what circumstances to have them before marriage. Children are important enough that forethought and planning should be a part of a couple's premarital agreement. I'm saying that before we talk about the "rights" of a child, we must talk about prerequisites to pregnancy: **The pregnancy should be wanted by husband and wife before it ever takes place.**

ISSUES IN PARENTHOOD

In preparing the nest for offspring the first prerequisite is that wife loves husband and husband loves wife. Of course this concept has different meanings to different people. But a reasonable degree of mature love is the best foundation to build a secure environment for the newborn.

MARITAL LOVE

The briefest description of marital love I can get by with is as follows:

1) The mate is accepted as a partner on the basis of shared interests: job, child training, in-law concerns, and pleasures.

2) The mate is accepted for what one is, along with one's failures.

3) The mate is forgiven and restored when sorrow and repentance are shown for mistakes; one's past sins and failures are not brought up again.

4) The couple share in successes, failures, and disappointments of each other.

5) Each is free to develop one's own potentialities along creative lines.

6) Each is free to show love to those who have a rightful claim upon one.

7) Each shares a satisfying sexual relationship, which respects one's feelings and desires; this accompanies a romantic, affectionate relationship.

8) Each is free to be alone at times.

9) Each is free to live and grow in a peaceful and harmonious home environment.

10) Each is respected, appreciated, and trusted.

11) The couple develops an interdependent relationship.

12) They share and practice religious convictions.

When a man and woman marry, they embark on the most difficult and challenging relationship possible. Typically they make what should be a decision for life at an age when their judgment is sometimes skewed. To be the most successful, it requires a reasonably mature and healthy personality. In my opinion, the majority of people who get married do not understand what mature love is all about. This is the tragedy of the modern home.

ADULT SEXUALITY

Neuroscientists, in analyzing brain scan images, know that romantic love is a complex biological urge similar to other basic functions, like eating and drinking, at the unconscious level. This is distinct from sexual arousal, which is deep in another part of the brain. Courtship and marriage bring these two powerful urges together. Under the right conditions the sex drive becomes intertwined with the love urge. And as the relationship deepens between the man and woman, the neural activity indicates that a (potential) long-term attachment develops. I summarize by saying that if one of the spouses is frustrated sexually, the "love" part of this equation is adversely affected. This problem should be solved before having a baby. The ultimate sexual relationship implies physical, emotional, and spiritual maturity. While this ideal is not typically present early in marriage, hopefully it is potentially present. David M. Schnarch in his text, *Constructing the Sexual Crucible,* quotes Peter De Vries in Augarde who says, "Who of us is mature enough for offspring before the offspring themselves arrive? The value of marriage is not that adults produce children but that children produce adults."

Schnarch proceeds to emphasize that the birth of a child challenges the stability of the marital relationship. He points out that, "When these stresses and challenges exceed the adaptive capacities of the parents, as commonly happens, marital intimacy and eroticism are affected."

Mature love and mature sexual relationship are intertwined and, while not necessary to procreation, being in this state is a definite advantage to successful parenting. The reason for this is that such a mature sexual relationship contributes greatly to a kind, tender relationship between husband and wife. And this kind of a relationship affects the overall atmosphere of well being for the entire family. It is known that women who are sexually fulfilled are more loving toward their children than those who are not.

EMOTIONAL MATURITY

Maturity, like love, is flexible and subject to definition. No one is perfectly mature; there are just varying degrees of progress along that scale. The summary I refer to is as follows: take note, however, that this list can and should serve as a goal of achievement also for your children. . .as well as for yourselves.

TRAITS OF EMOTIONAL MATURITY

1) Capacity to give and receive love

2) Capacity and will to work in organization and under authority

3) Reliability: a person that can be counted on

4) The quality of giving more than is asked for

5) Being able to endure difficulties, discomfort, frustration, and hardship; persistence in the face of these adversities

6) Having a sense of humor

7) To a degree, being able to act independently

8) Being able to size up a situation and make decisions

9) In relation with others: ability to communicate and be tolerant

10) Ability to be adaptable, flexible, and to arbitrate differences

11) Ability to stick to a job and finish it; stable; determination and will to succeed

12) Aspiration to spiritual matters

HOME STABILITY

Inasmuch as the infant is hypersensitive to its environment and is totally dependent on others to survive, home stability is vitally important. Home stability can refer to a wide range of traits with varying degrees of depth.

I have already indicated how important it is to have a consistent home environment for the infant and young child. Families who move around a lot contribute to the child's insecurity. Furthermore, the parents should have consistent schedules for being at home and work. Routine is an important trait for the infant.

Regularity of meals and bed time are important. Having a home that is quiet and free of confusion lends stability. The number of persons occupying the house or apartment space should be so comfortable that they can move about freely with a minimum of noise and turmoil. Likewise, the personalities of the would-be parents should be stable, and free of panic and anxiety.

It will be most favorable if husband and wife have similar cultural, religious/ethical, financial, and philosophical backgrounds. These conditions will enable them to agree more easily on the issues of life, which they will need to share with their offspring. If there are major differences between the spouses, they should be ironed out before having children, or at least outside the child's presence. And, it is vitally important that the parents compromise such differences for the benefit of the child.

Children have an intuitive grasp of what's going on between the parents. In spite of the fact that children do not catch on to conflicts like adults, they do have a brain that is so designed that it tries to make sense of things in the immediate environment. When husband and wife fight, the conflicting situation has a profound and negative impact. If parents only knew it, the quality of a marriage may be more evident in a child's sleep patterns than from a lengthy interview with a marriage counselor.

The other side of this coin would indicate that couples should NOT get pregnant in order to try to "save the marriage" or in order to be "cured" of emotional problems. Neither should they get pregnant because some of their parents are anxious to be grandparents. Such a move is rarely successful and is dreadfully unfair to the child. To say the least, the risk is too great to take the chance.

HEALTHY PRENATAL ATTITUDES FOR PARENTS

1) Both of you need to be committed to the marriage for "as long as you both shall live" (or at least as long as the children are at home).

2) Be prepared to let your children develop at their own pace without undue pressure from you, the parent.

3) You both consider the child(ren) is more important than business, recreation, extended family members, and all else.

4) With regard to attention to the child, a healthy middle ground will be found where there is neither over-solicitation nor neglect to the child and its needs and activities.

5) That you have open minds to let the child choose its own career and mate.

6) Be prepared to encourage the child's self-esteem in place of being too perfectionistic with your own standards.

7) Be prepared to include the extended family members (grandparents and other relatives) in the child's family circle (unless there is a real good reason not to).

8) The well prepared parents have adjusted their own moral character to such an extent that they are proper examples for a developing new life.

9) Be introspective enough that both of you as parents realize your self-sufficiency and maturity. It is possible for the parent, with an underdeveloped ego, to be overly solicitous of their children to such an extent that the child responds with an anxious attachment to the parent. Recognize that parental behavior should be such that it promotes a secure, accepting response by the child.

10) Recognize that as human adults you have both positive and negative feelings about yourselves, and, consequently, you will have ambivalent feelings about your children. There will be times when you will have

the urge to be tender and nurturing, but there will be other times when you will have urges to be aggressive toward them and will be in need of control.

11) Both husband and wife need to agree that when the child makes a mistake, they will ask encouraging and informational questions of the child. This is in preference to issuing rebukes, directives and commands to their children.

12) Be resolved to **listen** intently and frequently to your children no matter what your judgment is regarding the importance of their talk. If you will listen to them in early childhood, they will talk to you when they are older.

PREPARING FOR PREGNANCY

The time of year for some women is an important factor in determining when to get pregnant. For others it is not an issue.

A much more important factor is the woman's frame of mind. A woman with a happy, positive frame of mind is going to be more comfortable in her pregnancy than one who is not. Likewise, her husband should have these same traits in support. Severe tension has kept many women from getting pregnant in the first place. Certainly being optimistic and having an optimistic husband with a sense of humor as a partner will make life easier and healthier for all concerned.

Speaking of health, it's a foregone conclusion that the woman should have contact with an ob-gyn specialist BEFORE getting pregnant. And his/her advice must be respected. A complete physical exam will determine a future course of action for her in her physical preparation. A diet will be recommended. A dental exam is necessary as well. There may be reasons why her husband would have a physical exam before pregnancy, also. With our increased knowledge about chemicals and their effect on genes, there are circumstances warranting the male's check-up as well as the female's.

AN EXAMPLE:

Early exposure to nicotine, alcohol and certain other drugs in utero and in the postnatal environment are known to be hazardous to the fetus's brain. Nicotine is known to impact the brain's biochemistry and alter DNA and

RNA synthesis in the brain. Embryos exposed to smoke before birth are known to be at higher risk of developmental delays than others. Research has demonstrated that boys whose mothers were heavy smokers during pregnancy are eight times more likely than the sons of non-smokers to develop conduct disorders later in life. Even worse, is exposure to cocaine in utero. This could result in a neurological disorder such as severe infantile epilepsy, autism or schizophrenia. Less serious consequences are difficulties with arousal, attention, and reactivity to stress.

FINANCIAL FACTORS

Two may be able to live as cheaply as one, but, when the "two" have a baby, living conditions will change. A baby budget will be necessary. This will include doctor-medical considerations, clothing, nursery preparation, even insurance will have to be adjusted accordingly. Even mother's wardrobe will have to be modified. Check on family leave at work, if necessary.

SPIRITUAL HEALTH

Spiritual health is also important. A religious frame of mind that promotes a healthy, spiritual attitude is vital to one's total well-being. People, who are strong in their faith and have a secure loving relationship with spouse and fellowship with other such spiritually minded people, are known to relate better to their children and provide security and a wholesome environment for them. Yes, I take the position that religious training and morality training go hand in hand

A more complex issue that would-be parents need to consider is this: All too frequently a couple will become parents and be carrying extra baggage. I mean this: One or both of the parents may have a deep emotional hunger which has never been satisfied. He or she may come out of childhood with severe emotional deficits, which would prompt them as parents to make demands on the child in unconscious efforts to satisfy those emotional hangovers. There may be a grasping for attention or to receive love, or there is a deep inner need to "get even" for real or imagined wrongs done to that person. One or both of the parents may have been frustrated and impeded in their own career aspirations and so seek to fulfill these thwarted ambitions through their child. These people become emotionally constipated parents. In pronounced cases of that sort, it is impossible for them to fulfill the demands of the Bill of Rights for the child.

OTHER ISSUES FOR PROPER PREPARATION

A. "FATHERS ARE PARENTS TOO."

A high percent of our homes have been fatherless due to a variety of reasons such as divorce and abandonment. And the children of these homes are continuing to pay the price with frustrated behavior of wide variety. An outgrowth of the women's movement has been the feeling that fathers are not necessary in the home to the successful rearing of children. This simply is not so; and scientific investigations into this concept prove the idea to be utterly false.

John J. Hurley, acting director of the administration's bureau of family services, stated that assistance funds are helping to support 180,000 families with children whose fathers have abandoned them. This is a considerable expense financially and is much more expensive emotionally.

B. OLDER MEN AT HIGH RISK FOR FATHERHOOD.

Much has been said in recent years concerning the best years for pregnancy for women and how there is an optimum period in a woman's life for having a healthy pregnancy. A female's eggs are at their optimum when she is around 27 years old. Now a study reported in 2001 that fathers over 50 have three times the risk of having a child who develops schizophrenia as fathers under 25. Other earlier studies indicate that older men's sperm has been related to neural tube defects, nervous system cancer, dwarfism and prostate cancer in their offspring. It has been known for years that gene mutations take place in older men, according to Dr. Dolores Malaspina of Columbia University. Supposedly, the sperm of older men accounts for such results.

C. MOTHERS AT HOME.

At the beginning of this new century, there appears to be a trend among the 20 – 30 year old adults for women to be more interested than previously in emphasizing the value of relationships, health, and balancing work and home life. Catalyst, a New York-based research group, found that an amazing 86% of Generation X women say having a loving family is extremely important. Just 18% of those women said earning a great deal of money is what matters. It appears there is a fall-out from such a trend. In 1998 60% of women with a child under 1 year old were working or looking for work. In 2000 the figure was 55%, which, incidentally, was the first drop since 1976. There are many possible explanations for this, and hopefully it represents a trend which will continue. Women are apparently finding that there is too much stress in the responsibilities of home, marriage, children **and** job. Even part time jobs are full time stress on a woman, and unfortunately this is due, in part, to lack of cooperation from their husbands.

At any rate, it is a rare financial situation that justifies a mother's removal from a child under one – or even three, for that matter. I cannot emphasize too strongly that the couple contemplating pregnancy should plan on the mother's spending full time with the new-born. . . and, hopefully, breast feeding. However, I can't lay down a rule for you. Whether a child is put out to child care so mother can work outside the home depends on how good the child care facility is as compared with how well the mother can provide home care. These are important variables. It is safe to say, "Whatever is less stressful for the newborn is to be the deciding factor in this present day dilemma." Being in the baby's presence the first year has a high priority.

D. SINGLE MOTHERS

Women in Lesbian unions in recent times have had babies by artificial insemination, or vicariously by a mother substitute, and/or by adoption. They contend that whether single or with a female companion they can satisfy the maternal instinct with such a baby, and rear it as successfully as they could with a husband. This is another rumor propounded by the gay community, which is simply wishful thinking. It is known, should one want to know the facts, that children who grow up absent their fathers are five times more likely to be poor, two to three times more likely to fail at school, and two to three times more likely to suffer from an emotional or behavioral problem. And this isn't even considering the low risk such children have in getting along with a spouse in a mature relationship.

A recent Gallop poll indicates nearly eight in 10 Americans agree, "The most significant family or social problem facing America is the physical absence of the father from the home." This is not to deny that many a brave woman, who has tragically been left without her husband, has reared, under duress, children who have succeeded to prove exceptions to these observations. God bless them! According to the Census Bureau, women who are divorced or widowed have greater success with their children than single women who have never had a husband. Employment was an important reason for that difference, the report said.

CONCLUSION

I, personally, felt strongly enough about constant parenthood that I kept two jobs when going to graduate school so my wife could spend full time with our children. She took her role seriously and made it her career. I wish I had figured out another way at that time. I still have some guilt for depriving my kids of enough of my presence when they were in their pre-school years. But I got about as much time with the kids as the average man does today in those families where a husband in the professional or business world is struggling to succeed. And the children got more hours per day with a parent who loved them than they would have with a child-care substitute. As I look back on it now, I think the gain was not worth the loss (of my presence).

In the above list of prerequisites to pregnancy, I have been somewhat idealistic on purpose. You can make adjustments in harmony with your own viewpoint, but be careful. Perhaps the best summary of the philosophy upon which to build prospective parenthood is to be prepared to: 1) Avoid doing too little for the child which includes neglect, rejection, and coldness. 2) Avoid doing too much by over-indulgence, domination, seduction and/or cruelty.

POST SCRIPT

Consider Abram and Sarah, a couple who were desperate to get pregnant. Read in the Bible, Gen. 12:1-7; 17:1-8; 21:1-6. Here is an oft-repeated theme in the Old Testament. Key figures are unable to conceive at a time when having children was a vitally important factor in their lives. The ancient admonition to "be fruitful and multiply and replenish the earth" (Gen. 1:21), was a part of their culture, but this very early command was not the sole motivating factor in their desperate attempt to have offspring. The culture of Abram and his neighbors considered having children a matter of life and death: a matter of "Life" in order to carry on the "name" of the family. This was their view of "life after death." One's name must not cease from the earth. And the person bearing that name must inherit the family property and keep it in the family. A matter of "death," in that one's descendants must carry out the burial rites for the deceased forbears. This had to do with putting their spirits at rest as they were "gathered to their fathers."

There were a number of philosophies that grew out of this. One was that it was believed that, if a couple were childless, it was due to the woman's being sterile. Because a male could ejaculate and this was obvious, they didn't consider that the male might be the one who was sterile, unless, of course, he had been castrated. So, if a woman did not get pregnant, she considered herself a disgrace. She felt she let her husband down and was a "nobody." And many a husband blamed his wife and either divorced her or took another wife or concubine to have his children. This kind of thinking was behind Sarah's plan to have children vicariously by her handmaid. This was legally permissible in all of their surrounding culture and was looked upon as a viable substitute for natural pregnancy of husband and wife. In the culture from which Abram and Sarah came, it was the wife who selected the substitute, and she (the wife) would be present at the time of birth. It was said that the substitute would bear her child "at the knees" of the wife, and the child would be taken by the wife as her own. This same theme is repeated in the life of Isaac and Rebekah (Gen. 24; 25:21; see also 1 Samuel 1).

Of course our culture has changed radically since then, but the urge to have children is ever present. And the family, with husband, wife and children, is still the heart and core of our society. And as the family goes, so goes our nation.

QUESTIONS FOR MEDITATION AND/OR DISCUSSION

1) If you now have children, how did you and your spouse come to the conclusion to get pregnant? Was it easy?

2) In your group has there been a problem of infertility? How has it been dealt with in modern medicine?

3) How would you feel if you wanted to get pregnant and couldn't? How would you feel if you didn't want to get pregnant and did?

4) Do you know a single mother? What are some of the major issues of her life?

5) What is your opinion and feeling about single fathers? What are the issues of being a single father?

6) Modern medicine has achieved remarkable success with treating infertility. Do you think the example of Abram and Sarah would give us some basis for evaluating such procedures as artificial insemination or a woman having a vicarious pregnancy for another? How about ovarian transplants? How about so called "test tube" babies?

7) Do you know of couples, who were divided among themselves as to whether or not to get pregnant? How did they deal with it?

CHAPTER 3

ACCEPTANCE, The Child's First Right

A crucial turning point in a woman's psychotherapy came as she visualized her birth again. Due to profound rejection, she had serious emotional problems all of her 43 years. Now, in her therapy, she experienced vividly a rebirth. The memory impression of the original negative birth experience was replaced. Now she could picture a "welcoming committee" of relatives and friends of her parent's family surrounding her bassinet in the hospital. Now she could see their smiling faces and waves and now she felt she was wanted and welcomed into this world. Such an experience is somewhat like a receiving line where there is an honoree being greeted by well-wishers on a joyous occasion, perhaps a "welcome home" after a long absence somewhere. This visualization of a re-birth experience helped the woman to have a different view of herself now.

This woman was a grossly overweight, forty something person when I first met her for a consultation three months before this. She had an unsuccessful marriage some 20 years earlier. She had gone from one job to another and had very few dates and practically no friends. Her life was miserable. She knew her mother had not wanted to get pregnant with her and had considered aborting her. Throughout her childhood she felt rejected, and was treated that way. So, she acted this out in her relations with playmates and peers along the way, which, of course, further emphasized a self-fulfilling prophecy. A crucial need in her therapy was for her to be able to start over at birth. Doing this successfully, in her mind, enabled us to proceed to reconstruct the rest of her life in accordance with a feeling of being wanted, not only by her family, but also by friends as well. Furthermore, she needed to realize she was one of God's children and as such had an innate dignity of being. Her mental attitude about herself had to change as therapy proceeded.

DEFINITION

"Acceptance" basically means to be favorably received. But more than that, in this context it means to be wanted. Many marriages fail because one of the partners is "insanely jealous" and overly solicitous. There can be more than one ultimate cause of this, but usually the reason is that that person has "Separation Anxiety" and, perhaps, is emotionally dead. Such a condition nearly always starts with feelings of rejection received at birth or very soon thereafter. And the longer a person lives with that condition the harder it is to treat or (hopefully) cure such a disorder.

Acceptance is first because it is the first need of an infant. Almost all those professionals involved in maternity wards have now seen the light and no longer remove the baby from the mother at birth. What a break for the infant!

There is a relationship between the mother and infant, which no one yet fully understands. Because the infant is truly "bone of my bones and flesh of my flesh" (Gen.2:23; 29:14), there is obviously a strong physical relationship between mother and offspring. But that very developing relationship is more profound than merely physical. There is a spiritual union which is too mystical to be defined. Some women dream of a child or infant before they know they are pregnant, because the mystical union is there. During the pregnancy an unexplainable oneness develops between mother and fetus. There are exceptions to this, of course, particularly where the woman does not want to get pregnant. But in most cases a bonding that is greater than physical takes place. And it works both ways. When an infant is removed from its mother, both suffer from separation anxiety. Peace comes only when the new-born is placed in bodily contact with the mother -- either on her abdomen or at her breast.

Therefore, when the infant is removed permanently from the birth mother a psychological-spiritual scar is left for the rest of its life. Even when the mother plans to give up the child after birth to be adopted or has planned to give it up because she is a substitute mother by virtue of an implanted embryo, frequently she cannot bring herself to give up that baby. The emotional-spiritual tie has become too strong to break. **That tie is much, much stronger within that new-born infant**. If the baby is to be adopted, the ideal situation is that the adopting parents have contact with the pregnant woman before the birth of the child, talking to the mother and to the child and then to receive the baby "at the knees" of the birth mother at birth. I know a couple who did this and as of their ninth birthday the little girls (twins) are as perfectly adjusted as any children I have ever seen. The prophet Isaiah (49:15) puts this beautifully, *Can a woman forget her sucking child that she should not have compassion on the son of her womb?*

THE UNWANTED CHILD

There are many traits and circumstances which prevent parents from wanting a child. Some that are more prevalent are: the couple are unmarried; they do not love each other; they cannot "afford" a child; they have an intuitive feeling that they cannot "love" a child; they don't want to be bothered; they already have too many children. There are physical reasons why it is risky or even life threatening to get pregnant or to have the baby; living or social circumstances mitigate against it; racial or religious conflicts make it unwise.

There are other reasons, but where one or more of these reasons is present, it is hazardous for her to get pregnant. Why?

EMOTIONAL DISORDERS DUE TO REJECTION

The child that is unwanted is most apt to be neglected, mistreated, abused or even cruelly mutilated. I have treated many juveniles and adults who were unwanted at birth. Procedures in analytical psychotherapy enable us to take the patient back to re-live the birth experience, and a surprising number of emotional disorders have their ultimate origin at birth where the person was not wanted.

It is safe to say that most of the infants who are born to parents who did not want that pregnancy suffer the rest of their lives. If they are not just passively neglected, which is bad enough, they are abused either physically, emotionally, or sexually or some of all three. They are dehumanized.

At birth that unwanted infant starts the coping process to avoid the pain, which is instinctual. In childhood that is usually done by grasping for attention. Typically, the child regresses or engages in "naughty" behavior; in either case the situation is worsened. That is, the parent (or parents) react and simply treat the child worse, which in turn worsens the child's behavior.

CRUELTY

In not a few cases cruelty begins to take place. Some delinquent parents take to hot water scalding in retaliation for the pregnancy, while others take to physical brutality. Others resort to some form of sexual abuse. It should be said that these parents are usually ones who have been treated this way in childhood themselves. It is passed on to this generation who, in turn, will take it out on other children or on society in later years.

At every stage of growth, the neglected and abused children instinctively resort to some form of coping, and the older they get the more they resort to reacting and getting even. By early (or pre-) adolescence they get into drugs to salve the emotional pain, and they can carry a gun or knife and, thus, the delinquent pattern is well ensconced.

Mistreatment or defective treatment in the first months of life accounts for most of delinquency, criminality, drug abuse, school problems, and the most serious emotional disorders. The child does not just "out grow" or forget that kind of abuse.

It can further be said that the first years may be adequate for the child and that he gets off to a good start, but significant changes in the environment in preadolescence or adolescence can lessen or undo the good that has already been accomplished.

But serious and obvious aberrant behavior is not the only consequence of being unwanted. Where the rejection is not so pronounced or where subsequent treatment is not so severe or where the person has a strong nervous resistance to mistreatment, the personality is not so severely damaged. An example follows:

In treating people with marital problems where one is "insanely jealous" and makes life miserable for the mate because he or she is constantly asking, "Why are you late?" "Where have you been?" "Who were you with?" "When will you return?" etc. the diagnosis is "Separation Anxiety," and most of the time the ultimate start of the problem (the Initial Sensitizing Event) is the way the infant was treated at birth. It was too severely separated from its mother or rejected by her. The person is unable to form attachments with other people (notably a mate) and many other forms of insecurity are evidenced.

LACK OF SELF-ESTEEM

Lack of self-esteem is another consequence of birth rejection. It's reasonable that this happens. During the most impressionable period, the infant is not considered important enough by the parent(s) to be accepted, so it is not important, period! It does not see itself as having worth or value. So it spends its life trying to adjust to this despair. Of course, the person who feels like a no-body will have trouble adjusting to friends, school, or marriage. If this condition is serious, we diagnose it as an "Identity Problem".

Do you see why **acceptance** is the first need?

HOW ACCEPTANCE IS DEMONSTRATED

GRATIFY PHYSICAL NEEDS

When the baby is wanted and welcomed, the parents will most surely meet the need to be cared for and the need to be enjoyed.

The need to be cared for is fulfilled by supplying the basic physical needs to survive. The baby's needs are satisfied primarily around the mouth, esophagus, and stomach at this early stage. Taking food, being fed, and diapered are basic. In the first months the baby is held, rocked, and sung to. It's interesting to note that these days mothers and fathers are returning, at times, to an ancient method of carrying the baby, maybe by using a back pack and holding the baby against the mother's body. It's also carried on the hip or at the chest. Any way, the baby is transported comfortably, and against the parent's body is good.

Hopefully, the mother can, and will breast feed the infant. This is still best, especially from the emotional point of view. Even the Gerber's ads recognize that the mother's milk is to be preferred from a nutritional and prophylactic point of view, as they recommend their product as next choice. However, if there are good reasons why the mother can't breast feed, then she should hold the baby while giving the bottle. Remember the mystical attachment? This is the reason the mother should hold the baby while feeding. This is not to say that the father can't give some assistance very early, but his assistance should be manifested mostly by his doing other chores to relieve the mother so she can have the time and strength to "nurse" the baby herself.

Whatever the child's age, acceptance is demonstrated by proper care for that child's physical needs for appearance and comfort.

This is not the place to deal with the dietary needs, except to say that the parents will be concerned enough that they will be alert to the infant's and child's problems with diet and do something quickly when there is a problem.

Keeping the baby comfortable by changing the diaper (without scoffing or complaining about the "mess,") when needed is important, as is a sensitivity to changes of temperature in the room, so that proper cover in the crib can be maintained. Physical comfort is necessary, also, about the clothing as well as the temperature. And speaking of cribs, be sure that the crib and all baby items are safe. Many cribs have been found to be dangerous from several different causes.

GRATIFY EMOTIONAL-INTELLECTUAL NEEDS

The need to be enjoyed is just as vital to the physical needs in its own way as the need for physical comfort, for here we are dealing with the emotional welfare. The child needs to be cuddled; it clings to its mother's presence. Parents will play with the child, soft loving voices will talk to it, sing to it, and "coo" with it. Smiling faces convey this acceptance and reassure the child that mother and daddy will be back in its presence after they leave. Although these activities may sound superficial and as a matter of convenience, this is incorrect. Many studies have demonstrated the necessity of these activities to the total well being of the infant. By "brain scans" we can know that the infant responds positively to all of these activities.

I cited the research of Dr. Craig Ramey in Chapter One, and how he has demonstrated that the brains of infants and small children are capable of grasping an astounding amount of information in the first years of life, provided that they have appropriate, positive, and frequent interactions with parents and other caregivers.

Families and Work Institute report that when a parent lovingly comforts a crying baby or plays peekaboo and reads to a toddler, instantly there are these responses: brain cells are excited; other brain cells are strengthened; and new brain connections are formed. This kind of continued stimulation remains to influence that child *the rest of its life*. Only recently have neuroscientists recognized that, "the experiences that fill a baby's first days, months, and years have such a decisive impact on the architecture of their brains, or on the nature and extent of their adult capacities."

The parent who pays close attention to the baby's moods and expressions will respond to it accordingly. Then the baby is able to learn that it can trust the parent because that parent responds to the cues given by the infant. This is done by holding him, talking to her, singing, reading, (yes, I said reading), laughing, playing peek-a-boo, etc. By this interaction the infant learns that he or she can cause positive reactions in others.

GRADUAL SEPARATION

In the case of the newborn, it does not distinguish itself as separate from the mother-feeder. The process of emotional separation, and development of its own separateness as an individual, proceeds gradually through early childhood. This is the reason the infant grasps so for the mother's presence. The mother is also associated with the environment of the infant. The furnishings of the infant's immediate environment are also a part of itself. Thus, if the baby is removed from the home and taken elsewhere, something familiar to the infant should be taken with it. This may be a stuffed toy, blanket, or other item with which the child is familiar. This is called a "security object" for a good reason. But other objects surrounding the baby's crib or play pen play a significant role in development. That part of the brain that processes visual input has an optimal time for its influence. Thus, early on the parents should provide colorful pictures, books, and objects to stimulate that part of the brain development.

As the child grows older, the principal need for parental companionship, security, and regularity is still there but manifested by different means. After 14 months the child, who has had adequate mothering, can tolerate more separation from mother and its familiar environment because the need for that familiarity is not as intense for its security as it was earlier.

With the older child the play takes on a different aspect. But play is an essential ingredient to childhood, and it offers a means of companionship with parents. And there are many other ways that parents demonstrate acceptance. They all have to do with attention to the child's needs and desires. Providing time and opportunity for relationships with others is an example. This may be with other children close to the same age. It may be with relatives and friends who become familiar to the child and pay attention to it. Providing a variety of people and activity gives the child stimulation, which is good up to a point. However, be alert to situations that cause the child to show fright.

RESULTS OF ACCEPTANCE

SENSE OF BELONGING

When the child is accepted, cared for, and enjoyed to a reasonable degree, it will feel that it belongs. The sense of belongingness is an essential ingredient to one's self-concept. And when the foundation is laid early in life, the important sense of "we" and a feeling of being a part of a larger group strengthens the sense of selfhood. Without it one feels like he/she is on the outside looking in. The "loner" is an unhappy and often maladjusted individual. Furthermore, all of this activity contributes to the child's intelligence. For indeed, these experiences are "learning" experiences and lay the foundation for the way the child will associate with peers and learn at school later on. For self-confidence, responsiveness, and curiosity are just a few of the traits that develop as a result of such treatment, and these traits are essential to the total learning process as the child develops.

SELF WORTH

Belonging also has to do with the person's sense of worth. To be wanted by others means the person has value. If one is "valued" by others then one feels one's own value. To succeed in life one needs to feel like "I count" or "I'm good" or "I'm OK." We feel good about ourselves when we belong. **Acceptance** is one of the first building blocks to a mature, self-actualizing adult. And babies treated with warm, responsive, early care, which responds to their preferences, moods, and rhythms, stimulate the child to thrive and mature appropriately. The child that develops a strong feeling of being accepted and wanted early in life will not be so sensitive to feeling rejected later in childhood if others do not readily accept him/her into their own group.

THE TRAGEDY OF REJECTION

A few years ago on a cold (11 degrees) February morning an oil field worker in Texas going to work caught a glimpse of red cloth in a clump of bushes about one half mile off of highway #302. It was the body of 9-year-old Walter Butler, who had frozen to death over night. Four months previously Walter's mother, a single parent, left him in a boys' home ranch at Goldsmith, 30 miles away from Andrews, where they lived. Walter, in his desperation to return to mother and home, had started out walking the day before when the temperature was moderate. Five miles later a man offered him a ride in his truck, but Walter's mother had cautioned him not to ride with strangers. He didn't. He walked 15 miles, but never made it back home. A strong north wind on those Texas plains dropped the temperature suddenly. Walter apparently had sought shelter in the clump of mesquite.

Walter was quickly missed at the ranch and a search was made involving up to 100 persons. An employee at the ranch said Walter just wanted to see his mother. This is a tragic example of rejection and separation. No one had understood the internal pain of separation in Walter's heart.

When we talk about unwanted babies, we're not just talking about couples who don't want to get pregnant. We're referring to those who are born but are *refused* acceptance and, thus, literally become "human refuse."

AN EARLY SYSTEM OF CHILD CARE

This is not a new phenomenon. Not unlike circumstances in ancient Greece where unwanted babies were left in the open fields to die, we still struggle with these tragedies. And we say we have become civilized! In the more recent past since ancient Greece, foundling homes in Italy and France years ago had turning boxes in their outer walls. There a mother might, unseen from within, place her unwanted infant in a compartment. By revolving it so that the child was delivered inside the wall, a bell was rung summoning an attendant. No attempt was made to find the mother.

THE FATE OF THE UNWANTED

Today in many such cases the babies are taken in and cared for. But in others the unwanted child, unfortunately, is kept in the home where it suffers many times a fate worse than death. Our modern system of social work ferrets out a small percentage of these rejects, and a few of these are given loving homes. Some of the babies who are put out for adoption simply are passed from one house to another without feeling secure, while others go on into another abusive family. Some people make a business of taking in abandoned children for reimbursement from the state, but do not give them the kind of care they need, so the child goes from the frying pan into the fire. We haven't found adequate solutions yet, in spite of our emphasis on birth control to young people.

POST SCRIPT

Not too long ago a doctor in the Bronx was walking his police dog at midnight on a lonely stretch beside the Jerome Avenue reservoir. As they passed a refuse can, the dog whined and frantically pawed in spite of the doctor's efforts to continue down the street. The dog refused to follow, so the doctor went back and investigated. The dog was pawing a sizable paper bag rolled shut at the top. Instead of being garbage it was "human" refuse -- a red, wrinkled, baby boy. He was obviously only a few hours old but also dangerously near death. With the help of hurriedly summoned police, the doctor took the baby to a hospital where he was revived and later taken to a foundling home where a wristlet of beads bearing the number 1291 was put on its wrist. . . a human discarded with garbage and known only as "1291." It is an incidental tragedy on a public street in modern times.

It is obvious that the unwanted pregnancy is the one most apt to be aborted. And some of those that aren't aborted will be "destroyed" at birth, left in trash bins or sewers, abandoned somewhere, or suffer some other horrible death. When unwanted children are brought into this world and are reared in tortuous circumstances would they not have been better off aborted? This is a tough question for which there is no easy answer.

You can see why I say "acceptance" is the first of the child's natural rights.

QUESTIONS FOR MEDITATION AND/OR DISCUSSION

1) Are you familiar with a child or children who have been unwanted?

2) If you have been through the early stages with an infant, what did you find to be the most difficult physical need to satisfy in your baby? If you have not had that experience, what do you think it would be?

3) Do you know of mothers (or fathers) who want to just leave the baby alone till it gets old enough to be a "person".

4) At this point can you define "Acceptance" any more accurately than you could have before reading this chapter?

5) Can you see why I say "Acceptance" is the first and natural right of the new born?

6) In your personal experience have you observed children in a home that appear to be unwanted?

7) Do you remember knowing a "loner" when you were a child in school? How was that person treated by his/her peers? Have you noted the behavior of "loners" reported currently?

CHAPTER 4

LOVE, The Child's Second Right

WHAT PARENTAL LOVE IS

THE UNLOVING ENVIRONMENT

During my training, a psychiatrist referred a patient to me saying, "This man says he's possessed by the devil. You've studied theology, you take this case. He needs exorcism." The patient said he could not stop abusing his wife because Satan made him do it. His marriage was on its last leg. His wife had already left him several times, and each time she returned on condition that he change. He did not. Both wanted to save the marriage. Through visualization psychotherapy the man relived many incidents from early childhood, which laid the foundation for his abusive behavior. For one, his father had abused his mother. For another, whenever the child disobeyed, his mother in her anger yelled, "You little devil you; you're just like your father!" She was conditioning the child in several ways over the years that he was like his father, and that he was a devil. He grew up to fulfill that teaching. His home life was devoid of love. His parents did not love each other, and they did not love him. He and his wife suffered the consequences.

A major national news network opened its program this morning, in the context of a national tragedy involving children, with this statement, "Doesn't every child in America have the right to a decent start in life?"

The answer would appear to be a simple, "Yes, of course. Why not?" But the realities of life force a different answer upon us. What is meant by this question, anyway? One could start with the word "decent" and go from there. What is "decent" for one child in one culture or environment would not be the same for another child in another environment. What would be decent for one child would possibly be indecent for a child in another locality.

EXPRESSIONS OF LOVE

A little girl named Cindy, along with other children, was asked what love meant. Her reply was, "During my piano recital, I was on a stage and I was scared. I looked at all the people watching me and saw my daddy waving and smiling. He was the only one doing that. I wasn't scared anymore."

If we could say that one essential element in a child's beginning is "love" then we are off to a good start. For this need is universally essential.

When parents show "acceptance" sincerely, as emphasized in the previous chapter, this is prompted by "love." Thus, love is being expressed in all of those ways. But supplying the child's need for love involves much more.

LEARNING TO CONTROL EMOTIONS AND RESPECT AUTHORITY

I continue to emphasize that expressions of love in the early care of the child have a decisive, long lasting impact on how people develop, how well they learn, and what we are concerned with greatly these days: the capacity of children and adults to **regulate and control their emotions.** This is a delicate subject, and I will deal with it more later. First, I emphasize that parents need to accept their child's emotions, even validate them, "You're feeling hurt." "I can see you're angry." "You're afraid, and I understand." etc. This is important to let the child know you are in touch and understand them. But there is more to this subject of emotions than this. The human being experiences all kinds of emotions from time to time. Childhood is the time to recognize this fact and learn to deal with these emotions. The loving parent helps the child through these times gently and understandingly.

DEPRIVATION OF LOVE

You see, when we are dealing with criminal or even delinquent behavior such as social issues related to school beatings and killings and ask the question "Why?" too often people focus on current situations and superficial answers when the real, ultimate source of such devious behavior goes back to the nature of the individual(s) who perpetrate these heinous deeds. This nature or personality has its start at (or even before) birth. And a lack of love during this early period is a great part of the problem.

In seeking answers, editors plead for sanity. Politicians budget more money. Law enforcement sets up patrols. School officials install metal detectors. When a school tragedy happens, there is a feeling that we must do something to prevent the next one of a similar nature from happening. And this is fine. We need responsive leadership. But this is a long term problem. A fifteen-year old boy who shoots his class mates because he felt stigmatized or rejected, and shoots his teacher in anger because he doesn't respect authority, most likely had the origin of his problem in infancy or early childhood. And the cause probably was that his basic needs were thwarted by either neglect or abuse. And the first of those needs is "Acceptance" and the second is the need for "Love."

BIO-CHEMICAL EVIDENCE

Early in the first chapter I referred to the damage that prolonged childhood stress can do to the body due to the production of cortisol. When a child experiences repeated stress, later on it may take only one traumatic event, (called the Symptom Producing Event) such as being shunned by someone at school, for that child to "break."

There are likely others of his school mates who may also be shunned by "the football crowd" to the same extent, but they do not kill because they, for whatever reason, have not reached their breaking point. Perceptive teachers are aware of the differences in the "in crowd" and the "rejects" in every school. And among the rejects there are potential killers.

An example: a boy named Jim Myers, a junior in high school, was observed by the school principal. She had a feeling about Jim and took the time to talk to him and immediately called his father because Jim was on the verge of shooting up his class-mates. Jim identified with the boys who shot up Columbine High School. His parents were divorced and, due to being absorbed in their own upset lives, were not enough in touch with their son to realize he had a serious problem. His class-mates had made fun of him throughout his school career because he was "different." There were times when his father had seen that Jim was different or even strange, but he admitted he didn't know what to do. Well, he could have called a doctor, talked to the school counselor, or consulted a psychotherapist, and earlier his son could have been helped more than he will be now. Jim's father, like too many fathers, was too busy to take serious note of his son in the earlier stages of his growth. This is just one example of why I put so much emphasis on family relationship being more important than economic matters.

THE LONER

Many rapists and murderers upon being apprehended have been described by acquaintances or neighbors as "quiet," "loners," "strange" etc. Many of these have felt like "loners" all of their lives because they were not accepted with love in infancy. That is, they suffered the frustration of being "deprived" of love always, and hence their levels of cortisol were abnormal, and such hormonal imbalance prompted them to act on the impulse to ravage, rape, or kill.

Modern research demonstrates that babies who are treated with appropriate love in the first years of life are less likely to have abnormal cortisol levels which drive them to rebellious behavior.

Please take note: Due to the fact that the brain has a remarkable plasticity, a child who was deprived of love at the beginning, and in this regard is stunted, may be helped to overcome this deficiency by proper loving treatment and attention a little later. In other words, the brain can be somewhat reprogrammed, if parents start early enough.

REASONS FOR PARENT'S APATHY

CHILDREN NOT WANTED

Unfortunately, there are too many parents who didn't, and don't, want their children and, thus, treat them with disdain, hostility, or rejection in a variety of ways. They simply don't love their children; perhaps they don't have the capacity to love anyone. A deep subconscious reason for this attitude of rejection is due to the parents' inability to love. Their own background was unloving and rejecting, and because of this they are so frozen at a narcissistic level that they are incapable of giving an infant the outgoing love it requires.

RESENTMENT

A subtle cause of deprivation or abuse of the child is the parents' resentment toward each other. And resentment can have several motives behind it. One is that the parents feel there is so much expense with a child that they are being deprived of money for other "things" they need. These may be non-essential luxuries. If the parents are angry because of the money required for the child, they may take it out on the child in one way or another.

There is another, more subtle factor in this category. Mother may have had big plans for work, career, and the like. Taking time out for delivery and early natal care interferes with her career plans. This can cause resentment consciously or unconsciously. And such feelings subvert expressing the kind of love an infant needs from its mother. And if she does return to work (outside the home) she may feel guilty.

A wife may be terribly resentful of her husband for real or imagined mistreatment, or have some physical problem as a result of the pregnancy and, thus, be unable to give sincere, devoted love to her baby. She may come to feel it is the husband's fault she got pregnant, or he isn't providing support and attention for her in this new role as mother, or he isn't doing his share of the housework. She may have had to change her life style or living conditions, and, due to new stresses or discomforts, she blames her husband.

Likewise, a husband may be avoiding or neglecting his wife because he has resentments toward her. This whole birth process has interfered with their recreational or sex life. Or he may have to take two jobs for a while to meet expenses. Such situations breed resentment. Whether with husband or wife or both, resentment like this very often is taken out on the child in treatment attitudes which promote abuse or neglect. Needless to say, the relationship with other children or live-in relatives also can affect the emotional state of mother and daddy. Having a harmonious relationship among all the members of the household is vitally important as a prerequisite to being able to express the kind of love the newborn requires.

THE SYMBIOTIC RELATIONSHIP

MOTHER AND BABY

I have already referred to the mystical bond between mother and infant. Look at it as a kind of psychological "Siamese twin" attachment. This symbiotic relationship is one in which two organisms with essentially different needs mutually profit from the relationship with each other.

This is a natural spiritual oneness that males absolutely cannot have. And it takes this infant years to feel gradually separated from the mother. Newborns know their own mothers by the odor of their bodies, by the individualized odor and taste of the mother's milk, the sound of her voice, and in other ways not clearly understood. A new born infant can pick its own mother out of a crowd.

SEPARATION

In the period immediately after birth the interdependence of mother and infant becomes even more pronounced. Every time an infant is taken away from its mother or is deprived of the optimum attention and love that it needs, this severing is being forced upon it, and it is traumatic for both mother and child. As she feeds and nurtures, mother receives the satisfaction of completing the creation of her child; and as the infant receives the food and the other primary experiences of need-consciousness and gratification, the sensory nervous system matures a little more. I emphasize this mother-child bond because I have experienced mother-child separation anxiety with many neurotic adults who have returned to birth and early post natal experiences in deep hypnosis in their treatment. And when they have been so deprived of the mother either by being totally removed from her presence or frustrated by being deprived of her attention and tender, loving care repeatedly, they go kicking and screaming as if surgery were being performed without anesthetic.

This is a generality. There are exceptions, probably because of a genetic neural condition not clearly understood. But any given mother will not know this in advance.

THE ROLE OF FATHERS

Now, back to the question about the father: I have already alluded to the fact that about 180,000 males a year abandon their offspring. Fortunately, in the last few years efforts to find these men have intensified with increasing success. In the book, *Fathers are Parents Too*, English stresses the emotional responsibility of dads -- not just financial responsibility. It is known that children with caring dads grow up with higher IQ's and greater social skills than others.

In the latter years of this past century, more children than ever before were living apart from their fathers. This deprivation has serious consequences for the child. And, in part, it explains why there are so many environmentally induced homosexuals as opposed to those who are genetically induced homosexuals.

Our civilization is in a stage of growth, and, like the various stages of growth in individual development, it is awkward because new procedures and skills are being tried. We haven't arrived. One change we will see in the near future is that males will find themselves. Healthy strength, responsibility, and leadership needs to return to the family unit by way of the father. The need for love balanced between mother and father and bestowed freely and without reserve on their offspring will be always present.

MONITORING CHILD CARE

I must make it clear that I am not saying it is impossible for a mother to have a baby and work outside the home at the same time. Businesses more and more these days are coming to recognize this need of female employees, and in order to have them in their employ, they are providing nurseries, child care, insurance, appropriate time off, and greater understanding of the mother's and infant's needs and desires. At times a mother can make her own arrangements for adequate infant care, like working close to home. And in the future there will be portable electronic devices enabling a parent to look in on the nursery care facility from wherever she is and observe what is going on with the child at that time. It's hard to have ideal conditions. But all need to recognize that too high a percent of the child care agencies, nurseries, church, and social programs are inadequate and are proving to be detrimental.

Some parents have had video cameras installed in the home or place of care and have been shocked to discover how recklessly their infant or child has been treated by a trusted care-giver. Evidence of this is coming forward more than we expect. The best of such facilities are but weak substitutes for the kind of love the infant needs at the beginning.

RESENTMENT BETWEEN PARENTS

Having a baby is one of the most demanding of all situations, when a couple take the matter seriously. The child's demands place a responsibility on the parents that they don't usually anticipate until they have had one. They, therefore, need to be prepared emotionally to meet those demands. Giving **love** is of major importance. Love is defined as "a feeling of strong affection induced by sympathetic understanding." The desire for fusion or blending with the loved one accompanies that feeling. It is demanding and requires a great deal of human sacrifice to be done adequately. And the number of women who supply this need consistently has decreased. As we become more sensitive to gender issues, men are becoming more responsive to the partnership with mother in caring for the newborn. And it is vitally important that the parents form strong, secure attachments with the infant from the beginning. This is done by love.

BABY NEEDS TO SUCK

One of the first and most obvious needs is to fulfill the need to suck. Of course the child must be fed, but the very act of sucking is instinctual. I alluded to this in the previous chapter as a sign of "acceptance." But doing this lovingly is more than merely feeding the child. HOW the mother nurses and feeds demonstrates her love. These feeding periods should not be interrupted and limited in time. Preferably they should take place at the mother's breast, even if she has to give the baby a bottle.

THE MANY WAYS OF LOVE

Love is expressed to the infant in a myriad of ways, most of which are subtle and indirect. Of course at birth it isn't too early to use words such as "You're beautiful;" "I love you;" "You're precious;" "God's gift;" "Bundle of joy;" etc.. The very use of such expressions evokes from the parent a tone of voice, a facial expression, a touch, which conveys a positive, loving emotion, even before the words have a literal meaning to the infant. Such expressions are also made by singing to the child. Provide other forms of music, but when mom or dad sings to the child, it conveys a message of companionship, joy, and pleasure in each other's company, as well as presenting a soothing, calming atmosphere that breeds peace and relaxation for the child.

STORY-TELLING

In a similar fashion tell stories to the child and read to it. Of course such stories must be appropriate to the child of that age. There are a myriad of books with children's stories, Bible stories, adventure, fiction and non-fiction. Pictures and stories about animals are appealing to smaller children, and most children love children's poetry.

GIVE TIME

Giving time to the child is another way of showing love. The child is born requiring attention. It is more than needing to have diapers changed and feeding the child, which I referred to in the previous chapter. Attention must be paid to clothing comforts, temperature in the room, having a pleasant environment for the bed or crib as a part of showing love. Paying attention to the feeding schedule, which the infant sets up for itself, is vital. My mother told me that, when I was a baby in 1925, the doctors had a feeding schedule which they recommended to all mothers. I believe it was once every four hours. My mother said this schedule did not suit my needs. She knew this from instinct, and she soon fed me by my own individual schedule. I'm glad. Pediatricians know better now than to recommend that all infants eat on the same prescribed schedule.

HEALTH CARE

One of the essentials of filling the need for love is proper health care. "Shouldn't this be obvious?" you say. Yes it should be. But you'd be surprised at the number of proper parents who are slovenly about the baby's or child's health care needs. When the parents are taking the infant to the pediatrician, s/he will recommend the shots that are necessary in today's world. Periodically there is a wave of conflict about shots. There is a school of thought which discourages giving the infant a series of shots. There is a similar controversy over whether infant boys should be circumcised. And, while there are certain exceptions, most all of the prescribed shots are safe and certainly do a world of good in preventing disease and disaster.

While good nutrition in our country is available to most mothers these days, there are still too many families deprived of this. And even though it is not always convenient, the parents who love their child will see that they start out with a healthy diet. Remember, the child is getting the foundation for the rest of its life now. For example, it is known from many studies in the past that a lack of nourishing milk in the first months retards the baby's brain development.

RECOGNIZE IRREGULARITIES

Whatever the age of the child, attentive parents will recognize it when something is wrong. Disturbances in the child's sleeping habits, continuing nightmares, eating and digestion irregularities, sudden changes in behavior and/or mood, and, of course, a fever may be warning signs that something is wrong. This is NOT the time to let the infant "cry it out" alone and unattended. Furthermore, prolonged bed wetting, nail biting, and compulsive thumb-sucking may be indications of emotional problems. Different ages and varying family-sibling relationships may contribute to a variety of problems, some of which could be serious enough for professional attention. For example, a 24 month old who is quiet, talking little, would not be considered problematic as a 3 year old would be. Or the 24 month old may be depending on an older sibling to talk for him/her. At a different level, parents should pay close attention to children with these symptoms: the shy, withdrawn child who seldom speaks, the over-aggressive child always demanding attention, the chronic complainer, the one who fails in kindergarten or who fails in social adjustment. These behaviors may be just passing variations in personality. On the other hand, if symptoms rather suddenly appear after a sudden change or trauma in the child's life, professional help is called for.

More than ever before, disturbed children need to be recognized early by teachers and parents so that help can be given. It is perfectly in harmony with loving and attentive parents to feel OK with no disgrace to have a child with such disturbances as I have listed. But the parent who fails to get professional guidance is failing to love wisely. It has been tragic to hear many parents, as they are questioned about aberrant behavior of their child, admit that they observed certain changes, but they didn't give it any thought, or thought they would go away and didn't check with a doctor. This kind of picture has emerged from the shooting incidents in schools of late.

Proper care early may have saved lives. Thank God that children I have been talking about, in spite of their sensitivity, can respond favorably if they are given intensive and sustained physical and emotional treatment early enough! And an angry child, with proper help, can change.

BABIES RESPOND TO LOVE

Love is a learned response on the part of the infant. When a baby receives attentive love, it responds as babies are capable of doing. It may touch mother's face and breast, smile, or gurgle. The same kind of response would take place with father as well when he gives time and loving attention to the child. When the parents reciprocate and pick up on the baby's cues, these responses keep growing and expanding throughout life, being expressed in different ways appropriate to the child's advancing age. However, if parents neglect to respond to the child, it will become more distant and emotionally crippled, which prevents it from being able to form attachments later in life for itself and never will be able to love freely as it should. In fact, with little or no love from parents, the child may eventually lose even his desire to struggle. And this is a step toward suicide -- emotionally or in fact.

As the child gets older, some of the infant's needs for attention modify onto a different level. Of course, there is the same list of basics: food, clothing, attention to their wants, health, temperature, cleanliness, pleasant environment, ready availability of the parents, and the like. But, obviously, the way such demonstrations of love are made have to be adjusted to the age of the progressing child.

PROVIDE OPPORTUNITIES FOR PLAY

I have treated many adults, usually with the diagnosis of anxiety but sometimes with arrested development or immaturity, where a primary contributing cause to the disorder was simply that the patient never had a "childhood." Having a "childhood" is a stage of growth and maturing that, like other stages of human development, one must go through to be fully mature. Loving parents will provide the growing child with opportunities for play. In the earliest years the parents are the main playmates, unless, of course, there is a sibling. If there is no sibling, occasional visits with another infant are good. Then, as the child gains mobility, opportunities for play with other children should be encouraged. The interaction of play among children is necessary to maturation. Such activity is the foundation of getting along with others, and children deprived of this suffer in their interpersonal relationships when they become adults.

Regarding toys, a variety of colorful, safe toys is good, but there can be too many. This situation sometimes becomes a substitute for companionship with parent (or care giver). It also may lay the foundation for a materialistic view of life.

In the last few years I have felt pronounced disappointment to read of one school district after another canceling recess periods. Also, the school schedules are so demanding and full that children have less and less opportunity for free and unstructured play after school. This is lamentable. It is during such periods that kids are left to their own devices to set the rules, and make their own exceptions and penalties for infraction of the rules. If they are to play the game, they have to learn to give and take, cooperation, and other lessons. When they have disputes, they are forced into some form of arbitration and negotiation on their own, or the game doesn't continue. They learn more about sportsmanship and life than they usually do in today's structured team sports with its limited opportunity for participation and with an undue pressure to win and get to the finals. I'm sure you remember, as I do, that occasionally in childhood a kid who had not learned this lesson would say, "If you don't play it my way, I'll take my ball and bat and go home."

On the playground if they lose today, they will choose up and play again tomorrow, at which time they have another try at it. During the game if they mess up in some way, they aren't embarrassed because their parents and the parents of their friends aren't there watching when they fail. They don't have to go home and hear the discussion of parents as to why they lost and feel they let the family down. They can have the fun of playing even if they don't make the school team and wear a uniform. Kids need to have time to be just playing kids. And loving parents must see that this happens. Former Texas Governor, Ann Richards, regarding kids playing informally very pointedly said that in these days, "They play, 'I win, you lose' instead of, 'Let's all play and have fun together.'"

The necessity of play to the maturing process has been demonstrated in scientific experiments with monkeys and from observation of children of war torn European countries who were abandoned or orphaned due to the ravages of war.

ACCEPT CHILD'S LIMITATIONS

If a child in truth is limited in some childhood activity such as a hobby or sports, be honest about it but help the child to find a compensation for this limitation or deficiency. It's OK if a kid doesn't shine as an athlete. There are other things even more important that the child can participate in and perhaps excel in. One might say, "I know you did not succeed in doing that, but there are other things you can do successfully, such as..." Then acquaint the child with a variety of possible interests and activities that would captivate him/her..

UNDERSTANDING LANGUAGE

The baby/child needs to be talked to at every age. Very early the infant is learning language before it ever talks. Then, as it gets older, understanding along with expanding the vocabulary is important to the growth and development of intelligence, not to mention the emotional contact with the adult who talks to the child. Talk to the child while dressing it, while eating, playing etc. Keep the conversation going. "Baby talk" is acceptable if it is stopped in a few months. A two year old is perfectly capable of expressive language, including clear articulation and phrasing complex sentences, provided it has heard such talk up till this time.

Children need to feel free to express their inner feelings, needs, fears, and events at kindergarten or school. The adolescents who are open with their parents about their friends and activities when away from home are the ones who established the habit of talking to their parents when they were in the early childhood years. Loving parents must take the time to be receptive to their child's talk and encourage it. What the child thinks and how s/he feels may seem insignificant to the adult, but it is the life of the child, and the parents need to treat it that way. So the loving parent will strongly encourage two-way communication.

Some parents, when I suggest this, retaliate: "But my children don't talk." I say, find out why they don't talk and overcome it if at all possible. You talk to them. Also, ask them questions such as, "What did you do in kindergarten today that was interesting?" "You've talked about your friend, Timmy. What did you and he do today at play school?" "What did you do today that was fun while you were out playing?" There are many questions that the thoughtful parent can ask to prompt the child to start talking. Then let it become a habit. Encourage the kids to keep it up by your attentiveness. Start young and keep it up through childhood. You show love this way, and you'll be glad you did.

Being a good listener means paying attention. If the child considers a topic important enough to talk about, the parent must consider it important enough to give close attention without being distracted by the TV, phone, or something else. If there is a legitimate distraction, explain this to the child and come back to continue the conversation when you can take time really to pay attention to the child.

DEVELOPMENTAL CHANGES

As the infant develops into childhood, the methods of showing love will be modified somewhat in order to adapt to the growing child. For instance, the child needs the freedom to play with friends and needs to have some freedom of movement without constant warnings. It's as if as the child gets older, there is an invisible elastic cord between mother and child. The child stretches that cord a little more and a little more in its efforts to become more independent, but it always retracts to the parents' side. The constancy of shelter and warmth of parents at home is always vital to the child's security. But the ways that are expressed by the child are going to change as it grows older. The loving parent gradually lets go and lets the child take some risks. After all, that's life.

CAUTIONS FOR PARENTS

As the infant gets older, guidance is necessary. Please spare the child reproaches, intimidations, threats, warnings, and punishment regarding physical manifestations of his/her sexuality. Being human, we parents slip on these subjects from time to time. And even in our slip-ups a learning situation can be utilized. For example, the father who, in a burst of anger, threatens : "If you don't clean your room as your mother asked, I'll get my belt." When he has a second thought he can say something like: "I'm sorry. I made a mistake. Let's talk about this." Here the child learns 1) that people make mistakes; 2) that one can say, "I'm sorry;" 3) that talking about the situation can bring understanding; 4) that negative feelings are a part of the human experience, but they can be reckoned with.

One of the hardest lessons for us parents to learn is to understand the sensitivity of the child's feelings and the hurt that we can carelessly bring on by a few words spoken in anger. Parents who aren't getting along with each other are usually the worst offenders on this score. Mom and dad should make an effort to put themselves in the place of the defenseless child more often. A better understanding would probably emerge. Caution: Loving parents will not call the child names. Another warning: Loving parents will not compare one child with another, whether it is a sibling or an acquaintance. It's assuming the role of God to compare one with another because an adult does not know the mind of the child or the motivations behind his/her behavior enough to justify comparisons.

CAN ONE LOVE TOO MUCH?

This is a good question and the answer depends on how this is defined. From my point of view one cannot love too much. Healthy "love is patient, is kind; it is not envious; is not boastful, or proud. It is not rude, nor self-seeking; it is

JOHN A. SCOTT, SR.

not easily angered; it keeps no record of wrongs; does not rejoice in evil, but rather rejoices with the truth. Healthy love always protects, always trusts, always hopes, always perseveres." Does this sound familiar? It is from 1 Corinthians 13, verses 4 through 7. This doesn't sound like it is possible to love too much.

I think the afore-mentioned question intends to seek information like this. Some well-meaning people -- even including judges -- talk about parents giving too much love by not using discipline on the child. Some parents mistakenly say, " I can't discipline my child because I love him too much." Not so! Such a parent loves her/himself too much. A truly loving parent is willing to sacrifice his/her own feelings for the benefit of the beloved child. A parent will do loving things for the child, even though it is difficult to do; and that includes discipline and control. This has come to be called "tough love." A parent who exhibits "tough love" requires the child to conform, to obey, and to behave in an appropriate manner. This requires discipline and sometimes saying, "No.".

It is not always easy to say "No" to a child when the child asks for something it shouldn't have. Some children want to go places where they shouldn't. Some wish to associate with peers who are the wrong crowd. Small children are prone to play with dangerous play things. Some want to go into the street. Obviously, at every age children are in need of control and guidance. It isn't always easy for parents to exercise the kind of oversight and discipline that is needed. Unloving parents sometimes do not feel they should hurt the child's feelings by control. But the loving parent will do what is best for the child, even though it is sometimes not easy. More will be said on discipline in Chapters 5 and 6. Say "No," reluctantly, but wherever possible give a calm explanation as to why you have taken the position you have.

Always tell the truth to your child. Let him/her know you can be trusted. When they become adolescents, you will be glad you established this trust. It's too late to wait till adolescence to start telling the truth. Also, if you make a promise, keep it. Threats as such should rarely, if ever, be made. If one issues a caution or prohibition that appears to be a threat to a child, -- carry it out. But more will be said on this in Chapter 5 on Discipline.

In summary, take heart. You can be an excellent parent. If you want to boil these suggestions I've made down to the least common denominator, you may ask yourself these three questions:

1) Are you happy?

2) Is your spouse happy?

3) Is your baby happy?

If your answer is "Yes" to these three questions, you're doing great. Then, share your child's happiness with each other in close and prolonged companionship. Send out plenty of "love messages" every day.

Now the qualities that endure are these three: faith, hope, and love; and the greatest of these is love. (New Testament, 1 Corinthians 13:13)

CHANGES IN THE HOME

For discussion, consider if you know something about the way your grandparents reared their children and the way they showed their love -- if they did show it. How did the children feel their love? As recently as two generations ago, before World War II and before the electronic age of TV, CD, DVD, and computers, there was a distinct difference in the way parents reared their children. Here is a major difference: The Kaiser Family Foundation observes that children between the ages of 8 and 18 average an astonishing six hours and 43 minutes, every day, seven days a week, immersed in entertainment media. The foundation further found that for children between 2 and 7, 81 percent of TV watching was solitary; for older children it's 95 percent. The impact on their social skills is almost certainly not good, since what they watch is intended neither to educate nor to elevate, but to sell products. Further, almost 60 percent of the kids said the TV was on during meals.

The study warned that extensive media immersion could be a symptom of deeper problems. "Indicators of discontent, such as not getting along with parents, unhappiness at school and getting into trouble a lot, are strongly associated with high media use," it said.

Contrast this report with the typical way earlier generations showed love for their kids. (Courtesy of Enka Voice) they were not loved with toys and bribes; not by giving in to adolescent demands. But rather there must have been firm determination to show that love. And in return to demand that children honor and obey. Based on past experience compared with today's permissive and passive parenting, consider the following ways of showing love.

1) Create a home at home -- a place for joy and laughter, as well as a haven for sympathy, care, and understanding.

2) Correct and discipline wrongdoing. Good manners and good citizenship begin with you.

3) Praise that which is worthy of praise and let your child know how proud you are of an accomplishment.

4) Demand results, not excuses. Top performance at school is your child's primary obligation.

5) Be available for problem sessions. Let her talk. Ask her questions. Then talk with her about the right thing to do.

6) Set aside specific periods of time when your child must do homework and when it's OK to watch TV. There is no reason for a child younger than three to be in front of the TV.

7) Keep him properly clothed and restricted in activity based on his age no matter what your neighbor's child is allowed to wear or drink or do.

8) Provide books, magazines, newspapers, etc. Good taste is as cheap as the public library. Take advantage of it.

9) Determine where your child is in his free time without being ashamed to know. Meet her friends.

10) Make an effort to make a good living; be sure to make a good life.

A little girl named Claire, age 6, expressed a secure feeling of love from a child's point of view when she said, "My mommy loves me more than anybody. You don't see anyone else kissing me to sleep at night."

QUESTIONS FOR MEDITATION AND/OR DISCUSSION

1) Do you think you would be out of date to follow the above suggestions?

2) It's natural to want to be loved by your children. You also want to be tops with them after they are mature enough to judge. Do you see a conflict in these two desires? How would you reconcile them?

3) You, as the parent, are in charge of the home. What are ways that some parents have permitted their children to take charge of the home? How

is this situation to be remedied?

4) What is meant by the phrase: "The adult world is for adults?"

5) How can you tell that even the youngest child wants and needs your love and guidance?

6) What is meant by the phrase: "The physical, mental, and social differences between you and your child require that you be a parent, rather than a pal to your child?"

7) Are you and your spouse living in peace before your child(ren)?

CHAPTER 5

DISCIPLINE, The Child's Third Right

PART ONE; ISSUES OF DISCIPLINE

INTRODUCTION

In a suburb of Memphis, not far from where my wife and I live, our quiet, crime-free neighborhood was rudely awakened last year by these shattering words in our newspaper: "Collierville police have charged four Collierville Middle School students with aggravated rape after an incident at the home of one of the boys Saturday night." Three of the boys were 13 years old, and one was 14 years old. The girl was 13 years old, and all were part of a party gathering at the home of one of the boys where no parents were present. At some point these five were left alone in the home after drinking enough beer to become intoxicated. The boys were charged with aggravated rape. The parents of these boys were severely shocked upon hearing the charges. It was reported that a parent didn't think the children were too young to be left alone at home for a few hours. This brief summary speaks loudly for itself.

This reminds me of a statement I read some time ago: It has been said that the reason that so many children are found on the streets at night is that they don't want to be left at home by themselves.

PARENTAL MISSION

To so rear their children that they acquire family and cultural ideals; that their religious influence inspires the development of a code of ethics as a standard for their relationships; that the personal character of the children is developed to its fullest potential; and to develop standards of self-control for undesirable behavior. Such an ambitious program requires healthy discipline.

CHANGE IN THE LAST FIFTY YEARS

GROSS CHILD ABUSE AFFECTED THE WORLD

Alice Miller, Ph.D., gave a research paper in New York City, October 22, 1998, which explains, at least in part, the cruelty of Nazi Germany. The basis of her research was this question, "How is it that so many turn-of-the-century German children were born with such malignant genes that they'd later become Hitler's willing executioners?" She concluded it wasn't their genes. It was their environment. Her quest led her to a German teacher, Dr. Daniel Gottlieb Schreber, who was the "Dr. Spock" of Germany in the mid Nineteenth Century. Some of his books on child care ran to as many as 40 editions around 1860. His view would be called today the "systematic instruction in child persecution and maltreatment," according to Dr. Miller.

Schreber taught that newborns should be forced from birth to obey and should be spanked every time they cried. Of course, when a book was so widely read in Germany by adults in the last half of the 19th Century, their children would be the adults of the first part of the 20th Century —the time of the setting for the rise of Hitler, who was, himself, the victim of abandonment and abuse. Dr. Miller points out that Hitler's leaders, Eichmann, Himmler, Hess, Mengele, and others were all of the same type of background. Which explains the inhuman cruelty they perpetrated. The German children of this era were severely beaten repeatedly, subjected to the language of violence, and reared without love or being rescued by a bystander.

Dr. Miller further substantiates her position by studies in Romania of abandoned and severely maltreated children. There were lesions in certain areas of the brain, due to repeated traumatization, which increased the release of stress hormones. These in turn attacked the sensitive tissue of the brain and destroyed the new neurons. Dr. Miller's research uncovered many other individuals, well known from this era, who suffered similar deprivation and how it affected their writing or leadership.

FALLOUT FROM GERMAN CRUELTY

It is general knowledge these days that the crux of the Twentieth Century was World War II. This catastrophe changed American life as nothing else has. The home and family life as it had been known for centuries was turned upside down. Among other radical changes was the role of husband and wife and the total family unit. Families were no longer patriarchal. The roles of mother and father changed, and the result was a loosening of family discipline and a displacement of family relationships. This ultimately resulted in what some call the "child centered family." With so many men absent and so many families torn up, children lost their way. Too many male role models were gone, mothers were absent from home, and the little ones were shifted and left with relatives, friends, or strangers. Parental images, marital stability, and sexual mores were forever changed.

Dr. Edward M. Litin, head psychiatrist at Mayo Clinic, evaluated this situation a few years ago and said parents were afraid to say "No," afraid to give orders, and afraid to punish because they feared the loss of love. During and after the war, marriages became more unstable, and the shakier the marriage, the more marked the abdication of parental responsibility. This *laissez-faire* method with children was labeled "permissive" when applied to the home, and then it spread to many school systems where it was called "progressive education."

This story comes from that period: It seems that an amiable old gentleman walking in a park saw a youngster playing alone. With a smile he asked the child: "What school do you go to, little boy?" He received a terse answer: "What business is it of yours?" The old gentleman was surprised and replied, "Oh you go to a progressive school, don't you?"

As a result of sound research, we know today that a child has a variety of normal feelings which are expressed in ways which adults would call "wrong," "abnormal," "rebellious," etc. This is not necessarily so. Children are new to this world. And everything around them is new, strange, larger, forbidding, etc. They respond with fear, apprehension, self-protection, defensiveness, and other emotions which adults frequently do not understand. What they don't understand, they criticize. The child may take a spell of saying "No" to everything, may grab a forbidden cookie and run, or throw a toy impulsively, bite a sibling, hit a visitor, or exhibit other behavior that causes the adult to become angry and accuse the child of being "bad." Adult behavior (or example) may have provoked these strong expressions of emotions.

It is important for the parent to seek to understand such behavior before jumping to judge the child as being "willfully rebellious." There is a normal human need, perhaps awkwardly expressed in the small child, to be independent, to be assertive, to be strong, to be defensive, to be frustrated, and to express varying degrees of jealousy. This calls for patient understanding on the part of parents and care-takers that there is some "method in the madness" of the child. This is where intelligent discipline comes in.

Please understand, I'm not saying the parent can permit the child to do everything he pleases, when he pleases, without guidance and training. The adult must exercise control, or preferably "guidance," over the developing child without running rough shod over it. That's the reason for these two chapters on "Discipline."

In America in the last decade we have been impacted, even "traumatized" if you please, by the destructiveness of children and youth at school and on the streets - even in the desert. Everyone is getting in on the act. Government and school officials, law enforcement agencies, religious organizations, TV commentators, editors, journalists, talk show hosts, and others -- all are asking, "Why this surge of such delinquent child behavior?" Some of the more piercing questions asked, "Why do these kids not control their emotions any better?" and "Why do they have so little respect for authority?" "Why shoot to kill randomly?" **Control of angry emotions** and **respect for authority** are indeed basic, though not the only issues in this confusion. The growing child develops these traits beginning at birth and continuing through the first 5 years of life. And having the need for love adequately and appropriately supplied during this period is one of the main sources of developing these important traits. Whereas, having this need for love frustrated during this period results in lack of appropriate control of emotions and lack of respect for authority.

Of course, "lack of control" is a highly flexible term. No normal individual has perfect control over the emotions, nor should one be so "controlled," unless there are known and accepted standards for "emotional control" clearly understood by all. But no such state exists. Here is what I mean: There are some people who feel that, during grief or at a funeral, one should "control his/her emotions" and not cry. This is not necessarily healthy control of the emotions. Expression of grief by tears is desirable and usually a healthy response to the grief process. Jackie Kennedy was praised by many writers for not showing her grief when her husband was assassinated. This may have been OK for her under her circumstances, but it does not mean this is to be the proper behavior for everyone. Thus, the definition of "control" is variable.

"Respect for authority," likewise, is going to be flexible in its definition of what is acceptable behavior. Adolescents go through a period of disdain for authority during the process of becoming independent. The urge may very well be there normally, but one is expected to have the conscience so trained that one can restrain one's self from being verbally or physically destructive toward the authority. There are legal and morally acceptable ways of dealing with unfair authority figures – if indeed they are unfair.

BUYING LOVE

Usually the family that is run by children has parents who are preoccupied and negligent or who are trying to buy love. And they are usually trying to buy love because they don't understand what love is and do not have the maturity to give and receive love themselves. Such parents try to win the favor of their children by giving them everything they ask for and letting them do as they please. Typically, those parents most at fault for this are those who have divorced (and feel guilty) and trade back and forth keeping their children. I've talked with scores of them who are vying with each other for their children's favor and, in so doing, they do not discipline as they should. This results in permissive upbringing, which is disruptive to all in the family circle.

This is bad enough, but the worst of it is that children who take charge of the home, who sass their parents, talk back to, and curse their teachers usually manifest a flagrant disregard for law and order. Teens that have no respect for law and order are old enough to create havoc in a community, and more and more of them are being tried as adults for committing adult crimes and are ending up in correctional institutions. Furthermore, children reared this way at home are driving good teachers out of the classroom. And now the politicians are stumbling all over themselves talking about improving the teachers and the educational system. We have to start our improvement by starting in the home.

DISCIPLINE AND SECURITY

The way to prevent or interrupt this damaging situation is that many American children need to stop being pampered, stop being indulged, and stop being treated as if they were visiting royalty. Early on, rules must be established and limits set which are clearly understood by all. The child who knows just how far she/he can go will be better behaved, and relieved of a heavy burden and feel more secure. In short, "discipline" is the key word to solving this problem. And discipline begins with the infant. Naturally, we don't expect self-control of the infant, but as it grows older, gradually it must learn that certain impulses must be restrained and others encouraged. In fact, the child seeks to have its boundaries clearly laid out, and, when this takes place, the child knows the parent loves her/him and is interested in its welfare.

DEFINITION

DISCIPLINE NOT EQUATED WITH PUNISHMENT

Discipline is considered by many to be an unpleasant word. Somehow there are painful or distorted memories associated with it. Some people equate it with "punishment." And the two words are not synonymous. The root idea of "discipline" is "to learn" or "to teach." Webster: "Instruction: a subject that is taught: a field of study; training that corrects, molds, or perfects the mental faculties or moral character." In the rearing of children the concept of guidance or training must be emphasized. And when we approach "discipline" with this emphasis in mind, it is easier to understand. Shaping and molding mental faculties and moral character is what parents are doing with their children throughout childhood conditioning. Some parents believe they should let their children do as they please so as not to thwart them. This is incorrect. No sound psychologist or educator advocates letting children do as they please. Guidance toward certain goals is a necessary part of growing up.

Think of discipline as making corrections for staying on course. When an airplane is flying from point A to point B, a course is plotted on a map and by the compass. As the plane flies, the wind may change along the route and cause the plane to drift off course to one side or the other. Consequently, the pilot has to make a "correction" in his heading so as to arrive at point B after having been off course. Children in their behavior get off course - away from the proper heading - and corrections have to be made so as to head toward the goal. The procedure that the parent (or guardian) uses to help the child make the correction is "discipline." This helps the child later in life to have the judgment and self-control needed in order to make his or her own corrections and adjustments in living.

DISCIPLINE AS GUIDANCE

I have said that discipline is guidance, but it must be accompanied with affection. Without affection discipline is merely a show of authority, which is all right, except it is not enough by itself to give the child what it needs. At the same time effective discipline requires a good relationship between parent and child, but it also promotes a good relationship with the child. Parents need to know when and how to say, "No." They need to know how children grow and develop and why they do as they do. Parents must be consistent so that the child knows that what was permitted yesterday will also be permitted today. At the same time parents must be in touch with themselves and know when they are tired, angry, and frustrated, and be aware that tensions between mother and daddy should not spill over adversely into their relationship with the children.

Discipline is a complex subject not to be taken lightly. You may want to do further reading on the subject in order to make satisfactory decisions for discipline in your own home. The reason it is so complicated is that there are so many variables to consider. Some of them are: 1) No two children, even within the same family, are alike. 2) The section of the country where you live will be an influence. 3) The mixes of children in schools vary (by race, religion, socio-economic background), and this plays a part. 4) The age and gender of the child makes a difference.

These are reasons it is advisable for you to study this book in the company of peers where these variables can be discussed.

ISSUES AND GOALS IN DISCIPLINE

EFFECTIVE DISCIPLINE MUST BEGIN EARLY

As the child becomes older, naturally there will be other tasks equal to the child's age, and your family circumstances, which will be the challenges of the day. By five years old the child who was helpless is now transformed into one capable of climbing a ladder, shoveling snow and building a snow man, and other physical feats that may be surprising to some parents not prepared for this behavior. Furthermore, this child, having a mind of his own, is perfectly capable of resisting adult authority by hitting with his fist, calling names— even cursing (when previously exposed to it), and negatively refusing to do what he's told, whether its eating or going to bed.

Training is clearly needed before a child gets to the belligerent stage, for the period between 5 and 8 years old is the transition between early childhood and middle childhood. And the die is cast during early childhood as to whom that child will be. Thus, effective discipline must have already taken place in this period from birth to five, and, when adequately learned in childhood, the child becomes a *self-disciplined, self-confident, and self-sufficient adult.* Throughout childhood the training and guidance goes on with ever expanding tasks and responsibilities.

OBJECTIVE – ABILITY TO POSTPONE PLEASURE; GAIN SATISFACTION FROM STICKING TO DUTY

Please observe that there is a deeper objective to this childhood conditioning than simply accomplishing the routine tasks at hand whether in the toilet training or tasks around the house and about the child's room, possessions, habits, etc. The deeper objective is that the child learns responsibility and can derive pleasure from performing his/her duties. And by the same token, the child learns to postpone pleasure in order to stick to duty. In the younger years your praise and commendation as parents helps the child to feel good about his/her accomplishments. In some cases there will be rewards given; in other cases just the parental praise. But the parents can extend this praise by telling relatives and friends how the child has accomplished this or that. By talking in front of the child to a relative and telling how well the child is doing makes a favorable impression.

LOCALITY OF RESIDENCE

Earlier I said that methods of discipline would vary due to the locale of the family residence. For example, children who are reared in a sparsely settled or rural environment usually have all had the same or similar kinds of chores from early childhood. One family is living very much like the neighboring families. The children know this and thus accept that their responsibilities are like their neighbors. This is a way of life.

In the heart of the urban experience, there is a greater variety of family life and routine. Some of the mothers work outside the home; some don't. Some of the fathers are out of town a lot, or have long hours. Some spend a great deal of time working on their yards, or at ball games. Some are weekend athletes, etc. All of this variety influences what activity is shared with the family and what kinds of schedules and chores are available for the children to do. With the wide variety of backgrounds of the parents in a neighborhood, there comes a variety of expectations of the children. You parents need to consider and discuss these factors.

THE NEIGHBORHOOD

The neighborhood of residence becomes a factor in discipline. Even though small children are more flexible and adaptable than adolescents, they have a need to reasonably "fit" with their peers. There are neighborhoods which have a wide disparity of socio-economic levels or in ethnic or religion conditions. Your kids should not be held to greatly different standards than those of their close associates, either for strictness or leniency. If there is a wide disparity between what you require of your children and how their peers behave, then you should consider moving. A factor in making such a decision is the temperament of your own child and his/her feelings of being radically different. Such a situation may result in the child's feeling "left out" or "teased" for being different. Although some children can rise above this, others cannot. This implies that before a major move parents must investigate the neighborhood before buying/moving there. You cannot afford to alter greatly your own standards simply because the neighbors believe and practice differently. If there is social tension in the neighborhood, it can be stressful on the small child.

INDEPENDENCE

By the way, this is a good place to inject the idea (for children in mid-childhood) of strength to stand alone on your stable beliefs and teach your children to do the same. As a parent it may be necessary on occasion to say, "It doesn't matter to me what Sally's mother does about this, I believe so – and – so. Sometimes we have to be different because we believe differently than others, etc." There are matters of principle in behavior, whether adult or child, that are determined by your own system of right and wrong, and you can't vacillate on behavior simply because "others are doing it."

FAMILY SIZE

Families who have a large number of children (three or more) have to have a closer structure with a more rigid schedule than a family that has only one or two children. The larger family has more cleaning, more chores, more people under foot, and who need to be transported here and there than smaller families. Greater cooperation and higher respect for a time schedule is necessary in today's large family. Even a two-year-old can help with some chores, and needs to. And, however awkward it may seem to the parent, one should not take the position of, "Oh, let me do it. I can do it faster/better, etc."

Some parents are capable of dealing smoothly with many children and have enough love to extend to all of them and, thus, could be said to be a "four child" family. Other parents are capable of extending needed love only to one or two children, if any. When the number of children is greater than the parents can deal with acceptably, there will be problems with the discipline.

LIVING CONDITIONS

Living conditions today are just not conducive to families with three or more children, like they have been in the past. So, the rules and behavior expectations of the family unit must adjust to the number of people in the family, and even adjust to the size of the house where they live. Keep in mind adjustments need to be made so that there is a minimum of tension and strife among the family members and a maximum of smooth running, cooperative individuals with each carrying his/her share of the home responsibilities. Each needs to feel secure, loved, wanted, and needed; but also needs to have responsibilities that are routinely carried out. And in the midst of all of this, there must be time for the family to spend time together as a family unit from the children's earliest age up. I'm referring to eating together, going to church together, have family recreation time together. Then when the children reach adolescence and begin to go their own way with their associates, they have the background and foundation of your family tradition and mores that they need to stabilize their lives in the turmoil and turbulence of teenagers.

MALES AS DISCIPLINARIANS

Because of the male nature (larger usually, stronger voice, greater muscular strength and the like), children will basically see dad as the more dominate force in the household. Now, I say this with trepidation. But it is simply a fact of life that males have more male hormones, and these hormones determine coarser vocal cords, and greater muscular strength and aggressive traits.

Children feel this from the beginning. And little boys need to live with it.

Traditionally our culture has primarily left the subject of "punishment" up to the male. There is more than one reason for this. One is that boys are more rambunctious than girls and, thus, in need of greater control and restrictions coming from father. Since they have traditionally, in an agrarian context, been closely associated with their fathers, the fathers have controlled them. Obviously, our way of living has changed rapidly, therefore, we are more or less in confusion as to whether one parent or the other is dominant over the children, so some families will have it one way and some another. Regardless, the children need a father and a mother in the home who will train them to be emotionally healthy and prepared for their own family in the future.

Males, typically, do not hold newborns as gracefully or as often as females. The female arm is shaped to cradle a baby; her hands are usually more delicate, and her body, especially her chest, is softer, not to mention that the baby starts life suckling at her breast in many, if not most, instances. An infant in a crib can determine whether it is mother or daddy walking into the room before they can see which one it is because the walk is different. I refer to these physiological differences because such traits convey a subtle difference to the small child as to who is more dominant or perhaps can be more controlling.

PARENTAL EXAMPLE

Fundamentally, parents must set an *example*. I have alluded to the training or conditioning of animals as a source of basic principles of shaping behavior. In addition to what I said above, we have learned that an animal will learn its behavior faster when placed with other animals that already exhibit that behavior. By the same token children at the youngest age levels imitate siblings, peers, and their parents (especially their mothers; usually early they have more intimate and prolonged contact with her than with daddy, even if she works outside the home), and, as they get older, they imitate both parents.

If a mother keeps a neat house, it is easier to teach a daughter and son to do the same within their own limits for their own property. A father who speaks kindly to mother will find it easier to teach children to speak kindly to mother and not sass her. He, too, needs to set the example of cleanliness and neatness, personally and around the house, car, and garage. Both set an example of table manners from the beginning, of saying prayers, and standards of dress, and expressions of politeness, such as "Please," "Thank you," "You're welcome," etc.. And as the children get older, they will take note of other details, such as the way parents talk, the way they behave toward each other, their basic habits of life, and interaction with other people. From the beginning parents need to set an example of attendance at religious services.

LEARNING RESPONSIBILITY FOR ONE'S ACTS

In addition to heading toward certain goals, children need also to learn to be responsible for their acts. A lesson that is very important to learn early in life is that of "cause and effect." When one carries out a certain act, there will be consequences to that act. Theoretically, proper behavior leads to favorable consequences; whereas, improper behavior results in undesirable consequences. The task of parenthood is, during the early years, to convey to the child this basic lesson in life. This sounds so simple, but it requires patience, skill, and understanding to teach this to the growing child.

REWARD AND PUNISHMENT

The issue of *reward and punishment* is a tough subject because it can cover so much ground and leads into the issue of whether to spank or not. This means that within the household a system of rewards or commendations and praise should be used to reinforce required behavior. Likewise, a system of discouragement or suffering adverse consequences should be used for not minding.

Behavior modification has long been practiced with animals. Simply put, when the animal carries out the desired behavior, a reward is given. A part of this procedure is devising a way to prompt the animal to perform the desired act in the first place. When the animal diverts from the desired behavior, there is a painful or unpleasant consequence. These are said to be "conditioned reflexes." Thus, the animal learns the proper behavior and is said to be trained. If, however, these "rewards" and painful consequences are not applied regularly and consistently to the animal, the animal becomes confused and agitated, not knowing what to do. Keep this in mind.

REWARDS

When a young child puts his toys off the floor into a box or drawer, a smile, thanks, and praise from parent is the reward. It can be further emphasized by an offer to help the child move on to another fun activity. Now, when the parents desire certain behavior such as cleaning the room, taking out the trash, picking up towels, etc., as examples of early household tasks, the child may be encouraged by some form of recognition and thanks. As the child gets older, routine chores such as making the bed and "picking up" the room need no special recognition. But extra jobs can be associated with an allowance or special pay for a special job. The guiding principle here is that you are teaching the child to derive satisfaction (or even pleasure) from doing what he/she is supposed to do – and doing it consistently. And those acts vary with the advancing age of the child.

By the way children carry out household tasks early, and accomplish school work or extra curricular activities as they get older, they are developing a feeling of self-confidence and a feeling of importance. The very fact that they put forth a sincere effort and show determination, justifies your praise and satisfaction. Accomplishing their tasks also merits rewards of various sorts. What the "reward" or "pay" is depends on the age of the child and your circumstances in life. Giving the child an allowance has a lot in its favor. And there is an overriding principle in this procedure. Susan Molinari, former member of congress and now chair-person of the "Americans for Consumer Education and Competition," takes a strong position on educating children early in "Financial Literacy." Her point is well taken that in today's world survival with a fulfilling life requires good financial planning. This does not come automatically and is not a required subject in school. This training should start early at home. And a regular "income" by allowance is an excellent way to start. There are other ways parents can find to "reward" their children for a job well done. The allowance should be consistent and not used as a threat over the child's head.

If you give your child a regular allowance, establish a basis for it that is clearly understood. There needs to be regularity and consistency. But under extreme circumstances, the child could be docked, but not for minor or rare infractions. Consider this like training for a job later in society.

Some well-meaning parents cause a child to feel a sense of failure and futility because the child did not do a job to perfection enough to please the parent. When the child is doing his/her best, she/he deserves the reward of praise, commendation, and/or thanks. Maybe the parent needs to give a little help.

In many cases more tangible rewards are given, such as extra privileges, a second dessert, or permission to do something the child especially wants to do. A comic once said, "I learned very early you can get what you want in life if you just keep your room clean for a week."

CHART OR BULLETIN BOARD

Parents can have a chart on the refrigerator or on a bulletin board or in the child's room, whereon a record with stars or grade points are displayed for others to see. This can be a source of pride to have such information on display for visitors. Of course, if the child is not accomplishing the tasks, this may be a source of embarrassment. In some cases when the child is hypersensitive about others seeing his "failures," the chart can be moved temporarily to a corner out of direct sight of others. Here again is a need for parental judgment to be used wisely in handling the display of "failure" or "success" in the matter of child behavior. Severe or shocking embarrassment to the child is unwarranted. Some children can tolerate some embarrassment and profit from it by being encouraged to make improvements. Other children can't tolerate embarrassment without being completely discouraged by it. Keep in touch with your child's feelings about either too much display of success or failure regarding chores, grades, and other forms of behavior. Be alert to your child's feelings!

A 2-year-old can learn to empty the trash and pick up toys. Once our son, John (about 2), was playing in my office and accidentally turned over the wastebasket and scattered papers all over the floor. I asked him to pick it up, which he promptly did. Then I praised him lavishly and encouraged him for helping me keep the floor so clean. Promptly he turned it over again looking for this extended praise. When such lessons are learned at two, the parent can be confident of a reasonably cooperative behavior at 12.

POST SCRIPT

The following vignette is anonymous but true to form for a child who has been well guided:

"Last week I took my grandchildren to a restaurant. My six-year-old grandson asked if he could say grace. As we bowed our heads he said, 'God is good. God is great. Thank you for the food, and I would even thank you more if mom gets us ice cream for dessert. And liberty and justice for all! Amen.'"

"Along with the laughter from the other customers nearby, I heard a woman remark, 'That's what's wrong with this country. Kids today don't even know how to pray. Asking God for ice cream! Why, I never!'"

"Hearing this, my grandson burst into tears and asked me, 'Did I do it wrong? Is God mad at me?' I held him and assured him that he had done a terrific job, and God was certainly not mad at him."

"An elderly gentleman (a preacher-like person) approached the table. He winked at my grandson and said, 'I happen to know that God thought that was a great prayer.' 'Really?' my grandson asked. 'Cross my heart,' the gentleman replied.' Then in a theatrical whisper he added (indicating the woman whose remark had started this whole thing), 'Too bad she never asks God for ice cream. A little ice cream is good for the soul sometimes.'"

"Naturally, I bought the kids ice cream at the end of the meal. My grandson stared at his for a moment and then did something I will remember the rest of my life. He picked up his sundae and without a word walked over and placed it front of the woman. With a big smile he told her, 'Here this is for you. Ice cream is good for the soul sometimes, and my soul is good already.'"

QUESTIONS FOR DISCUSSION AND/OR MEDITATION

1) What is meant by "buying love?" Evaluate this.

2) Have you heard people give a short, one sentence description of their discipline procedure, such as, "I always deal with my children's misbehavior by....?" How do you evaluate such over-simplification?

3) How would you distinguish "discipline," "guidance," and "punishment?"

4) When a parent says, "I never say 'No' to my child," what do you think?

5) As you observe your neighbors and their children, how does this influence your philosophy of discipline?

6) Take note of how the adults in your house talk to each other. Are you all polite, kind, expressive?

7) What do you think about giving "rewards" to children under certain conditions?

CHAPTER 6

DISCIPLINE, Part Two: The Child's Third Right

INTRODUCTION

In March, 2005, the media were full of vivid pictures of a little defenseless 5 year old girl, being handcuffed by two burly police officers and taken into custody. There was a video tape played over and over showing the little girl having a tantrum. I've seen tantrums in many public places but, I have never seen one as raving crazy as this one. This was more than screaming, hitting, and stomping. Little Ja'eisha Scott was shown going to a shelf and sweeping items off on the floor. She raked photos off the wall. She picked things up off the floor only to smash them again. As if she were following a written list, she went from one place to another, methodically wrecking and destroying everything she could get her hands on. The administrator kept saying (as if taught by Super Nanny), "That's unacceptable." The little girl didn't appear to hear her, and if she did, she didn't know what it meant. She responded by punching the defenseless matron.

Every time I saw that tape, I wondered to myself, "Why doesn't someone swat her on the back end and shock her into reality?" Then in private moments I felt sorry for the little girl because she had obviously not been disciplined during her previous 5 years of growth. How sad that it had become necessary for someone to call the police, and that she had to be taken away in handcuffs! Of course that was extreme, but it was a tragedy that the police had to be called because no one controlled a little 5 year old girl.

Little Ja'eisha's mother, Inga Akins, betrayed the root cause of this display when she gave an explanation. Her daughter's outburst was excused by saying she didn't like the assistant principal. The mother was doing what so many parents do these days when their kids misbehave at school: excuse the behavior, blaming someone else without disciplining the child. She also threatened to sue the school. In this one case we have a macrocosm of most of our childhood behavioral and learning problems.

So, here we have fallout caused by a little 5 year old girl in an uncontrollable tantrum, creating an outrage at school for the second time, prompting school meetings on policy for uncontrollable children, and causing a disruptive investigation in the St. Petersburg Police Department,

Teachers in child care facilities, kindergartens, and schools are aware of other, similar misbehaviors that disrupt the classes, but are ignored by parents. Predominant conditions seen daily are: insolence, sassy retorts, sullen silences, eye rolling impertinence, interrupting adult conversation, destroying public school property, screaming, cursing, complaining, impoliteness, poor manners, disrespect for adult authority, and such like. What's happening anyway?

PARENTS MUST BE IN CONTROL OF THE HOUSEHOLD

A fundamental principle of any household is that parents should be in control, rather than children. Parents have control at the beginning All they have to do as the child grows older is to KEEP control. If they do it a day at a time, it is not difficult to do. One of the earliest conditioned responses that all parents have to deal with is toilet training. I'm going to describe this in some detail and draw some deductions from the process that are applicable to the wide variety of behaviors that parents endeavor to teach pre-school children.

TOILET TRAINING AS AN EXAMPLE

Dr. Edward Strecker, Head, Department of Psychiatry at the University of Pennsylvania Medical School fifty years ago, used to refer to the "Potty Culture." He meant the neighborhood talk by mothers who were bragging about how they trained their child to use the pot in a shorter time than anyone else. Such mothers, typically, put too much pressure on the small child when trying to break records.

Some parents are too eager to get the infant toilet trained and, thus, place unrealistic demands on the child, which frustrate both parent and child. At the opposite extreme there are parents who are so laid back that their distance and lack of concern are interpreted as not caring about the child. In summarizing basic principles of toilet training with the child, attitudes and procedures, which can be learned by the parents, will be applied for the next ten years or so in their discipline.

The role of the parent is to be a **guide** in conditioning a response by the child. This procedure was described in Chapter Five. I'll illustrate.

The first principle in guiding the child into a desirable form of behavior is to recognize the age and the natural abilities of the child. In the case of toilet training, traditional authorities maintain that there should be no attempts at bowel training until toward the end of the baby's first year. Some are shortening this. Training for bladder control should not start till later than that. Training that starts too early, *for that particular child*, will simply frustrate the baby and parent.

THE CHILD SETS ITS OWN SCHEDULE

It is important that parents realize that periods of activity and regression are a natural phase of healthy development. The child is not just resisting. There are many other revolutionary changes taking place in the baby's life during the second year, such as walking, talking, and dealing with the urge to explore and leave the mother's sight, but also feeling some fear at leaving. So much is happening in the developmental process that it's as if the child cannot learn everything at once.

Surely every parent realizes that regularity and consistency on the part of parent or guardian is a part of the training process *when the child is ready*. That is, the parent puts the child on the pot at the same time each day, say upon waking up or after breakfast and other meals, etc. Some studies have been made with identical twins by leaving one to its' own devices for excreting, and the other by encouragements by the parent in various, traditional forms, most notably by putting the child on the pot at specific times during the day. The conclusion was that the child sets its own time for conforming, based on the development of muscles and muscular coordination. The child's own development has more to do with the timing of its' responses than did the training itself. Putting the child on the pot is fine…when it is ready.

An interesting pattern was observed over a period of time with the twins. The children that were being trained initially showed an increase in the number of successful responses to the potty in the first weeks, then a decline in successful responses set in. Then, later they were least responsive between the ages of six months and ten or eleven months. The reason for the initial success was physiological at first, in that urination is reflexive and automatic in character. Merely handling the baby in getting ready to be put on the pot stimulated a physiological reflex and caused the infant to void. It only *appeared* that he was responding to training. And this is where some parents find cause to brag that their child has been trained earlier than another.

NO PUNISHMENT OR COERCION

Punishment and coercion are definitely out of place in the potty training at this time. In those situations where well-meaning parents have endeavored to train the child too early or to punish the child for not conforming, the child becomes anxious or frustrated, which usually delays the training that one so desires. Tenseness caused by such pressure on the part of the parent may cause the child to need to urinate much more frequently than the normal pattern, and, thus, the whole process has become counter-productive. Also, tenseness may cause constipation. No harm is done if training is delayed until the child is more mature and better able to understand what is expected of him. Remember, tension causes retention. (I should mention that periodically someone comes up with a plan to hasten this process, but I have not seen evidence yet of a successful program.)

Remember, also, when the child is in a loving atmosphere, it sincerely wishes to conform to the parents' wishes, and will usually do its best to live up to their expectations. Thus, when the child is appropriately praised when using the pot successfully, there is an infantile pride in achievement. And when this phase in training is complete, parent and child, as a partnership -- a successful team, if you please -- are ready to move on to other challenges of growing up. Coercion or punishment can cause long-term harm.

GENERAL PRINCIPLES OF DISCIPLINE

Keep in mind the two basic phases of discipline: namely, the need to reinforce good, positive behavior and the need to discourage unacceptable behavior.

Now, based on the toilet experience, we can make some deductions and observe these principles of discipline (training) and apply them to the rest of childhood.

1) A task is not prescribed until the child is mature enough emotionally and/or physically to accomplish said task.

2) The parents or others in charge, must be consistent and regular in their expectations placed on the child.

3) It is far better to encourage the child than to coerce or threaten the child to conform. Exaggerate praise and happiness when the child successfully complies with, or makes an effort to accomplish, the desired task.

4) Recognize that the child may have some failures at first, but as long as there is a trend toward improvement, accept that the child is making an effort. Any new task is usually not learned to perfection immediately -- if ever.

5) Adult standards cannot be fixed on a child. Recognize that the child does not think in logical terms as the adult. Give the child credit for its efforts even if he/she does not seem to meet adult standards.

6) Jean Piaget, called the giant of the nursery, stressed that the child does more than reflect what is presented to his senses. HIS image of reality is, in fact, a portrait or reconstruction of his *interpretation* of the world around him, not just a simple copy of it. This must be taken into consideration when imposing rules on the child. When the adult understands that the child's view of things is different from the adult interpretation, it requires **patient understanding.**

7) At the appropriate time the parent can exhibit disappointment if the child does not seem to put forth an effort to comply with parent's wishes.

8) Recognize that when a child continues to pester mother, after she has told him she has a headache and wishes to be left alone (or has some other legitimate distraction), it is because of the child's immaturity that he cannot put himself in his mother's place and understand. Children are not just small adults, they have to learn they cannot monopolize mother's or the caretaker's attention.

9) Anticipate, whenever possible, when a child is going to misbehave and what may happen and steer the child away from the potential misbehavior. It is a worthy challenge to parents to develop the skill of "distraction." Thus, you avoid the unwanted incident before it takes

place. And you also avoid just another scene of stopping the child's impulsive behavior. For example, some children always "run wild" when taken into a public place, like a restaurant or church. Don't wait till running starts. Hold or confine the child before it starts, and, as the child gets older, verbal warnings in advance should suffice.

Disapproval is given when the child does not obey and does not act responsibly, no matter what the age. This may be voiced in a number of ways. Simply saying that mother or daddy is disappointed for some children will be enough said. I've suggested above that a series of penetrating questions, calmly asked, may accomplish a great deal to help the child come to its own conclusion, that disobeying was a mistake. Calling for "time out" not only can be helpful in stopping wrongful behavior, but also help the child to calm down and let anger be assuaged.

SHOWING DISAPPROVAL

Small children do not always understand that certain behaviors are unacceptable, so this must first be clarified before administering any form of "punishment." In fact, the parent may ask, "Do you understand that is not acceptable?"

Jon Oliver, at a Boston study group, talks about *self control time*. He suggests that children stop, when angry or too excited, to do some deep breathing. This helps them control their impulses and understand that anger or rebellion need not always be acted upon. Another procedure for slowing down the emotions is to help the child make a large stop light out of construction paper. This can be hung on the child's wall or closet door. When the child has misbehaved, send him to his room to look at the red light – and *stop*. When his time is up, tell him he can look at "Go." Or give her x number of minutes, and then she can look at "Go" herself and come out.

For some it may require scolding to get the point across. In other cases it may require depriving the child of certain privileges. The parent will know the rank order of the child's fun activities and, thus, will know which one to prohibit to show disapproval. In my opinion, there are some children who just get out of hand and, consequently, must have some corporal punishment in order to calm down and learn the basic lessons of life. But this should be rare, carefully administered with love, and just enough to get the point across that you mean business. It is rare that parents feel so helpless with a pre-school child that they feel they must rely on corporal punishment, but, if they feel that way, the child can be spanked with a rolled up newspaper or given one swat with the palm of the hand to make the desired impression. Two dangers of spanking are that some parents over rely on it, and that in anger they become too rough. But keep in mind when you use corporal punishment in place of verbal correction and explanation, you may be stimulating a response on the part of the child "to get even," rather than engaging the mind to grow and learn.

A few rules of thumb in behavior control are: Don't over react; don't issue vague warnings. Depending on the age, you can give extra chores, deny TV privileges, prevent friends from coming over to visit, blend flexibility with firmness, deny privileges, stop and give breathing exercises to help regain focus and distract from the behavior at issue.

The above suggestions apply also to the misbehavior of sibling strife. Due to age, temperament, gender, physical and other differences, many children do not get along well together. This becomes an object of disciplinary concern. An entire chapter could be written on this subject. It requires unusual patience and skill on the part of parents to deal successfully with this problem. There are a number of root causes for sibling rivalry. A frequent cause is real or perceived favoritism on the part of parents. This provokes jealousy on the part of one or more of the children. If the child is older, it becomes a form of bullying the younger or weaker sibling. If the jealous one is younger, that one will subvert the older one, usually by "setting him/her up" to get in trouble. If the parents resort to spanking and one becomes the main receiver, then that one will be prone to get even by more bullying of another sibling. If a parent spends more time or money on one child than another, the one left out is prone to feel "left out" and retaliate with siblings.

The "ounce of prevention" the parents need is to nip conflict or bullying in the bud when it begins, whatever the age. This should be done by loving reason rather than by "punishments." This is an opportunity to teach the children the "How would you feel if. . ." lesson. Trading places and gaining a sense of compassion and understanding can be taught, and should be taught, at an early age. See Chapter 9, "Sensitization of Conscience" for more detail on this.

SOME CAUTIONS

First, never, ever threaten a child with a loss of love. "Love" by the parents is NOT conditioned on doing a job. Some well-meaning parents say, "Mother won't love you if you do so-and-so." Or, "If you do a good job, mother will love you." Wrong! It is imperative that children NOT feel that parental love is so fragile that it depends on their accomplishments or can be removed on a whimsy. Everything the parents do must be in a context of love. And where some form of discipline is administered, it must be followed with assurances of parental love. Discipline should not be interpreted by the child to mean the child is not loved or is being rejected by the parents. The old cliché that "this hurts me worse than it does you" has some meaning. They ARE loved because they are your children and part of the family!

Second, when the child disobeys, before issuing rash judgments, ascertain *why* the act was committed. Some children will take money from a purse, even though they know it's wrong to steal, to buy candy for a friend *in order to be popular.* The bigger issue is why does the child not feel popular? This feeling needs to be examined. It may be a symptom of a personality problem. Did he tell a wild story in order to be the center of attention? Does the child frequently get involved in bullying other younger children because there is on-going hostility? Ascertaining if the misbehavior is a slip-up or a spur of the moment mistake is one thing. But if there are underlying emotional factors which drive the child frequently to commit the same or similar unwarranted acts, this is another thing and deserves investigation and attention by the parent. Caution: restraint has to be balanced with an overall demeanor of the child's feeling a general sense of freedom.

Third, physical restraint is necessary in some cases. If a child is on the verge of activity in which he might harm himself, physical intervention becomes necessary. The child may have to have scissors taken away from her, or a child may have to be bodily removed from a counter top, etc. One form of restraint that is practiced at an early age is "time out." The child is required to go to a certain place and remain there until told he can leave. But physical restraint may be necessary to keep one's child from harming others. In the case of scuffling, it is hard to know when to intervene, but when boisterous behavior is too often or too vigorous or in the wrong locale, the contestants must be separated. The welfare of others must be considered all of one's life, and the child must learn this as early as possible and in small ways. By "physical restraint" I am NOT referring to tying or chaining a child to a chair, stool, or bed. When parents start having urges like this, they MUST seek professional help immediately.

Fourth, never lock a child in a closet or, worse, in a trunk or chest. I had an adult patient once who had acute agoraphobia. She was in her late thirties as self-confinement became so pronounced that her husband was threatening to leave her. We went through the usual behavior modification procedures with the hope it could be cured quickly, but without success. During her therapy we discovered that the first event that set her up for this fear was being shut up in the quilt box for punishment when she was about two years old. It was a death like experience in which she thought she was smothering to death. And indeed, she possibly was on the verge of that very thing. In therapy she abreacted in re-living that terrifying experience and, thereby, started on the road to recovery. The childhood punishment was cruel and too traumatic. It had become buried in her unconscious and was being replayed unconsciously in her adult life more frequently when she left her house.

Fifth, keep up with the maturing child. Parents have a tendency to lag behind the development of their children - especially with the oldest child. Here's what I mean. Parents may successfully control a child's activity at one age, for example at four. But that control may need to be relinquished or altered by the time that child is six, etc. An adolescent has privileges that a 12 year old should not have. All too frequently a parent will get fixated, say, with certain habits or treatments when the child is one age, and will continue to think of the child as that same age for the next several years. The child will resent it.

Sixth, where possible, it is good for parents in the same neighborhood or of the same class in school to meet and together determine the standards of behavior they will expect of their children within certain bounds. For example, Susan tells her mother that her friend, Margaret, is permitted to go down the street to a play ground by herself. Meanwhile, Margaret tells her mother that Susan is permitted to go to the play ground by herself. Both mothers would prefer that their daughters not do this. Each mother does not wish to go against the reported more liberal standards of the other. Of course, the simplest solution is for the mothers to contact each other. This doesn't happen very often. The kids -- even at five or six years old -- gain control by using this means of manipulation. Parents should not let this happen.

Seventh, Communicate your wishes and standards clearly. Avoid issuing vague warnings.

Eighth, there are some parents who must be cautioned about "perfectionism." They may be prone to make too many demands at too early an age on the child. Or they may be too rigid at all ages. These parents must be reminded that children are NOT capable of ADULT behavior. Reading on the subject of discipline will be helpful to parents who slip into that fault. Looking at the standards of other children of neighbors, friends, relatives, etc. may give a hint to a parent that he/she is too demanding or punitive. Parents can talk together and perhaps gain some insight. But if the child is continually unruly and flaunts the parents' guidance, seek professional help.

Ninth, generally the parents of newborns and small children are in their twenties and/or early thirties. Because their experience and training with children is limited, they may make mistakes in judgment on discipline. Ask most grandparents if they would rear their grandchildren today in the way they reared their children a generation ago, and most will say, "No." The point is that young people will make more snap, dogmatic, or less well-thought-out decisions than those same people would when they become more mature. Therefore, caution is needed at this age.

Tenth, both parents need to have frequent talks with each other privately on the subject of what they expect of their children so that each one will require the same behavior of the child. For example, the child needs to know what time to be in after school and that both mother and father will hold to that requirement. For week-end sleep overs, parents need to know who their associates will be for unusual, non routine activities, etc., mother and father must agree. If among themselves parents have major disagreements on the child's behavior, they must seek counseling from a neutral source and come to a compromise of some kind. The child absolutely must have consistency between the parents for their rules and regulations. An exception to this would be where the child is made privy to a difference between the parents, and the child is appraised of the difference, and then all three work out a compromise. This is not only resolving the issue at hand, but, also it is teaching the child indirectly an important procedure in problem solving.

Eleventh, parents must be cautious in making rash "punishments" during the heat of anger on the spur of the moment. I know of parents who have caught the child in some gross disobedience and rashly said, 'You can't go back to grandma's house for 6 months" (or such-like). Then, after cooling off, realize that period includes special holidays when the whole family would be affected. When the parent realizes such a mistake, an apology to the child is called for. If the parent cannot bring himself to make such an apology, the child will be resentful or "provoked to wrath," which is damaging to the relationship. Or, in other situations, the child will recognize that the parent has gone back on his/her word and changed the "punishment" without explanation. This inconsistency is harmful. If painful decisions are needed, they should be prompt and thought out. It isn't fair to the child to postpone a decision to discipline, unless a reason is given, such as having a conference with the other parent. It is easier for a child to accept a hard decision if it is given promptly. Any "punishment" to be fair and effective, must be the logical outcome of the child's act, or be the outcome of the parents' warning and commitment, known in advance.

Twelfth, in the case of step-parents, the age of the children involved will determine how this relationship is handled. But if the children are old enough to be reasoned with (four or older), before second marriages the children need to be talked with a great deal; help them to understand your point of view, and you come to an understanding of their point of view. When a home is broken because of death or divorce, it is traumatic to the children. In most cases of divorce the children harbor deep guilt, resentment, anger, frustration, bitterness, and other negative emotions. And they are hesitant or afraid to express these feelings. It is very important that these emotions be dealt with. Usually professional counseling is advisable. It is highly desirable that the step-parent be gradually introduced to the children over a period of time during courtship, and that good rapport be achieved prior to marriage. This is not always easy. But the children's feelings must be considered and dealt with gently.

Thirteenth, authorities say specific restrictions should be as few as possible, enforceable, and consistently observed. When, on the other hand, the child is brought up on too much self-expression, he is likely to be a pest at best and a hoodlum at worst. Such loose child care has turned mothers and dads and teachers into nervous wrecks, and the child into a major national problem. To

"Never say, 'No,'" is being unkind to the child. However, the opposite extreme is for parents to issue forth with too many "No's" and "Don't's." An over-abundance of negative suggestions and warnings has the opposite effect from what the parent intends. Example: "You're a poor reader. Why can't you do better?" will surely make the child do worse. It's the same with other negative suggestions. "You never do pick up your room. What's the matter with you?" "You always leave your toys out." etc. The child lives up to these negative expectations.

Fourteenth, do not burden the child with recriminations, which "brand" the child inwardly. Judgmental epithets such as "You are a big boy, and big boys aren't afraid," "Only babies are afraid," "Don't be a sissy," "You little devil," "Daddy won't love you if. . ." etc. Also, do not call the child names.

Fifteenth, please note that there is a difference in helping a child to feel satisfaction for doing a good job and *bribing* a child to do a good job. A bribe is set by a remark like this, "If you clean your room before school, I'll give you money for ice cream after school." First, cleaning the room would be a standard requirement, a routine job. It has its own reward built in. Note the word "if." The parent is setting her/himself up for failure on occasion because, if the child wants to rebel or isn't in the mood for ice cream that day, then he feels he doesn't need to obey. In this situation if the parent needs the room clean before the child leaves for school, then give a kind request in plenty of advance time. There should be a good enough relationship with the child that s/he will comply gladly. Gratitude can be expressed afterwards. When the relationship is thus cemented, similar requests can be followed with extra expressions, favors, activities, etc.

Sixteenth, giving limited choices gives the child a sense of freedom within your own control. For example, when he is getting dressed, say, "Do you want to wear long pants or short pants today?" Give the child a choice of what to wear. Then he must live with the consequences of his choice. This is not the time for the child to make one choice and then the other at a whimsy. A kind response can be, "Sweetheart, if you don't decide, then I will decide for you." It's over. That's it. Small children can learn this very vital lesson. Children respect a sense of structure, which you're building kindly but firmly. You have to mean what you say and say what you mean.

SUMMARY AND CONCLUSION

Discipline is a form of guidance which will enable children to live a more satisfying and fulfilling life. It gives them confidence and security and is a great factor in their ability to live a productive life in society. Furthermore, inappropriate behavior during the adolescent years is largely prevented by proper training early. If children are not taught these lessons by 6 years old, their moral judgment will be damaged forever.

When children complain of having to face the consequences of their actions, remind them that all of us have to do something every day that we do not want to do. This is life. And the sooner we learn this lesson the better off we will be, and the more comfortable we will be in our total life experiences. This lesson is primarily learned from disciplinary procedures for disobedience, but it is also learned from the discipline of work and carrying out one's responsibilities and doing them on time. And on this subject, when children ask "Why?" they have to do a chore or some other responsible task, there are times when the parent should give an explanation in answer to the question. But do not feel you have to explain every time. Many times I told our children, "I have to do something every day that I don't want to do. You can learn that, too." At times the parent may have to respond, "You do that because I say to."

During the first 12 months remember that the child is exploring a new world. This means that delicate bric-a-brac, like harmful objects, should not be left within that child's reach, and it is too young to understand that it is not to touch it.

Two-year-olds are capable of understanding basic reasoning; so use it. "When climbing, one can fall." "When you hit your friend, it can hurt."

Three-year-olds, by virtue of better communication skills, are capable of understanding more reasoning. Since they are more gregarious than earlier, they respond verbally to your requests and reproofs. For example, "Toys are to play with rather than to hit with."

Four-year-olds can understand simple rules about taking turns, trading toys, being quiet when taking a rest, etc.

THE ISSUE OF WHETHER TO SPANK OR NOT

This subject continues to be unsettled among authorities on child rearing, and it is because it is so complex. One cannot give a yes or no answer that applies to everyone because of this. Dr. Dennis Lowe, of the Center for the Family at Pepperdine University, in summarizing late research on this, lists these issues for parental consideration. In brief, he states:

1) What is the general philosophy of discipline and control management by the parents in the first place? This refers to how rigid and exact do the parents look at control; whether the parents were spanked as children themselves will influence this overall view of corporal punishment.

2) What does it mean, "to spank"? There are many different procedures of applying corporal or physical discipline to the child, from the very mild, such as a tweak on the ear or spanking with a rolled up newspaper, where there is no actual discomfort involved, to the extreme of beating with a cane and the like, which inflicts pain and bruises or even bleeding and bodily injury.

3) What are other criteria for effective parenting? This refers to other procedures that the parents may have at their disposal to help in control of the child, for example, using "time out" or deprivation of privileges, etc. in place of spanking. It is easier to control the pre-school child, and when the pre-schooler is obedient and compliant happily, that child will be easier to manage in adolescence.

4) What does social research recommend on this subject? Unfortunately there is not a wealth of empirical research on this subject. There are some articles and sections in books, but little scientific investigation. Besides, some authorities say that once a parent's mind is made up, for whatever reasons, research is not likely to be effective in influencing that person. And I agree.

5) Lowe cites one authority, Oosterhuis, who, like others, refers to Biblical passages as a possible source of guidance, but, like many, not being a Biblical scholar, she is not prepared to give definite interpretations.

MY PERSONAL OPINION ON SPANKING

Many counselors and parents cite passages from the Old Testament to justify spanking, but such justifications for today are not legitimate. The decision on whether or not to spank should not be made on the basis of what one has read in the Old Testament. I have written at length on the subject of "The Bible and

Child Discipline," and this appears in the Appendix, if you are interested.

In my own opinion, there is not a dogmatic answer, "Yes" or "No," to this profound question. Most parents who have reared both boys and girls in their family have observed that boys are harder to control during the childhood period than girls. Thus, some parents will feel a greater need to exercise a firmer control over boys than with girls. The parents are going to have to make that decision for themselves, considering the peculiarities of their own circumstances. A strong-willed boy can get out of control as a small child, and this will usually indicate more severe trouble as he gets older. In other words, such a child needs understanding and highly skilled disciplinary procedures, and for some in this category that means controlled spanking.

It is not in the child's best interest for him to be out of control. Children cannot be reared without control to some degree or another. The most desirable situation in the home is that the parents are so skilled in control that they induce the child to mind, and that the child grows up obeying the parents without any form of corporal punishment. I believe it can and should be done this way. If some form of corporal punishment is necessary for the child to learn to mind reasonable parents, then it should be carefully administered. But the parent should devise a list of other disciplinary tactics to use before relying on corporal punishment. However, it must be said that the *parents' standards of behavior are reasonable and appropriate and within the bounds of standard parental expectations.*

Fifty years ago I felt occasionally that I needed to spank our boys (not our daughter). As I look back on it, it wouldn't have been necessary. I was spanked in childhood. My father was spanked. And my grandfather was physically abused by his father who hit him with his fists. And that man was in the Civil War as a teenager and was acquainted with strict rule by corporal punishment. I say this to illustrate the principle that corporal punishment is usually passed from one generation to another. On my mother's side, she was reared as the oldest with three brothers. Her parents were weak emotionally and physically and did not control her brothers. None of those boys was able to create a stable home and marriage. I am glad to say that one of my sons used no corporal punishment, another used very little (having four girls), and my daughter (and her husband) have used none with their children.

A leading opponent against spanking is Jordan Riak, who lives in the

California Bay area. Riak, who is a retired arts instructor, has battled the practice of spanking from Australia to America, especially in the schools. He doesn't mince words and asserts that spanking is an assault on a helpless person, and that it should be a crime. He wrote the 1987 law against corporal punishment in California schools and continues to campaign against any form of corporal punishment. Personally, I feel he overstates the case when he says spanking is like slavery, child labor, and wife beating, because some forms of corporal punishment are not brutal and help some children to learn self-control and respect for authority. If you desire to contact Riak, he is at *(www. nospank.org)*. A swat on the backside with an open hand serves to get attention and is not "brutal," nor is it "violent." I've seen it stop hysterics in a small child.

In case you're interested in what your neighbors think about it, 90% of parents admit to spanking their children. Before 1968, 94% of parents considered a "good spanking" a necessity. While 85% say they would rather not, but resort to it when all else fails, according to a 1998 study in the journal *Pediatrics*. Furthermore, researchers report that in one-quarter of all middle-class, two-parent homes children are spanked weekly. It is also reported that for most families spanking is neither routine nor abusive and that it should be limited to certain conditions -- to punish persistent defiance or deliberate acts of willful disobedience by children old enough to know better.

In my personal opinion, those children "old enough to know better" were probably NOT shown proper Acce*ptance, Love,* and *healthy Discipline* sufficiently in the early years to gain a respectful, loving relationship with the parents. And because of this poor start in life, they exhibited their frustration by "defiance and deliberate acts of willful disobedience." In other words, they had already gotten "out of hand." Furthermore, I personally believe it is not the *act* of spanking, but *reliance* on spanking as a substitute for reasonable communication, that is what we ought to fear. When all is said and done, if, or when, a child persists in potentially dangerous behavior toward himself, a spank will be necessary to get the point across. Such behavior would include playing with scissors, running in the street, playing in the car alone, playing around lawnmowers, machinery, and the like.

AN ABHORRENT CASE OF INCONSISTENCY AND ABUSE

A few years ago in Rockwood, Michigan, police, acting on a tip, entered the suburban home of Donald Coffman, 32, and his wife, Marilyn, 31. They found a frail little girl, Debbie, 11 years old, tied to her bed in the basement. She was the oldest of 6 children and had been treated like an animal for at least four years. Judge Douglas W. Craig stated such a case was "unbelievable." Debbie had subsisted on a small bowl of dry cereal each day and was forced to use the back yard for a lavatory. Also, she was forced to stay outside in the cold while her five brothers and sisters went to bed. Police said the brothers and sisters (aged 2 to 9) were allowed to play upstairs while she was tied so tightly to her bed that the ropes had to be cut off of her when the police entered.

It was determined that the girl, years earlier, had been an all-A student in school, having above average intelligence. Authorities speculated that her parents could not cope with her intelligence; so they used force rather than understanding. Neighbors reported that Debbie had been sent into the backyard each night after her brothers and sisters went to bed and made to stay there until late. "The little kid would crouch by the door whimpering with cold," one neighbor said.

Police reported that, although the Coffmans lavished love and affection on their other children, school authorities complained that Debbie was always dirty and poorly clad. Each day she was forced to walk three miles to and from school, crossing a busy intersection and railroad tracks, while her brothers and sisters rode a bus. One relative told police Debbie was once punished by being forced to sit in a tub of scalding hot water until she fainted.

Mr. Coffman's brother, Troy, said that after the deaths of two younger children the treatment of Debbie gradually changed for the worse. Mrs. Coffman's only explanation about Debbie's treatment was, "She was different."

And where were the neighbors who obviously observed much of this mistreatment? And the teachers? And the relatives? "They didn't want to cause trouble in the family by reporting it," a relative said. The parents were charged with "child-torture." It's also obvious they had too many children for their capabilities.

I wonder what it is about scalding water that appeals to some warped parents as a means of discipline. I recall a case where a mother held her small boy in a tub with scalding hot water pouring in on his genitals as punishment. It is likely she had some inner hostility against the male genitalia for some real or imagined harm she suffered from some man.

It was reported on NBC "Dateline," April 17, 2000, the case of child abuse and punishment in which a child was starved to such an extent she ate crayons and garbage at school. She appeared at school with bloody fingers, and upon investigation it was discovered that her fingernails had been pulled out. The teacher reported this, but a Social Worker did nothing. Obviously, this child wasn't wanted by her parents.

ARE YOU A PERFECTIONIST ?

Most perfectionists share these characteristics. It is not so much a case as to the value of these points per se, as it is the degree to which one is made uncomfortable by them and dedicated to enforcing them on others, as to whether any or all of these traits are desirable:

1) Place excessive demands on themselves;

2) Become obsessed about the details of a task even though it may not be that important;

3) Have a mental list of things they should be doing;

4) Become upset with themselves if they make mistakes;

5) Believe they are never doing enough;

6) Become annoyed when others don't act or behave as well as they do;

7) Notice imperfections in themselves or others rather than the positive qualities;

8) Are overly organized in one or more areas of their lives; or

9) Have difficulty making decisions.

Caution: Perfectionists usually are overly strict on their children, and this tends to create anxious adults.

QUESTIONS FOR MEDITATION AND/OR DISCUSSION

1) How were you disciplined in your childhood? How would you have changed it? How were your friends disciplined?

2) Do you know how your parents or grand parents were disciplined? Has there been a family pattern of discipline? Has there been a reaction

between two generations of your family in discipline?

3) What was your position in birth order among your siblings? Was there a difference in the way you were treated as compared with your siblings? Or, if you were an only child, how were you disciplined?

4) Did you have trouble when you went away to college or got married keeping your room clean? Getting lessons? Being on time?

5) Has an employer ever complained to you that you are too often late to work or late with an assignment?

6) Examine and review your relationship with your own children. Have there been occasions where you have been too demanding? Too lenient? How do your children feel about your disciplinary methods?

7) What do you know about the disciplinary methods of your friends or relatives? Have you discussed it with them?

GAME POINT

If you gain loving control of your children from the beginning, your problems with discipline will be minor.

CHAPTER 7

APPROVAL REPEATEDLY, The Child's Fourth Right

DEVELOPING AND STRENGTHENING THE EGO

One of our missionaries in Germany a few years ago sent this message back in reporting a funeral he had recently conducted. "The second of January began with a horrible calamity for a Munich family. In their apartment the father discovered their only son, 17 years old, poisoned with gas. It was suicide. The suicide note named the reason as being 'sick of life, lonesomeness, not being understood, and loss of hope.' From a 17 year old boy! The father was sent to me from the city burial institute, because no clergyman of the state churches was willing to conduct the funeral. . .

"The father cried by me. He saw his guilt greatly. He had striven for position and knowledge, and had no time for his son. Now it is too late. He can never forget the boy's arms folded under his head, lying on his side. He had to witness his stiff body being placed in a large box and transported to the judicial inquiry. How unimportant the amount of the monthly income becomes; how unimportant the comforts of the apartment; how insignificant whatever position he had reached! How important the time he had previously not had -- did not want to have. Now, he would have plenty of time. He conceded, too, that it would go differently. 'How foolish I was,' he said to me, with tears in his eyes."

That boy's ego was dead inside; so all he did was to conform to his inner feeling by taking his physical life. Not only was he rejected in life, "lonesome, not understood, etc.," but he was even rejected in death. How tragic for one of God's children! E. Kent Hayes, of the Menninger Clinic, reports that suicide is the second leading cause of death among young people; an average of 18 youths between the ages of 15 and 24 kill themselves *each day*. "One suicide can lead to an epidemic if not properly handled by parents, schools, and other community agencies," he reported.

THE EGO

An innate desire of all of us is the desire "to be somebody." This means different things to different people, but the fundamental thought is that the inner person, or "ego," needs strength to survive. The people in despair who say, "I'm a nobody," usually mean they do not consider they have worth as a human. They feel they have no talent or ability to take a place in society. They usually mean that others look down on them as being without value as a human being. No one wants them whether to love, respect, to work, or be able to contribute anything to society. A "nobody" is a shell of a human having flesh and bones but nothing inside. Technically, we sometimes refer to a person who feels like this as being in an "Existential Vacuum" or being dead internally. A few are glibly diagnosed (incorrectly) by some as being "depressed."

Usually when people have this problem seriously for very long, they commit suicide. They say they have nothing to live for, or "What's the use of living anyway?" If they don't take their own life, they act as if they are partly dead -- and they are. Such people usually dress in dark clothing, are inexpressive, retiring, gloomy, and negative in their thinking. Their vocabulary includes words of death or despair in a pessimistic setting and negative attitude. Their body language is "cowed," head down, retiring, slovenly. Frequently they are struggling to survive and don't know it. They are walking zombies.

It's tragic to see a person in this state. There are a variety of different possible causes for this condition, and I am not going into them now, but the child who never receives approval will tend toward this condition. If there are other deficiencies in their rearing at home, and a child doesn't get approval, s/he will slip into this condition. A basic need that all children have is to be approved of -- all their lives. It's most unfortunate if a parent says, "My child doesn't do anything to be approved of, so how can I show approval?" Then that parent is admitting, in a sense, that s/he has not been able to be a successful parent to this point.

All too often children no longer feel they make a vital contribution to the family -- or to anything. Children in those circumstances mostly are the ones who give up and say, "What's the use?" If parents don't give them home tasks or insist that they perform those home tasks, where does the child learn self-confidence? Perhaps he learns in school. But that is not necessarily so with that type of personality. Mediocre school performance simply reinforces the feeling of uselessness, and the child sinks deeper into self-criticism, which often leads to self-destruction in mind or body.

IF YOU APPROVE, THE CHILD WILL IMPROVE

Too many parents have so much to say that they become fault finding too easily. Well-meaning parents can slip into this as a habit and not realize what they are doing. For example, dad says to five year old son, "You left your toys outside again. They could get stolen or it might rain. I've told you a thousand times to put up your toys at the end of the day." This is pretty blatant as a fault finding routine. But the same feeling can be engendered to the boy by saying, "I see your toys were left outside again today, just like yesterday. You always leave your toys out." A father who makes the statement this way appears to sound softer, but he is still criticizing instead of approving. And the effect on the boy will basically be the same, namely, "I can't ever please dad. I never do it right," etc. So, the boy gives up, and he leaves his toys out again the next day. He feels: "What's the use?"

LIFE BECOMES FUTILE

Picture his mother who, the same afternoon, reminds the boy that his room is still dirty. "You can't keep a clean room. Its always filthy...," etc. This may be just two admonitions from the parents, in the same day, of rather insignificant infractions. But in many homes there are other admonitions about the various conditions of the child's life, and soon the week is nothing but a series of "failures." And if this continues very long, the child will develop a sense of futility. Depending on the child's age, some means of defense will be found to escape these negative criticisms, like running away, trying drugs, acting out at school or among friends, etc. Note that both the father's and mother's criticisms included the word "always." This popular mistake should be understood as if it were a command to "continue *always* to do the undesirable action."

These, and other parents like them, have good intentions. They want to rear their children to be responsible adults. And some of these parents will be reasonably successful. But for the most part they are not doing their best for the child. For example, in the above situation the dad could simply say, "Did you play outside today?" This might be enough to remind the boy that he did not put his toys away, so he goes to bring them in. Then dad could praise him for acting responsibly, and tell him that one day he will have a bike to take care of.

That same mother could say just enough to bring up the subject of his room to the boy by some such statement as, "Have you been in your room since you got home from kindergarten?" This is non critical and non judgmental, but it brings up the subject, and the boy, provided he has been taught before, will know what to do. Later, mother can brag on him. This is approval.

An alternate way of dealing with the toy situation or similar circumstances where the child's behavior doesn't quickly change, is for the dad to say nothing after repeated conversations on the subject. He simply, quietly gathers up the toys and locks them in a closet until the boy talks to dad about it, and they have a gentleman's agreement that dad unlocks the toys when the boy is sure he has learned he will put them away properly. Then when this begins to happen, giving praise and commendations for taking good care of his toys earns the boy privileges he desires.

ENCOURAGMENT

If the problem of the room is worse and/or of long-standing, mother can say, "When can we straighten up your room?" By offering her help, it can be a shared experience, after which she can give him praise and mention the blessings of having a room that is neat. At the same time she is showing him what she means by a "clean room." Some such blessings may be having the clean clothes he wants at a certain time, finding the things he needs more easily, and being proud if a friend comes in. Again, talking it up is the way to go.

Speaking of a child's room, it is important for children to have their own space. Usually this would be the child's room -- even if it is shared with a sibling. Each can have his/her own desk or CD player. Help the child have pride in having his own spot. A desk doesn't have to be bought. A simple desk is easy to make. This is a task which a parent can share with the child. Once approval is given, it can be reinforced with giving permission for favorite activities.

I have referred previously to the impact of "Negative Suggestions." When parents focus on what is wrong, the child will focus on what is wrong and be inevitably drawn to act that way. When I was a beginner learning to ride a bike, I was on a sidewalk, and a neighbor woman by-stander warned me, "Don't hit that lady on the walk." In spite of the fact I had plenty of room, I hit the lady. Fortunately, I wasn't going very fast, and she was not hurt. My pride was what was hurt. The neighbor woman should have focused on the positive by saying, "You've got plenty of room to go around on the grass." I would have seen it that way. Focus on the positive. Focus on strengths.

VARIATION IN THE KIND OF PRAISE

It is not advisable to give equal praise for everything. The varying degrees of praise depend on the child's age. For example, for the young child lavish praise is usually OK for most of the tasks achieved. But for the older child the simple task deserves acknowledgment, whereas, the complicated or prolonged activities would deserve higher commendation. The child will see the difference in praise levels according to the tasks achieved. The child will realize that one does not achieve a great deal of recognition for performing a routine, simple, daily task each time it is done. He doesn't expect to. But, occasionally, recognition for repeatedly performing a task is certainly justified. Then when a difficult task is performed, lavish praise is in order. It is good for the child to see the parents thank each other for various deeds done for each other or for the household.

Dr. Haim G. Ginott reviews the goals of such praise and commendation. They are to build confidence in the child, increase security, stimulate initiative, motivate learning, generate good will, and improve human relations. But he also points out that we still don't have enough children who have accomplished all of these fine goals. It will help parents to understand a little more about what wholesome praise is and what it can accomplish.

ELEMENTS OF PRAISE

First, praise is not flattery. Generally, "flattery" is insincere, and this is felt by the receiver. So, it doesn't do good anyway. Considering the age and capability of the child, praise must be sincere. When it is a sincere, positive evaluation of the accomplishment by the parent, it is encouraging and provides a strong motivation for the child to try harder and to continue.

Strangely, however, some praise may not have the desired effects on the child, rather the opposite, from what the parent expects. For some children praise may cause discomfort, anxiety, guilt, or even misbehavior. Just as an adult may not be able to accept a compliment graciously, so a child or adolescent may be hypersensitive and feel ill at ease when praised. For example, a boy is told he has done a good job, and this may inspire him to keep on doing a good job or even improve. Another boy, doing a similar task and being praised for it, may deny that he has done anything good or praise-worthy. Some girls, if told they are pretty, will blush and deny it in spite of the fact that most girls wish to be pretty. Those children who can't handle praise are put on the defensive and have not learned to take a compliment graciously by simply saying, "Thank you."

A part of the problem with those children who can't handle praise comfortably is that they are frightened or anxious in the situation. A part of this situation is due to the fine points of detail regarding HOW the commendation is expressed by the parent or adult. Remember, I stated earlier in the context of "discipline" that the parent could focus on the **deed** which has been done, rather than the **person** who did it. For example, a small boy makes a Valentine's card for his mother. His mother "ooh's and aah's" over it and tells the little boy enthusiastically that he always does such a great job making cards; he's a natural born artist; he knows his colors, etc. The child then grabs the card, tears it up, and says, "No, I'm not," and stomps out of the room. Mother is stunned, wondering what she said wrong. The boy spent a long time working on the card, trying several plans and discarding them. He had a hard time choosing his final colors and what his design would be. Now, his mother tells him he's an expert and a "natural born artist." The boy feels that a "natural born artist" would not have had the trouble he had making the card.

The preferred nuance would be for mother to compliment that **card**, its color pattern, etc., rather than telling the child what a great talent he has. The boy worked so hard; he probably wished he had talent and could accomplish his task quickly. This seems like a pointless detail, perhaps, but children often build on details and their own interpretation of details. Remember, I have already said in another context that children reason differently from adults. In any given situation the child will see the situation and interpret it through the mind of a 4 year old or 6 year old, and that interpretation will be different from the adult's. Therefore, the parent needs to be alert to the child's temperament and respond accordingly.

APPROPRIATE AND INAPPROPRIATE EXPECTATIONS

The parent who says, "You are always so neat. You are always so good," etc., causes some children to feel they are expected always to be perfect, and they know they can't do that. It is too formidable a task that the parent appears to be putting on the shoulders of such a child. So the parent needs to be sensitive as to HOW the approval or praise is given. And the way to do this is to be alert to the child's responses. Can the child receive your praise gracefully, or does the child become upset and deny the very thing you are commending?

Praise that evaluates *the personality* or *character* is unsafe, uncertain, and perhaps unpleasant for some types. Praise that describes *efforts, accomplishments,* and *feelings* is helpful, encouraging, and safe. An appropriate example will be helpful: Suppose a 5 year-old boy is asked by his dad to clean up the yard and prepare it for guests for a cook-out. So the boy spends several afternoons working diligently on the yard; he rakes leaves, picks up sticks and toys, and flower beds are cleaned. Before the cook-out the father, being greatly impressed by what the boy has done, says, "The yard is great. It looks like a garden out here." The boy says, "It does?" Father continues, "It's a pleasure to look at it, the grass, garden and all..." The boy tersely says, "Really?" Father says, "It's the best looking yard on the street."

Note how the father *described the yard* and specified details that pleased him. He dealt with the **task** and not the boy. He described his feelings about the yard -- now the yard, being an extension of the boy, was the means by which the boy received his own self-gratification. This was a successful venture for him because what he did was successful. His dad did not evaluate the boy's character. He evaluated the yard. Give a realistic picture of the *accomplishment* rather than glorifying the person.

CHILDREN INTERPRET WORDS OF PRAISE

You see, there are two parts to this, approval and encouragement. One is the *words* of the parent, and the other is the *child's conclusion* about the situation. The child's *interpretation* of the parent's observation of the task is what he can handle on his own. He will not over-burden himself or conclude with excessive demands on himself when it is only the task or efforts or achievement of the moment, which the parent has commented about. The parent makes statements of praise about the (non personal) task, and the child draws his own conclusions about himself personally. His own inferences will be positive and constructive when the parent makes statements that are realistic and sympathetic. The boy's ultimate conclusion, partly conscious and partly unconscious, is "I am liked. I am appreciated. I am respected. I am capable. I'm somebody." And that's exactly what the parent or the teacher is trying to achieve.

The above principle needs to be emphasized. With every event there is the person's *response* or *reaction* to that event, and that usually determines the outcome. Disappointing -- even painful -- events happen to people all the time. One person can see it as a challenge and look on the bright side and profit from a catastrophe. Another person, involved in the same event, may see it from a negative point of view and be defeated by it. The event, plus your response, determines the outcome.

When I was about 10 years old, after gradually working up to this, I got the job of mopping the kitchen floor about once a week. Mother bragged on me to dad when he came home. She told visitors and relatives in front of me how the floor was cleaner than it had ever been, even than when the maid did it. Of course, I worked harder to get it cleaner and keep up the record. I got a sense of accomplishment and pride at my skill (?) each time I mopped. I was more impressed with how good I was than how hard the work was. Maybe it's a wonder I didn't turn out to be a house cleaning specialist. The focus from mother was on the accomplishment of an extra clean floor.

APPROVING THE PERSON

Now comes the difficult part of "How to give approval." There is also a place for approving or praising the person of the child. If the child is not getting the message intended by praising a task well done, and, thereby, becoming self-confident, the parent must take another step, that is seeing that the praise for the job is so accepted by the child that the child grows. It is inadequate for the child to conclude that, "My parents love me because I make good grades." Or, "My parents love me because I did a good job cleaning the yard." If the child draws such a conclusion, then he or she may push his-herself unmercifully to keep doing better and better in order to be loved. Such a system leads the child to equate self-worth with the accomplishment of tasks. This is *not* to be desired as a result of "approval."

Can you see the type personality of the child who would fail to feel that the parent loved him, in spite of the fact the parent is giving repeated approval? It is because, *for that child*, there has not been enough of a base or foundation of love laid early enough. The child just described, who can't interpret that his parents love him, is one who has not received enough love early enough in life. This is the reason I say you have to evaluate your child as to how he/she receives praise.

Praise and approval should be honest, even though at times exaggerated a bit. Certainly a parent does not want to call the child a super star athlete when the child knows in her heart she has a hard time holding the ball. But the parent can find something for which honestly to praise her efforts. Start with the preschool child and continue with the older child.

For those who may have to hunt for something to complement the child about, look carefully into all phases of the child's life. There are many school activities, both curricular and extracurricular, that you can explore. Talk to your child about what is going on at school. By finding something good to say, you are also encouraging communication with the child, which is good. Consider music as an area where you can find an excuse for praise. What about church activity, Scouts, or other child group activity which may be available? Encourage the child to participate in some activity that he/she has never tried before. This may include dance exercises at nursery school, hobbies, crafts, etc. There are many sources of participation for your child where encouragement may be needed, but it will also be valuable as a source for your child to learn confidence and build a variety of interests.

Another suggestion: Encourage your child to articulate his/her own desires for accomplishment. "Have you seen something your friends do that you want to try?" Also, encourage your child to lead into an activity of interest. Then encourage, or provide encouragement or instruction. Be responsive to your child's needs, wants, requests. Then respond with, "That's a good idea." Friendly guidance promotes self-esteem. The confident child learns he can positively affect others.

CAUTIONS: LEARNING BY LOVE IN PLACE OF FEAR

Keep my over-all message straight. Every child has his or her own individual nervous system and personality. That personality will effect how he or she receives your words of praise and commendation. The child who got a good foundation of love and acceptance will blossom more when approved of repeatedly, and the details of how you do it will not matter so very much. If the child at an earlier age has become a little insecure or anxious, you will have to be careful how you phrase your praise. Evaluate how your words of praise affect the child and alter your procedure or points of emphasis, if it is necessary to achieve your desired goal.

Parents should never take their wrath out on a child. So, they need to get enough rest and relaxation to maintain a good humor around the children. They need to be enough in touch with themselves that they are aware when they have had an unusual amount of adult stress, or are fatigued, or had quarrels among themselves.

Obviously, the opposite of "approval" is criticism and negative approval. The day must NOT be filled with "Don'ts." The first grader who is told, "You can't spell." will not be able to spell. The child who is criticized by evaluations about appearance will live up to the criticisms, such as "You're awkward," "You're shy," etc.. If the child does not overcome the weakness of poor spelling or reading or being awkward by loving attendance, it will surely not overcome those factors by negative criticism.

The children who are starved for words of approval will unconsciously seek out some way to get approval from some source. This is where adults must be alert. The pre-school child will seek attention by acting out with boisterous, even aggressive behavior. Older children follow a different course. They are the ones who take guns to school and shoot class-mates. Such action gives them a feeling or importance or control. They have never felt important to anybody. They felt rejected at home and act out at school. The rejects at school band together. They find one another because they have this common ground. They dress differently. By their own code, their tattoos, jewelry, skin penetration, hair styles and color set them apart. Yes, they are different. In neighborhoods where the kids are turned loose on the streets to grow up on their own, with no legitimate accomplishments of any kind, they form their own clubs, gangs and do their own thing. They have found acceptance by their peers. They will accomplish something, but it will be in gang wars, shootings, or belligerent attacks on those who have looked down on them. They are all hungry to accomplish something for which they can be proud -- even if it is in a distorted way; they are seeking to "be somebody."

SIBLINGS SHOULD NOT BE COMPARED WITH EACH OTHER

Some well intentioned parents will compare one sibling unfavorably to another in an effort to motivate a child to improve. When siblings are compared in such a way that one is set up as an example to another, rarely, if ever, does this produce the desired effect. The lesser child is bound to feel discouraged with hopelessness and may say, "She always does everything right and they don't care when I try."

If a parent feels constrained to refer to a child's short-comings, focus on that child alone. Don't compare that one to another child whether sibling or an acquaintance. Now, children will inevitably compare themselves with each other. OK, but don't you parents get caught up in this kind of situation. If one of your children has a weakness or fault, work to strengthen that weakness between the two of you without comparisons. And, at the same time, find some trait, habit, or attitude to compliment as a strong point by way of compensation for that child. Your goal is for the siblings to accept themselves and each other with confidence.

POST SCRIPT

A LITTLE PARABLE FOR MOTHERS (AUTHOR UNKNOWN)

The young mother set her foot on the path of life. "Is the way long?" she asked. And her guide said, "Yes. And the way is hard. And you will be old before you reach the end of it. But the end will be better than the beginning."

But the young mother was happy, and she would not believe that anything could be better than these years. So she played with her children, and gathered flowers for them along the way, and bathed with them in the clear streams; the sun shone on them, and life was good, and the young mother cried, "Nothing will ever be lovelier than this."

Then night came, and a storm, and the path was dark, and the children shook with fear and cold, and the mother drew them close and covered them with her mantle, and the children said, "Oh, Mother, we are not afraid, for you are near, and no harm can come." And the mother said, "This is better than the brightness of the day, for I have taught my children courage."

And the morning came and there was a hill ahead, and the children climbed and grew weary, and the mother was weary, but at all times she said to the children, "A little patience and we are there." So the children climbed, and when they reached the top, they said, "We could not have done it without you, Mother." And the mother, when she lay down that night, looked up at the stars and said, "This is a better day than the last, for my children have learned fortitude in the face of hardness. Yesterday I gave them courage. Today I have given them strength."

And the next day came strange clouds, which darkened the earth -- clouds of war and hate and evil, and the children groped and stumbled, and the mother said, "Look up. Lift your eyes to the Light." And the children looked and saw above the clouds an Everlasting Glory, and it guided them and brought them beyond the darkness. And that night the mother said, "This is the best day of all, for I have shown my children God."

And the days went on, and the weeks and the months and the years, and the mother grew old, and she was little and bent. But her children were tall and strong, and walked with courage. And when the way was hard, they helped their mother; and when the way was rough, they lifted her, for she was as light as a feather; and at last they came to a hill, and beyond the hill they could see a shining road and golden gates flung wide. And the mother said, "I have reached the end of my journey. And now I know the end is better than the beginning, for my children can walk alone, and their children after them."

And the children said, "You will always walk with us mother, even when you have gone through the gates."

And they stood and watched her as she went on alone, and the gates closed after her. And they said, "We cannot see her, but she is with us still. A mother like ours is more than a memory. She is a living presence."

QUESTIONS FOR MEDITATION AND/OR DISCUSSION

1) Do you remember, during your childhood, times when you were encouraged and praised for your tasks? Think about your feelings at times when you wished for praise or when you got praise and encouragement.

2) Do you know people who cannot accept a compliment? If one is paid to that person you hear a reply like, "Oh you can't mean that." Or, you praise a person's looks, and you hear, "Oh, no, this is nothing. It's just an old thing I drug out of the closet." How do you feel when a person rejects your well-intentioned compliment?

3) When you receive a compliment, can you be gracious and reply with thanks and a smile and show your genuine appreciation for their thoughtfulness?

4) Apply these adult situations to your relationship with your children. Be alert to the way they receive your praise. Take note: if they can't tolerate it comfortably, then talk with them about it. Help them to learn early to accept a compliment instead of rejecting it.

5) Can you think of situations at home, work, church, or elsewhere where someone has done a good job and received no notice for his/her hard work? Have you ever heard one say, "I really worked hard and sacrificed to do that job, and what thanks did I get for it?" How does that person feel? Have you been in that situation?

6) Have you observed a person or child improve greatly after being complimented?

7) Have you visited in a house where there was chaos all over? What caused it?

CHAPTER 8

SATISFACTION OF CURIOSITY, The Child's Fifth Right

CHILDREN ARE INTENSELY CURIOUS

When our boys were about 6 and 4, they found a beetle-like insect at least two inches long crawling on the sidewalk and hastened to show it to me. Question: "Daddy, what kind of bug is that?" Answer: "I don't know boys, but I'm curious about it, too. I'll find out what it is." Well, this was one of those situations that parents get themselves into where one wishes the event had never taken place, or that one had not made a commitment to a child. To find the answer, I tried several possibilities from the dictionary, then, from an old zoology text I had, but to no avail. My boys continued to ask, and I said I would have to find the answer at the university where I was doing graduate work. It was only after some research in the biology lab, that I got the answer to the question of two little boys who expressed a natural child-like curiosity.

The youngest one had forgotten the question by the time I got the answer. The older one was glad to know, but I think soon forgot. . . and so did I. But the principle was that I didn't know and told them truthfully. Second, I committed myself to finding the answer to their question. Thirdly, they saw that I was determined to do what I said I would do and that it took time, but there was an answer. They learned a principle and that was what was important. All three of our children did post-graduate work on professional degrees. Inquiring minds must be started early.

It has been estimated that, from the time a child is born until he graduates from high school, he is awake 105,000 hours. The child spends nearly 10,000 hours in school from the time s/he starts in the first grade until s/he graduates from high school. If this child is taken to Sunday school every week, s/he will spend about 2,100 hours in Sunday school.

However, during these 105,000 hours, parents have him/her under their direct influence and supervision for approximately 93,000 hours. If a child is lost, parents are more to blame than either school teachers or Bible School teachers because parents have him so much longer than these others.

JEWISH PARENTS INTIMATELY ASSOCIATED WITH THEIR CHILDREN

The Jews have achieved many remarkable accomplishments through their long history. One that is most unusual is that, in spite of being scattered all over the face of the earth and being persecuted endlessly, they have kept their national cohesion and ethnic individuality. There is a reason. The parents of each generation have, according to the plan of the Torah, taught their children. And note the circumstances, required by the Torah, under which each generation was taught: it was whenever the parents and the children were together, whether sitting at home, or taking a journey (mostly on foot), working in the house or in the fields; in fact, from the time they got up in the morning till they went to bed at night, the children were being taught by their parents. The children were encouraged religiously to ask questions about the major events of their history, and the parents or teacher gave the answers. This pattern was repeated year after year. (Deut. 4:9; 6:4-9; 11:19; Josh. 4:20-24)

Of course there are different kinds of questions. Some are ritualistic, as they were frequently with the Jews. Some are rhetorical, and some are out of plain curiosity. In this chapter I'm referring primarily to the latter kind because this type of question is the normal, natural consequence of the child's growth. But I must give some background to the child's development.

THE CHILD'S INTELLECTUAL DEVELOPMENT

New parents many times will stand looking at a sleeping infant in profound wonder of this new human being that has blessed their house and, thereby, helps to make it into a "home." As they look in amazement, they will question what is in store for them in the near future. This little person begins now to take in the world of humans and the world of things, and he is starting from scratch. "How much does she have to learn and in what time frame? How can we as parents facilitate the total learning process? In these early years the child needs help -- but of a certain type. The job before us is totally awesome. Are we up to such an immense challenge?"

CHILDHOOD CURIOSITY

Yes, the job is awesome, but guess what? You've got built in help right from your little one. In the course of development, the natural stages that that child will go through in the development of its body and brain will let you know along the way what it is ready for, and what it needs at any given time. But you parents must pay attention; be alert. Questions will come from that small bundle directly, verbally. And questions will be asked indirectly and non-verbally by actions, expressions, and by interactions with yourselves and others, which will let you know what is on the child's mind, and what it is curious about. The developing child has a right to answers and guidance, which help to pave its way in life. During the first few years any kind of response to the questions is OK. As the child approaches ages 4, 5, or 6 a truthful, factual answer should be given. The parents can provide an environment and resources which are conducive to the total learning process. This is a big order. Here's a rule of thumb for the questioning parents: Your child comes into this world knowing nothing about it, but needs to learn all about it. So teach her/him anything and everything, and the chances are you won't start out too soon about anything.

"Satisfaction of curiosity," then, means that the developing child from birth through about five years old has a deep need for gaining, absorbing, and engulfing information of every description. Remember, I said earlier that the brain of the newborn develops much more rapidly than has ever been expected, so that with the brain cells multiplying at a logarithmic increase, and the interconnections between those cells multiplying by the millions times millions, that child's brain is ready to gain all the world around it. The brain, like soft clay, can be easily molded, shaped, impressed, programmed, and filled with all that life has to offer.

So, when I talk about "Satisfaction of curiosity," I'm not merely talking about a child asking questions that come to mind on the spur of the moment. I'm referring to the child's total quest for information. Sometimes she will ask questions reflecting her obvious curiosity at that moment; but much of the time the curiosity is inward, and she may not verbalize in the form of a question, but the curiosity is still there. Even though the quest for knowledge may remain unexpressed, the parents must see that it is satisfied. Boy! What a challenge!

STAGES IN SATISFYING CHILDHOOD CURIOSITY

All children grow in stages of progress. We are concerned about what aspects of the world the child is taking in, say, at 2, then later at 3, at 4, at 5. Permeating each of the stages of growth and maturing, there are two overall aspects of the informational input. I admit that I am oversimplifying this, but I want to make it as easy for you as I can. First, recognize that the child's task is to become separate from the mother and, thus, develop self-awareness. Then, just as you would expect, the child becomes aware of *things*. They, too, are to be tested, tasted, tossed, and tumbled. What an experience! What excitement!

HOW THE CHILD LEARNS

Note that the baby is prone to respond to emotional stimulation with its entire body, in place of verbalization, as adults would do. He laughs and cries with his legs and arms in motion. This expression of emotion by motion gradually decreases through the age of six. So, don't expect small children to keep very still any time. Another way the child is getting into the swing of things in this world is by *experiencing*, as well as observing, its environment. In essence, this is what is happening when the child watches his hands and feet so intently. First, he looks as if to admire his hands and toes, which is to say this is **intake** of information. Next, he acts and grabs at his extremities, and this may be said to be the **outgo**. Actually, all of his learning, and indeed adult learning as well, goes through these two basic phases.

In order to "learn," adults must take in information and, next, be able to use it in practical application. That's education. We know about adults. Let's look more closely at the child.

Learning by the "law of association" means there are two major avenues by which the developing brain absorbs knowledge of the surrounding world: **intake** and **outgo**, absorption of information and utilizing that information in practice. The way the child takes in information is by the utilization of all its senses and all of its muscles. For example, note that the small child uses its fingers, nose, body balance and even its tongue and mouth to learn what's new with the world around it. We adults can understand what's going on here. We attach certain memorable events to the music that we heard at the time of an original, special event and conclude "they are playing our song." By this we mean when a particularly significant event took place and a certain song was being played, the two were connected. Now, it can be 50 years later when that same song is played that the event and the accompanying emotion is recalled.

On a simpler scale this type of learning is taking place with the child. My grandsons and I took a hike into the woods where there was a platform from a burned out cabin of long ago. All three of us let our imagination run away with us as I told a story about how in the old days Indians were on these hills and in these canyons when the first settlers came in. When I asked over a year later if they remembered our hike the five year old remembered that that was the place where he scratched his leg climbing the mountain. He remembered it in his leg.

A child at play will remember events by sound images, such as whistles and bells; also remember by muscle images such as being sore, tired, or scratched. The intake is the impression formed, and the outgo is the play or other activity of the event. Such activity can be simultaneous with the event or later. Observe a child playing by itself. There are sounds of engines, whistles, horns, conversations, and various other noises and movements as previous events in the child's life are repeated, according to the interpretation that child has made of the original event. This is a review in **outgo** of earlier events that were registered as **input**.

THE WORLD OF THINGS

At the youngest ages the infant-child's world is composed of simple things with which to get acquainted. In the "pre-me" stage, the child is caught up with a simple world of things that make a noise, something with color, or small movable objects that she can experiment with. Even without computers, this is a complicated world of inanimate stuff. Toys and furnishings in the nursery are to be used, waved, explored, torn up, put together, used as weapons, thrown, banged, and destroyed. They are tested and tried for taste, sound or noise, shaking, throwing, pulling, or grabbing. The play experiences taking place here utilize muscular movement and sense reception. He kicks his legs, waves his arms, twists, and turns. All of these actions repeat the overall process we recognized earlier, namely, **input** and **outgo.** In the world of *things*, as in the world of *people*, by trial and experimentation the child is developing. This blurred distinction at a very young age between people and things is well illustrated by the fact that young children believe that anything that moves is alive, and that the names of objects (things) reside in the objects themselves.

The same basic structure continues as the child gets older, even though the surrounding elements become more complicated. The new stage shifts from the self-centered activity to an ever-widening circle of materials. These include autos, planes, boats, fire trucks, earth-moving equipment, and the like. There are also household items like chairs, furniture, dolls' tables with dishes. Oh, but this learning and testing is not limited to the nursery. When the child, in crawling, discovers the kitchen, here's a whole new world of shiny, noisy instruments that are available behind cabinet doors and can be pulled out with reckless abandon. Gradually, the world of CD's, video, and TV encroach on the nursery. This brings in stuffed toys he has become familiar with from the media, such as Ernie, Big Bird, and others.

The child who has been confined to the city is separated from the world of animals, both wild and domesticated. In time, these also will compose the world of things that are becoming a part of the child's knowledge. Whereas, at 2 and 3 years old, dolls, chairs, trucks, and the other toys are tasted, examined, thrown, crashed, and broken, by 4 and 5 the stuffed toys are alive and talking, while other pieces are making other sounds of various sorts. Parents need to see this as trial and error experimentation. She doesn't know that an object of play can be broken and fall to pieces, until she sees it happen. There is no need for adults to give warnings. It won't matter.

PEOPLE AND THE WORLD OF THINGS

People now enter the world of things. There is the fireman for the fire truck; a captain for a boat; a mother for a doll. These associated people are only vaguely human to the small child. The child may wonder if the fireman has a house; if teachers go to bed; if a doll feels it if an arm is pulled off.

Take note of the play table that has been in the room since the child was two. If there have been crayons, there will be marks where the child learned that these things make a change in the table's surface. Then, there will be paper to draw on or with outlines already on it, and the child learns it can add to its world of things and colors by its own creativity. The child doesn't understand that to mark on the wall with a crayon will damage the wall. It only understands that this is adding something to the ever-increasing world of things in the environment. At a later age parents can look at the drawings. Ask the child what the object is. Let the child explain to you what is going on there. You may be surprised at what all has been observed by this inquiring child. The adult may be surprised at the ability of a two or three year old to produce symmetry or design. Furthermore, the crayon and the paper are means of reproducing intake experiences which help them to "seat" in the total learning process.

Just as the motor development of the child is expressed in the drawings, however crude, so the verbal development is likely to be expressed by rhythmic sounds of songs or a kind of metric poetry. Rhythmic sounds combined with nonsense syllables in a kind of humming are made as a part of this discovery. Again, here is the outward sign of what has already taken place inwardly. Furthermore, the increasing skill of verbalization will indicate some of the imagination that is taking place. Parents sometimes make the mistake of once again taking adult standards to the child's world and correct or, worse, rebuke, the child, for "telling stories." The child's stories have no concept of deception, any more than the art work should be judged by "reality" concepts.

Wandering around to see each child's artwork, a kindergarten teacher was observing her class while they drew. As she got to one little girl, who was working diligently, she asked what the drawing was. The girl said, "I'm drawing God."

The teacher said, "But no one knows what God looks like."

The girl replied, "They will in a minute."

In the widening world of experience, the child is taken to the zoo and rides a train while there. The experience is taken home with her, and she becomes the animal keeper, if not the animal. He's taken to church and returns home to stand on a stuffed chair, and the back of it becomes his pulpit while he preaches. The memory of the intake of experiences is now combined with the imagination to produce the outgo of application. True learning has taken place.

In summary, then, we have these new little people enter on the family scene and, like foreigners, their task is to learn all the ways of this new world. In time they struggle through the stages, localizing their intake through sensations, emotions, sounds, and experimentation, to where they discover themselves and the world around them. What an exciting thing to do! How exhilarating all these experiences are! And each level becomes the platform on which the next level is built. Let's hope that the adults in their environment can contribute and stimulate the child's own contrived experiences and add more by their contributions, so that the learning experience continues to have the interest and excitement for the child that the child started out with within itself. Parents cannot maintain a "hands off" relationship by their absence or ignoring the child's world. Parents must provide the laboratory environment where the child's experiments with life take place. But they must do more. They provide themselves as foils for much of this learning, as well as being a resource for contributions to the process.

Details of the stages of social development at later ages will be taken up in a later chapter.

CONTRIBUTIONS OF PARENTS TO THIS LEARNING PROCESS

We've been discussing the child's developing view of *people* and *things*. Young children believe that anything that moves is alive. The child's innate concept is the same as that of the early civilizations of the Mesopotamian valley, that to give a thing a name gave it existence if it did not give it life. Similarly, objects like clouds, sky, thunder, and lightening are imbued with motives, feelings, even activity like being alive.

In some primitive societies there was a tradition whereby early shamans or wizards gave explanations about the natural world in which they lived so closely. Such basic questions about their lives had to be answered. Some were: "Why is there always smoke around the top of that mountain?" "Why do the spots on a deer change?" "Why do the shapes of the star patterns change?" "What makes thunder?" etc. Such questions have found their way into our civilization and have been titled, "Just So Stories."

Piaget brought out that the child's animism and artificialism help to explain his famous and often unanswerable "Why?" questions. Children in this stage, like the primitives, believe that everything has a purpose. For example, they ask, "Why is grass green?" "How do birds fly?" "Why do stars shine?" Parents need to respond to such questions, but do not necessarily need to give a properly correct scientific answer. That, indeed, misses the point. The child is making contact, and you, the parent, make contact with some sort of response. Then the child continues to "pester" the parent with more questions that appear to be repetitious or senseless to the adult. But to the child they are the means of communication. Two children in the nursery room may be talking at each other on two very different subjects, and this satisfies them both. They talk *at* each other, rather than *with* each other, which is probably due to the young child's inability to put himself in another person's position.

It is at a later age (5, 6, 7) when the child starts asking questions based on an expanding and enlarging world view, that the questions take on a different form and, thus, need to be answered by the parent much more realistically. And realistic questions require realistic and truthful answers. Of course, some children's questions cannot be answered; then they have to be told and an explanation given. The questioning mind has a right to some kind of response from the adult. The parent that doesn't take time to listen to the child's questions and respond in some way is doing a great disservice. Yes, some children have more questions than others. That's good. The parent knows what to shoot at. Other children do not ask many, if any, questions. That's not so good, so parents must anticipate what is on the child's mind by observing the child carefully, knowing about what level the child is on, and giving answers anyway.

I emphasize again the importance of showing a child that answers may be found in books. If the home does not have a good library including encyclopedias or child's education series, then make frequent trips to the children's section at the library. This is like taking a trip to the zoo. There are many subjects, lots of colorful pictures, movies, and other decorations, which appeal to small children. Such a fun experience makes a deep impression. There will come a time when that child is in high school and college that it will be natural for her/him to go to the library for research.

PIAGET'S OBSERVATIONS OF DEVELOPING STAGES

Piaget made two discoveries pertaining to the child's learning that will help the parent here. He observed that current education procedures tend to focus upon life and its events being stationary and fixed in place, rather than upon its constantly changing scenes. The child is customarily taught how and what things **are** but not the conditions under which they **change** and modify. And, yet, the child is constantly confronted with change and alteration in its daily life. The surrounding world is constantly changing: seasons come and go, trees leaf out and drop their leaves later, snow and sleet fall and then melt and disappear. People change; appearances change; the house is redecorated; families move to another locality. The point is that the child typically receives a flat, static education while living amidst a world in transition.

Very well, how does the child become reconciled with such alteration between the static and the dynamic elements in its learning process? As the child grows older, it is prodded into using reason to grasp and understand the inconsistent world around him. And this happens in stages.

The point of all of this information is this: Parents must recognize that all children go through sequences of "stages" in their intellectual development. Not all children go into each succeeding stage at exactly the same age, but they typically go through the same order. And, that a major change comes at about age 6 or 7 when reasoning starts. But the ability to reason must also develop through a series of stages to reach levels anywhere near the level of adult thinking. Adolescents still don't reason like adults.

But there is another factor that must be understood with the above. In some middle class homes, where the adults are well educated, children will develop language skills and a vocabulary that make them appear to be more advanced in their intellectual development than, in fact, they are. That is, their vocabulary makes them appear that they could comprehend information and answers at a higher intellectual/educational level than they really can. At the same time, children from lower level homes, having fewer verbal skills, may have better thinking abilities than their lower level vocabulary would indicate. Thus, when adults take this into account, they will answer their children's questions and give out information much more accurately for the child. The point is that the vocabulary and language of the child can be deceptive with respect to thought. Children need time to develop systematic, orderly patterns of thought.

PRACTICAL APPLICATIONS

I've already mentioned that the parent needs to teach the truth in everything, and they teach, also, by example. They realize the child is always receiving and absorbing, like a sponge, what is going on around him/her. So the adults must be careful about their behavior toward each other and their language among themselves, even when not speaking to the child.

Talk to the child on/at his own level, rather than down to him. Your child will make greater progress if you do. But don't expect the child to understand your words in the same manner that you do. Remember that your child takes in your words and thoughts and then interprets them in accord with his own level of thinking, which for years will be below yours. So, because you think you have made something "clear" doesn't mean that you have. Furthermore, be consistent and honest with all that you say to your child.

One Sheldon M. Gallager, a few years ago, reported on the work of Margaret S. Woods of Seattle Pacific College. Ms. Woods has a reputation for brilliant leadership in creative education. She has operated several children's centers, where children are present in the center for only a few hours. Her job was to teach them as much as possible in a short period of time. Years ago as a neophyte high school teacher, she was challenged to instill a thirst for knowledge into the minds of football players. After some experimentation she discovered the idea of exciting their imaginations first, before attempting to fill their heads with facts. Little by little, almost magically, her students began to show a genuine interest in learning. Thereafter, Ms. Woods' theory has been if you can inspire football players to like schoolwork, you can teach anybody anything. The foundation of her success is the principle that "education that is not accompanied by an imaginative and emotional experience is merely a collection of sterile facts packed into an unwilling child."

Furthermore, Ms. Woods believes there are five powerful catalysts that help to make a learning experience meaningful and enduring. They are "curiosity, courage, confidence, creativity, and compassion."

LEARNING BY DOING

Although you parents are not involved directly in a classroom situation, you are deeply involved in the education of the most important children in the world to you -- your very own. You can make good use of these learning principles. I believe that, unfortunately, most parents in our society--consciously or unconsciously --believe that their children, educationally, are in a holding pattern until they start to kindergarten. That is, the parents feel that their children are to be cared for all right, but their education will take place after they start to school when they turn them over to teaching experts who will do the job. Not so!

You have learned from the preceding pages that small children take in the world around them (i.e. learn) and they start with a natural-born *curiosity*. God intended that children start their education at birth. Parental *compassion* follows with the shared process of *doing, seeing, touching, smelling, and hearing* real things. This is just what Ms. Woods recommended, as cited above.

Obviously, this has to be the natural procedure by which children learn. Use it yourself. Let -- no encourage --your child to make her own discoveries, and to fire up his own imagination, and they will learn more, faster. As a parent with many other things to do in the house or outside of it, you want to be the most effective teacher you can be in the few short years that you are the main teacher. Remember that it is in the first five years that your child learns more than it will in any succeeding five-year period the rest of its life.

OK, you know that the "learning by doing" method is the natural way a child learns. Now apply it. Cooperative let's-do-it-together projects are tremendously effective. You can see why this is so when you remember that the child starts out feeling unified with you, the parent. Then gradually it separates into its own individuality. So, sharing in the discovery process is always good. Select activities, which are exciting in themselves, but at the same time get across more complex ideas of life.

One good idea is to make ice cream or cookies together. There is first the fun of mixing ingredients. The small child loves to play with mud, clay, play-dough etc. Mixing ingredients in the kitchen is right down his line. Then, when freezing the ice cream by churning, the child can learn that the cream freezes because salt melts the ice, and the cold is transferred to the cream mix -- a very good, advanced lesson. Basics in physics, chemistry, social customs, history, and geography can be taught with simple projects shared by the parent and child. And there are books available to give the parent resources for this kind of teaching. Now, I'm aware that cranking ice cream is a little out of date, but do it anyway, or make fudge. When you and your child have done projects like this a time or two, you will realize that more is taking place here than just the procedure of making ice cream or fudge. Sharing an exciting activity with you accomplishes a stage in strengthening your relationships and instills confidence and the thrill for learning something new.

Such learning is exciting. A blind boy felt a baby duck hatch out in his hand and excitedly exclaimed, "I can see! I can see it happen!" Another child who was deaf and could not clap her hands in rhythm was taken to lean against the piano. Suddenly she could sense the vibrations and could feel the music and join in the clapping.

I cite these examples to stimulate your own imagination and ingenuity in exciting your own child. You can help your child gain confidence on her own by occasionally coming up with giving her some *choices* of activities to do on her own or to share with you. When the child enters on a project or activity on her own, there is something inside her that says she is ready for this experience. She enters the activity with interest and, thereby, learns from it because it was her choice. Interest begets interest. Success stimulates the child to more of these exciting new experiences. When children participate in activities that excite and arouse them (emotional stimulation), they are more likely to remember. Remember the "our song" example above ? Same principle!

We remember from the earliest years what children get excited about: blocks to build with, paints to color, a drum to beat, a truck to roar. Four year olds quickly learn the difference in silk and wool because they feel the difference. Many modern zoos have "touching" zoos, where children *feel* bones, fur, skin, leather, feathers, etc. Go and observe. (But be careful for cleanliness; keep hands clean and away from face.) Ms. Woods found that children learn to tell time quickly by having a large clock face that they can look at right in the eye. They are looking at time.

CURIOSITY ABOUT THE BODY

Recently, I observed how my grandsons were enthralled to watch a chick hatch out of an egg. I knew it was making a deep impression. But as I thought about it, I speculated that deep in their unconsciousness there was a repetition of their own birth experience -- the time their own life started not long before this. No wonder there was a seeming naturalness to the revetment of their focus. And this kind of thing is true of much of the child's natural curiosity about life, about the human body, about the mother's breasts, and about food. Look at their curiosity as a matter of "life and the struggle for survival." If, as a parent, you are on your toes closely to observe your child, you will see what excites your own child the most. Then capitalize on that and use it to satisfy its curiosity in a learning experience.

I've already alluded to an infant's discovery of a hand, a foot, a flailing arm. This is a prelude to a discovery of the "self" as a separate entity from the mother after a while. A parent or caretaker can ask a 2-year-old a series of questions like, "Where is Brennan's nose? Where is Taylor's elbow?" etc. These body performances are reinforcing the sense of self, which is so very important.

Very young children also discover their genitalia. It is perfectly normal for small children to feel of the genital area when the diaper is down or gone. It's OK. Just keep your cool. Say nothing and remove the hand as you replace the diaper or clothing. After all, if it were to be harmful in some way for children to touch themselves, God wouldn't have made them sensitive at this early age.

AWARE OF "GIRLS" AND "BOYS"

Children gradually develop an awareness of the presence of other children and by around two see them as separate people, rather than just other "things." Pretty soon the child hears a distinction between "sister" and "brother." Is there a relationship between these words and "girl" and "boy?" For little girls what does "boy" mean? This distinction is vague at first. If they are small and bathe with a sibling of the opposite sex, they develop so gradually with the awareness of differences in the anatomy, that they do not usually ask about it. They just "know."

When I, personally, was a child and heard talk about "girls," I realized at the first stage that the difference was that girls had long hair, and boys had short hair. That was all there was to it. Then, in due time, I saw there was a difference in my sister's body and mine, just as mother's body was different. We boys had equipment girls didn't have. This awareness comes gradually and usually comfortably, though not always. But the awareness of the naked body is accepted matter of factly to the very young child, and as it grows up with this knowledge, there is no shock at later references or pictures.

A little boy got lost at the YMCA and found himself in the women's locker room. When he was spotted, the room burst into shrieks, with ladies grabbing towels and running for cover. The little boy watched in amazement and then asked, "What's the matter, haven't you ever seen a little boy before?"

At about 8 or 9 years old, a boy I played with, who did not have a sister, asked me once what girls looked like down there. In my wisdom from experience, I described her as looking like a bobby pen. He looked at me quizzically, and that was that. This was my first experience at teaching sexuality (little did I dream that one day I would become a certified sex counselor). Some children can be very open with their questions in this quest for knowledge. At a church camp in a class of 12-year-olds, we had had a lesson on Abraham and Isaac and his circumcision. Several of the girls were unaware of what that was and asked. I told them and described the prepuce, etc. After which one girl turned to the boy next to her and very calmly, innocently, asked if he were circumcised. I wish all of sexuality education of children could be this calm and this natural and matter of fact.

If they do not grow up from early childhood with the opposite sex, at 2 to 3 years, or thereabout, the time comes when they want to know what the difference is. The parent needs to get picture books from the book store that show drawings of boys and girls, and when they ask questions, give them the simplest explanation: "That's the way God made us." Some children, mostly females, at young ages perhaps will ask boys if they have that thing, or they want to see it. They can't imagine having a penis and testicles between their legs if they have not seen daddy or a brother. Perhaps they have had occasion to watch a visitor change the diaper of a male infant. Mothers of girls need to provide this opportunity as early as possible because the earlier they begin to see the male genitalia, the easier it is for all concerned. Of course, boys have a similar curiosity about the girl's anatomy, also.

For mothers with children who have not had the opportunity to start out gently in this way, they can get together and find an excuse to let the children see each other. This has happened many times with mothers who are friends, and they have put bathing suits on their children together or have changed dirty or wet clothes. Such a scene, of course, presupposes that within the home the parents have not rushed to cover everybody up while bathing or dressing. Private nudity in the home is OK. Let it be natural, casual, and comfortable at these pre-school ages. Please, this should be acceptable that doors aren't slammed or that one doesn't holler to "shut the door." God made the body this way. The human body is a work of art. It is the "temple of the Spirit of God," and we should care for it as such. Humans' attitude about the body has made it dirty, not God.

A WHOLESOME ATTITUDE TOWARD THE HUMAN BODY

It is natural and normal for small children to want to take off their clothes at times. Frequently, this takes place in public. Sometimes a small child is discovered playing naked outside with neighbor children. They do not feel shame for this and should not. It has to do with a natural freedom, and at times is an expression of their curiosity about their playmates. I saw a small boy starting to take off his clothes after Sunday School in the hallway. His dad very calmly told him not to do that and helped him as the child obeyed. It was handled beautifully. Parents should not shout and create a scene over such an innocent bit of natural behavior.

Children have a natural acceptance of the human body. This anecdote is a good illustration of this: A woman reported, "I was driving with my three young children one warm summer evening when a woman in the convertible ahead of us stood up and waved. She was stark naked! As I was reeling from the shock, I heard my five-year-old shout from the back seat, 'Mom! That lady isn't wearing a seat belt.!'"

A parent may ask, "What if my child does not ask about the body differences?" First, I would say, does your child feel free to ask personal questions? Or, have you kept your body so private, that the small child has a kind of fear of seeing you exposed? Have there been remarks made in the child's hearing that disparage the body or nakedness? If any of this applies, then you have to overcome the so-called modesty within yourself first and help the child to overcome his/hers also. Of course, there is a place for calm modesty in the home, depending on the ages of children, but not at the expense of creating fear about the body.

There can be other reasons your child may not verbally ask about the body. The child just may not have enough curiosity at the asking age, say at 3 or 4. If so, you can watch for the opportunity to bring up the subject yourself. Get the picture book and tell the child you have a new book, which may interest her, "Let's look at it together." This will likely prompt an expression of the child's inner curiosity and wonderment. Let your answers and explanations be made calmly, naturally, and gently for the unknowing child.

WHERE DO BABIES COME FROM?

At around age 5, 6, or 7 comes that question, "Where do babies come from?"

I well remember asking my mother that several times when I was about six. Once my little sister was present, and a couple of times I asked mother in front of my grandmother. All of those first few times I asked, she said she would explain it to me, but "now is not a good time." When we were alone, she said she had not told me earlier because in her mother's day they didn't talk about it. And it would embarrass her mother to tell me in front of her. So she wanted to tell me by myself. I still remember how important I felt.

Then she told me the mystery of birth. I asked her if it hurt when the baby came out. She said it did, but you don't remember the hurt. You are thinking about the new child that has come into the world. I asked how the baby started. She said daddy planted the seed inside, and God made it grow. I don't remember asking about how he planted the seed. I think I was so impressed with this new knowledge that I had the whole story, and I was caught up thinking about the baby coming out of her insides. I also remember wondering about food in her stomach at the same time the baby was there. I went about my play satisfied in this, also.

I think I was about typical, although for 1931 my mother was not typical. Not too many mothers were answering their children's questions so frankly in those days. Her hesitancy to talk in front of her mother was typical. Often, since then, I've wondered about the advanced knowledge my mother had about that and other questions, like masturbation, that she and my dad educated me on. I think her deep spirituality motivated her to answer my questions and to tell me the truth in doing so. I know that when I heard the "stork story" from some source, perhaps a friend, and asked her about that, she explained that some children were told that, but it was not the truth.

What if your child does not ask the question about where babies come from? Then, you have to set up the circumstances so that the child feels free to ask. This can be done by talking about a friend who is pregnant, or who has a new baby, so that your child overhears. Pictures in the magazine or other allusions to pregnancy or babies may provoke the question. If you still don't get an expressed question, start explaining when your child shows interest or fascination in a picture or a doll or a baby. And explain as if the question had been asked. Probably you should not wait any longer than about 7 years old, unless your child is very immature for her age. Typically, children show this curiosity around 5 or 6.

I think it is best always on the mysteries of life and death to bring God in on the answer or teaching. Stories from the Bible like Abraham and Sarah are a good starting point. A Bible story book with stories from both the Old and New Testaments give a wonderful base for telling the story of life. This is good evidence that the story of life and birth and the sexuality that accompanies such facts and mysteries is from God, and, thus, is worthy of our respect and openness.

HELPING YOUR CHILD REACH POTENTIAL

As you look ahead to your child's school experiences, you will be impressed, if you aren't already, with the highly competitive system our education has become. Dagburt Runes makes a strong case when he states that our competitive educational system is ancient in which the allegedly gifted are rewarded, and the less fortunate are set back, despised, and exposed to public ridicule. For instance, a lot is made by our government of raising the scores and making more pupils have higher grades. This presupposes that the philosophy of making grades is the best system for educating our children. There are some educators, that I highly respect, who feel that the system of competition, which turns the class-room into a tournament, is a radically wrong concept to start with. But, until there is a fundamental, radical change in this philosophy, we have to live with it. So, what I have been saying will be the best groundwork you can lay for your children for today's educational system.

Some have said that geniuses are made, not born. I'm not in a position to evaluate this assertion scientifically, but I do believe there is an awful lot to it. And the thing that is on your mind as a parent is, "What can I do to help my child be an "A" student?" I reply, instead of waiting till the child is in school to worry about grades, start at birth. After all, this is the running theme of this whole book, that the first five years are the most important. And you parents are in control of that. More specific information on "The Making of an "A" Student" will be presented in Appendix.

POST SCRIPT

MAKING A DIFFERENCE

Mrs. Thompson, a 5th grade teacher, stood in front of her class the first day of school and told her pupils she loved them all. This was difficult, because there on the front row, slumped in his seat, was a little boy named Teddy Stoddard.

Mrs. Thompson had watched Teddy the year before, and noticed he didn't play well with the other children, that his clothes were messy, and that he constantly needed a bath. And Teddy could be unpleasant. It got to the point where Mrs. Thompson would actually take delight in marking his papers with a broad red pen, making bold X's and then putting a big "F" at the top.

At the school where Mrs. Thompson taught, she was required to review each child's past records, and she put Teddy's off until last. However, when she reviewed his file, she was in for a surprise. Teddy's first grade teacher wrote, "Teddy is a bright child with a ready laugh. He does his work neatly and has good manners...he is a joy to be around."

His second grade teacher wrote, "Teddy is an excellent student, well-liked by his classmates, but he is troubled because his mother has a terminal illness, and life at home must be a struggle."

His third grade teacher wrote, "His mother's death has been hard on him. He tries to do his best, but his father doesn't show much interest, and his home life will soon affect him if some steps aren't taken."

Teddy's fourth grade teacher wrote, "Teddy is withdrawn and doesn't show much interest in school. He doesn't have many friends and sometimes sleeps in class."

By now, Mrs. Thompson realized the problem, and she was ashamed of herself. She felt even worse when her students brought her Christmas presents wrapped in beautiful ribbons and bright paper, except for Teddy's. His present was clumsily wrapped in the heavy, brown paper that he got from a grocery bag. Mrs. Thompson took pains to open it in the middle of the other presents. Some of the children started to laugh when she found a rhinestone bracelet with some of the stones missing and a bottle that was one quarter full of perfume.

But she stifled the children's laughter when she exclaimed how pretty the bracelet was, putting it on, and dabbing some of the perfume on her wrist. Teddy Stoddard stayed after school that day just long enough to say, "Mrs. Thompson, today you smelled just like my Mom used to."

After the children left, she cried for at least an hour. On that very day, she quit teaching reading, and writing, and arithmetic. Instead, she began to teach children. Mrs. Thompson paid particular attention to Teddy. As she worked with him, his mind seemed to come alive. The more she encouraged him, the faster he responded. By the end of the year, Teddy had become one of the smartest children in the class, and, despite her lie that she would love all the children the same, Teddy became one of her "teacher's pets."

A year later, she found a note from Teddy under her door telling her that she was still the best teacher he ever had in his whole life. The same thing happened six years later after high school and then four more years later after college, where he graduated with honors, in spite of having a struggle. But she was still his best teacher.

Then four more years passed, and yet another letter came. This time he explained that after he got his bachelor's degree, he decided to go a little further. The letter explained that she was still the best and most favorite teacher he ever had. But now his name was a little longer. The letter was signed, Theodore F. Stoddard, M.D.

The story doesn't end there. You see, there was yet another letter that spring. Teddy said he'd met this girl and was going to be married. He explained that his father had died a couple of years ago, and he was wondering if Mrs. Thompson might agree to sit in the place at the wedding that was usually reserved for the mother of the groom. Of course, Mrs. Thompson did. And guess what? She wore that bracelet, the one with several rhinestones missing. And she made sure she was wearing the perfume that Teddy remembered his mother wearing on their last Christmas together. They hugged each other, and Dr. Stoddard whispered in Mrs. Thompson's ear, "Thank you, Mrs. Thompson, for believing in me. Thank you so much for making me feel important and showing me that I could make a difference."

Mrs. Thompson, with tears in her eyes, whispered back. She said, "Teddy, you have it all wrong. You were the one who taught me that I could make a difference. I didn't know how to teach until I met you."

SUGGESTIONS FOR MEDITATION AND/OR DISCUSSION

1) Have you been on picnics or other excursions or visits with another family where you could observe small children playing together? What did you observe?

2) In the preceding chapter what bits of information were new or strange to you? Were they clear? Discuss some of these thoughts with others in your group.

3) Do you have a child old enough to have gone from the "world of things" to the world of "people?" If so, at what age did this happen? Have you observed this with friends' children?

4) Through your own experience can you see the differences in the "stages" of the child's growth? How has your child compared with what has been said? Remember the ages are highly flexible for entrance into a given stage of growth.

5) What are some of the strangest questions your children have asked you?

6) In your family or among your friends, have you observed how free small children are to undress in public without any embarrassment whatsoever? How did you and any other observers react? Discuss this.

7) Have you had the experience of explaining to a child where babies come from? How did you feel about that?

CHAPTER 9

SENSITIZATION OF CONSCIENCE, The Child's Sixth Right

THE MEANING OF COMPASSION

Author and lecturer, Leo Buscaglia, once talked about a contest he was asked to judge. The purpose of the contest was to find the most caring child. The winner was a four-year-old child whose next door neighbor was an elderly gentleman who had recently lost his wife. Upon seeing the man cry, the little boy went into the old gentleman's yard, climbed onto his lap, and just sat there. When his mother asked him what he had said to the neighbor, the little boy said, "Nothing, I just helped him cry."

Can a small child learn "compassion?" You bet he can! And note that "Compassion" is the central theme of the ministry of Christ.

A CURRENT SOCIAL PROBLEM

The American Psychological Association observed that children are glued to the TV too much of their time. They should have this time limited because of these following figures. It is estimated that the typical child spends 27 hours each week at the TV (many spend much more). By the time s/he finishes elementary school, s/he will have watched 8000 murders and 100,000 acts of violence. The movie and TV producers are kind of like the gun lobby in the blindness and prejudice of their defense, and claim that it has not been proved that there is a relationship between children perpetrating acts of violence and the influence of TV (or the availability of guns).

I maintain that there is a direct relationship for *many* children, because those that are from an inadequate home background have a predisposition for violence when they turn the TV on; they are already waiting to be shown how to carry it out. If there were a direct relationship for *all* children, then more children would be committing acts of violence than do now. Most all children fall into the above statistic for watching TV and having their minds infiltrated by violent acts. And the procedure of desensitizing the mind to acts of violence and mayhem could not be more effectively done if it were planned. But the reason most of the children do not follow through with acts of violence is that they have been taught at home to behave in a more civilized way. That is, their consciences have been taught that such acts are wrong.

Children who are emotionally neglected or abandoned very early in life often have difficulty with such brain-mediated functions as empathy, attachment, and emotional expression. It should grieve us that this is so.

DEFINITION

The word *compassion* means "sympathetic consciousness of others' distress together with a desire to alleviate it." To be conscious or aware of another person's distress means that an individual has had his or her conscience sensitized, or alerted sufficiently to pick up on the distress or discomfort of another. How does this come about? The foundation is laid by the parents. A child's native capacity to reckon with its emotions is found to hinge, to a significant degree, on biological systems shaped by its early experiences and attachments with parents. But the tragedy is that 20% of children are at risk of not developing a stable conscience at all. At the same time, it has been determined that *if a child is not taught by 6 years old, moral judgment is forever damaged.*

THE CONSCIENCE

To keep things simple, picture graphically that there is a section at the top of the brain called the "conscience" (technically called the "Super Ego). When a baby is born, this is like very soft, malleable clay. It is smooth all over, except possibly for a very small area. From the day the parents start teaching that baby that some things are not permissible, that are prohibited, it is like the orders have been etched in that clay. The parent spends time each day saying, "You can't do that," or "It's OK to do that." These simple admonitions accumulate as impressions on the soft clay of the "conscience" and, thus, become standards by which the child lives. As the child gets older, that clay begins to dry out and harden. Impressions made in it become "set" and are harder to change, and, in hardening, it is more difficult to add new concepts of right and wrong and standards of behavior, as in, "You can't teach an old dog new tricks." Thus, the conscience is *trained*.

Above, I said the clay has a small area that is not perfectly smooth. I say this because I believe the child's conscience at birth has an innate "sense of the fitness of things," as C. S. Lewis calls it. There is a sense of propriety that humans are born with that is the heart and core of the conscience. It is an integral part of being human. It is easiest described as a sense of fair play, and this is theoretically already inscribed on that soft clay. In other words, at birth I believe the child already has a start on the sensitization of the conscience, albeit in a very rudimentary way, and it does not ripen until the child is older. As the child grows, parents and others in the immediate environment begin to add to that innate sense, and the list of "do's" and "don't's" gets longer and longer. The conscience has the *potential* of being shaped and formed as the infant grows. As in other situations I have mentioned, by the age of 5 or 6 that child's sense of right and wrong is pretty clearly formed in a global sense. The lessons, that there are some things that one just cannot do, have been learned in a broad way. In addition, one learns to understand what another person feels. Now, the details and specifics of some of these broader categories will be picked up later.

THE PLEASURE PRINCIPLE

In the newborn infant there is a basic human attitude that "what is pleasurable is good, and what is painful (uncomfortable) is bad." Technically this concept is what psychoanalysts call "hedonism" or the "pleasure principle." Simply put, this trait is a natural characteristic of the infant and is a symptom of immaturity in a grown person. It is recognized by the manifestation of the attitude, "I want what I want when I want it, or I'll throw a tantrum if I can't get it." Many immature grown ups (not "adults") broadcast their immaturity by wearing T shirts with the slogan, "If it feels good, do it." Currently, some CEO's of large corporations may not wear the T shirt with such a slogan, but their actions in cheating their employees and share-holders out of millions of dollars and benefits, are living the same immature way. They want what they want when they want it and will do anything to have their own way. In spite of their exalted position in the business and financial world, they never had their consciences sufficiently trained in childhood. It's tragic that so many suffer the consequences of their hedonistic dishonesty.

Now, this basically "selfish" urge is characteristic of the infant, and any requirement that does not fit with this attitude is resisted. So, there is an early struggle within the infant over whether to continue to do only what feels good, or what it wants to do, versus what is required to do, which may be uncomfortable. It is a pleasure to please the parent, but it is unpleasant to be potty trained, and so on. This helps you see that the wise parent uses the pleasure principle of showing love and affection to the child while at the same time conditioning it to do what is right and proper for that age.

THE STRUGGLE BETWEEN RIGHT AND WRONG

This struggle between "what I have the urge to do versus what I should do" goes on all of one's life and is discussed thoroughly at the spiritual level in the New Testament by the Apostles John and Paul under the title of the "lusts of the flesh." At the psychological level it is described as the struggle between narcissism (childishness) and maturity. Therefore, it is important that during the early, formative years, the infant-child learns to manage these conflicting feelings. And that these issues become not only a struggle for the infant, but also a struggle for the parents in guidance. It is vitally important, then, that the parent, step by step, guide the infant-child in such a way that the conscience is conditioned so that the child understands the difference in right and wrong. Also, beyond this, that the child is able most of the time to follow the guidance of its own well-trained conscience.

There is not enough space in a book like this to go into the detailed structure of the human mind and the development of personality. But I do want to clarify a couple of issues, which may make all of this a little easier to understand. First, there should be a distinction made between what are popularly called moral or ethical values and cultural subjects. Moral, ethical values that are inherent in our American Judeo-Christian tradition include **honesty, courage, love of truth, loyalty, sexual fidelity, devotion to duty, unselfishness, respect for just authority, and concern for the rights of others.** It has been said that these traits are the "soul of democracy." They are standards of behavior, which have been a part of our historical tradition. They are considered to be desirable traits of character for a citizen and are taught as standards of Christian behavior.

Second, in addition to the above list, there are cultural traditions which are not viewed so much as a part of moral/ethical behavior as the above. In the religious sectors of our society, there are broad categorical distinctions of Jews and Christians. For example, Jews have a heritage which they wish to pass on to their children at an early age and proceed in their own way to do this. Not only that, within Judaism, there are three major divisions, each with its own peculiarities, which these respective groups teach. Similarly, Christendom is divided into two major groups, viz., Catholics and Protestants. Likewise, there are sub-groups within these large Christian bodies. And the families who are a part of these respective bodies are frequently concerned with passing on to their children the peculiarities of the group in which they were reared.

In addition to the above, there are certain spiritual issues, that I will deal with in a later chapter, which are, for the most part, peculiar to Christianity.

Before going further, it will be helpful to list briefly the characteristic natural elements of the child's maturation process, because the training or conditioning of the conscience should coordinate with these natural developmental characteristics.

NATURAL MATURATION

I have already referred to the importance of the first five years of life as being the period of fastest development of the child's life. For convenience, look at the child as growing physically, mentally, and spiritually from zero to, say, 50%. Of course, this is just an arbitrary figure, but I emphasize that in stages day by day and week by week, there are developmental changes in progress – for the child, that is typical and healthy. Some children mature faster than others, so be careful about comparing your own child too closely with that of friends or neighbors. For this reason I give the following abbreviated list of approximately what to expect as the child matures.

During this period there is what Havighurst calls "the naïve hedonism of infancy, when pleasure is good and pain is evil." So the child must learn the concepts of "Yes," and "No," "Good," and "Bad." As the years go by, the child picks up on the warnings and punishments of the parents as these issues are accompanied by displays of affection and loving guidance, approval, and disapproval. Thus, the basis for the conscience is developed. Upon this foundation the structure of values and moral character will be built.

RESPONSES WITHIN THE FIRST NINE MONTHS

The typical, healthy infant begins to smile about 6 weeks old, and at 8 weeks old it responds to its mother's smile. Then by 12 weeks the infant will spontaneously initiate a reciprocal social smile with its mother. After a few more weeks the infant becomes sensitive to frowns, and by 36 weeks he responds to a "No! No!" as both a nursery game and a serious command. Note that what appears to us adults as a blend of playfulness and seriousness becomes a learning experience for the child.

THE INFANT AT ONE YEAR

It becomes apparent that the baby likes to please others. And at fifteen months he has acquired a will of his own sufficiently that he no longer heeds, "No!" In becoming more self-assertive, he lets his parents know that he has a will of his own. By 18 months old, there is a primitive sense of what we call "guilt," although it is what specialists Gesell and Ilg refer to as a "primitive shamefacedness," which denotes a simple form of "shyness and withdrawal," usually linked to the function of elimination. But this illustrates how the beginning of the sense of being approved of by the parents, or disapproved of, is beginning to develop. By this age the child is going through the process of separation and individuation from the mother. As this takes place, the child's "self-hood" becomes noticeable.

THE CHILD AT TWO TO TWO AND ONE-HALF YEARS OLD.

By this time the child likes to try out alternative choices and to choose according to his limits of maturity. At this time the child may begin to ride a tricycle, refine the use of fork and spoon; refer to self by name. The child practices saying, "No," and, at times, may have tantrums. Significantly, the sense of shame more fully develops upon which the parents can build constructively. At this age, the child should not be expected to share willingly, but s/he does enjoy being around people. Some are afraid of the dark. Physical maturation progresses enough that the child is toilet trainable.

Literal thinking is characteristic of this period, and it is self-centered. Also, there is some confusion between reality and appearance (use of the Halloween mask illustrates this). The child does not understand the passing of time, and it has poor memory strategies. S/he does not take intentions into account and is confused about the relationship between cause and effect.

TWO AND ONE-HALF TO THREE YEARS OLD

The child is riding a tricycle by now and is toilet trainable and dressing itself. There is less scribbling and more drawing within lines. In speech, it uses adverbs and prepositions, and there is a virtual vocabulary explosion, which may be made more impressive, provided the parents have been talking a great deal to the child since birth. The child says, "No," and may have tantrums. The child still cannot share very well and sometimes has fear of the dark. Pretending is a form of play. The early stages of "learning to please" are obvious and are manifested in the toilet training.

THREE YEARS OLD

The child is dressing herself now, has fewer tantrums, and remains toilet trainable. Also, now she has motor skills sufficient to cut paper and hair, draw crude faces and shapes, and can hop on one foot. Significantly, the child is playing better with its peers and shares better with them; fantasy is included in the play. Sentences have become more complex.

Cognitive aspects are the same as at two. He likes to make choices and to please the parents. By this age the child is capable of assuming responsibilities, as he is becoming aware of "minding and not minding."

FOUR YEARS OLD

Progress is evident in that this age can carry out a sequence of two simple directions in the order given. Also, this child can give a connected account of recent experiences and can understand the concept of 2 and 3 days in the future and into the past. Motor skills have developed enough that the 4-year-old can print "letters," draw figures, handle zippers, buttons, and snaps. Significantly, for our purpose, this age is capable of sharing and social play, but can be oppositional as s/he asserts his/her own individuality more. Fantasy play becomes more evident. Also, typically there are more questions, and here we see the beginnings of moral reasoning. For example, "I should get my own way." "I am good to get rewards and avoid punishment." "I will lie to avoid punishment." As the child's individuality becomes more pronounced, he will be less anxious to please than he was earlier. But at times he will readily obey and show pleasure in doing so.

By this age, there is an increasing affinity for the parent of the opposite sex. Parents can view this period, which may last anywhere from a few months to a few years, as a kind of "infantile romantic attachment" to the opposite sex parent. Look at it as an early training period by which the foundation is laid for future adult relationships with the opposite sex. Parents need to respect this very important period by the father's taking special time to be a companion to his daughter and the mother's doing the same with her son. In my opinion, it's the worst period for parents to separate. It is a serious deprivation to the child who is in a one-parent home. It is a badly informed rationalization for a lesbian couple to think they can rear a little girl through this age as well as a normal couple can. The same principle is true of the gay couple, who take it upon themselves to rear a little boy through this age. And the principle also applies to the single parent who feels that a boy-friend or girl-friend can take the place of a true parent for their child. If, by chance, it *appears* that such an arrangement is successful, I respectfully ask to interview the child when it becomes "of age."

Cognitive aspects of this age child include: egocentrism is fading, four is beginning to understand cause and effect patterns better, but is still literal in his thinking. Further, this child is better able to separate fantasy and reality.

FIVE YEARS OLD

By this age some interest is shown in reading, writing, and more complex drawings. Grammar is more nearly adult and complex. Speech is noticeably intelligible. Physically, the child skips, skates, and rides a 2 wheeler without training wheels. Socially, there is interest in mutuality of friendship, and goal oriented play is beginning. The affinity for the parent of the opposite sex continues typically.

Cognitive aspects of this age are similar to the four year old. Significantly, moral reasoning is developed to the extent that he can say/think, "I should do what I am told in order to stay out of trouble."

SIX YEARS OLD

Six is self-centered; possessive; impulsive; and has wide swings in behavior and mood. S/he also tends to blame others; has brash reactions and bursts of activity. In an effort to remember things, events, and people, this age has some primitive memory strategies. An attitude at times is: "I should look out for myself but be fair to those who are fair to me." Typically, this child learns to read at this time (if not before). Also, the child by this age has learned to defend itself by denying having done forbidden activity.

Behavior patterns and learning comprehension depend on a child's stage of development. When you know what to expect, you will not ask too much or too little. Natural growth factors, listed above, should be taken into account as the parents train the child's conscience. And, the parents, knowing the typical levels of children at a given age, can know approximately what to expect of their own child in this learning process. They must admit to themselves that a certain child may be a little ahead or a little behind the levels that have been listed above. Variations are normal. With that in mind, we shall consider the matter of *training* the conscience.

TRAINING THE CONSCIENCE

And why must the conscience be trained? We have already seen that every child is born with certain "hedonistic" impulses or the drive for pleasure, but it does not have the ability or incentives or understanding within itself to control or channel those basic impulses, appetites, and temper. His parents provide the incentives, which he will gradually incorporate into his own system, and then will call these incentives his own. This is training the conscience.

So, when I speak of the "ethical sense and moral values," I am talking about training the conscience. The core of the conscience, which is constantly developing, consists of an understanding of justice, obedience, punishment, and guilt. These are harsh words of themselves, but the elements of these are a part of life; and loving, affectionate parents are the ones to begin the teaching of these precepts gradually from birth. Patterns of parental control establish patterns of self-control as the child grows up. It is a natural human trait that we become like those we admire. In most cases, children admire their parents and follow their example in all things.

Further, there are specific traits that accompany that infrastructure, such as awareness of the suffering and the rights of others; that teasing hurts; the principle of the "Golden Rule," truthfulness, kindness, and fair play. These principles can all be started in the child's youngest years. As the child gets older, the teaching and guidance continues with such principles as courage, loyalty, and devotion to duty. And, as all of these principles are taught day by day by devoted parents, the child will pick up others' principles automatically and not even be aware of what's happening. For example, as the child identifies with the parents, it learns respect for just and fair authority; how husband and wife treat each other; how to communicate; how to go about solving problems; how to control instinctual drives, etc. Why? Because the child wants to be like his parents and imitate their actions. The following are some examples of how parents convey some of these vital lessons to the child's conscience.

AWARENESS OF SUFFERING IN OTHERS

Previously, I said that, by 3 years old, the child is much more aware of others. Probably having a pet at an earlier age is one of the best ways to introduce the concept of thinking of pain in others. Unfortunately, small, inexperienced children are prone to mistreat their pets because of a lack of understanding of hurting others, but when the cat squalls or the dog yipes, an adult can tell the child the animal is hurting. When told enough, the child begins to understand the pain of animals because he has fallen and hurt himself many times by now, at which time you, the parent, have said, "I'm sorry. You fell and hurt yourself. I know that hurts. Let me kiss it, and it'll feel better." The word "hurt" begins to take on meaning which the child comprehends. And such an example by a parent goes a long way toward impressing the child with a concept of empathy. We have already seen that small children learn early that activities that arouse and excite them cause them to remember.

Then, the next stage is to help the child learn that when he kicks the dog and pokes the cat with a stick, it "hurts." The parent needs to learn early to keep on saying to the child, "How would you feel if that had been done to you?" Even though these words may not mean much at first, they will gradually take on meaning, which gets the lesson across.

If there are siblings in the home, the same principle can be extended to them. Then, it widens out to playmates and to others. Parents help, also, by exaggerating their "pain" if a child pokes them or hits them. A loud "Oh!," followed by an explanation that that hurts, will have its effect in due time. Frequently, a statement, such as, "I know you did not intend to do that, but that hurts," will be understood.

As the child gets older, lessons can be extended. Very early the parents can begin to say, "Wouldn't that hurt if someone did that to you?" The child is prodded into reasoning about his actions to others. Even before your child can reason, the idea will be taking root and bear fruit later on. On occasion, when someone else is hurt or disappointed, the parent can suggest that the child go put his arm around that person. "That will help him feel better." The child soon understands this because she is glad when someone gives her comfort when she hurts herself. Physical acts of pain and physical acts of comfort are understood first.

TEASING HURTS

With the parents' help, a child learns there is more than one kind of pain. The pains of disappointment and hurt feelings are recognized in due time, if the parent helps. The child is crying because he can't go out with someone. Mother says, "I know you're disappointed that you can't go." Or, "I know that hurts." In the first place, it's good for the parent to acknowledge feelings, especially negative feelings. Second, the child learns that the way he is feeling is labeled "disappointment," "hurt feelings," or "anger." The next step is that the child can learn that others have those same feelings. He learns that his own feelings are assuaged when someone pays attention to him. He learns that he can identify with another by being told, "How would you feel if that happened to you?" etc.

Still later, certainly by kindergarten, the child learns that taunts, and jeers, and name-calling hurt another person. The child has already learned that there are some things you cannot say to your parents. The child may have a tantrum at 2 1/2 years old, which can be ignored at the time. And later a parent can say, "I know you are disappointed, but you cannot play with the scissors," etc. There comes a time when the parents say, "You cannot speak that way to me. I am your father," etc. Eventually the child learns that there are some things you cannot say and some acts of anger that must be limited.

THE BULLY

Wherever children gather, whether around home or at pre-school, church, or child care, there will be some child that is already on the road to being a bully. This starts at the younger years, mostly by name-calling and an effort to control others. Pushing and hitting can become verbal assaults. And the language the would-be bully hears at home will be repeated to other children, such as racial and sexual slurs. Frequently the younger or weaker or meeker child will be the target. And once it starts, the bullying behavior escalates. Pushing, shoving or cutting line is a part of it. Grabbing items which are being distributed by an adult ahead of others, and pushing kids around is all a part of younger bully behavior.

After such treatment a child returned home from a pre-school saying, "Nobody likes me, I don't have any friends." A small girl returned from school and reported that a popular girl began intimidating a group of girls on the playground. If a girl disagreed on what game they would play, the popular girl would exclude the first girl from play and try to turn the other girls against her. The little girl complained to her mother that, "If she teased me in front of everybody else, I felt embarrassed. If she teased me alone, I felt sad." All the girls were scared of the bully because she had already exerted control over the others. This is the way it all starts, a day at a time and one child at a time, and gradually the bully takes over. Then, unless it is stopped, "it tends to increase during elementary school and peaks during the seventh and eighth grade," according to Nancy Mullin-Rindler, associate director of the Project on Teasing and Bullying at Wellesley College. When such behavior continues into the adolescent stage, the result may be a "Columbine type" of tragedy, when the kid that has been the receiver of mistreatment feels he's "had enough" and decides to get even.

Since the Columbine shootings in April, 1999, authorities are starting programs for schools to counteract this bullying type of behavior. Heretofore, programs have not been formally started in the school until about the fourth grade. Now they are starting in kindergarten, because they are needed by this age in order to prevent such behavior getting worse. It's interesting to note that European educators have been combating the problem for 25 years, whereas, we are just now starting. I think I am justified in putting another statistic with this. President Clinton, in Palo Alto, California, in March, 2000, said that "American children are killed by gunfire at a rate nine times higher than the combined total of the next 25 top industrial nations." It has also been observed that here in the U.S. more and more children *under twelve years old* each year are being accused of "murder." Nearly 300,000 high school students are physically attacked, and 125,000 high school teachers are threatened each month, according to Richard Lieberman's report in the *Los Angeles Times*. He further reported that bullying affects approximately 5 million elementary and junior high students a year.

The pre-schooler may be reluctant to go to school, "Because they don't treat me nice," or "He hurt my feelings." Yes, there will always be some of this behavior, and children need to learn to stand their ground. But some don't, and those are the ones who end up taking guns and threatening others. A gun gives this type of child the power that it lacked when being oppressed. The ultimate prevention is that little children learn to be compassionate of others at an early age and this attitude becomes contagious to their peers.

Some parents told Dr. Joyce Brothers that their child came home from school making biased remarks about other children. This was not something that was learned at home, and they were disturbed that the child had picked this up. Dr. Brothers' reply was, "One way to combat this is to build a person's own sense of value and worth so he has no need for this irrational ego boost. Try to establish the point that this particular bias is a first cousin to all other biases, and that one prejudice is just as destructive as another."

Parents' attention and expressions of confidence in the child are ways to convey that. Another way is to teach the child to say, "I like myself. I like myself." This is associated with neatness, cleanliness, personal grooming, etc. And, here, it is a case of which comes first, the chicken or the egg? Liking oneself and neat appearance go hand in hand and help convey this sense of personal value.

THE GOLDEN RULE

Very early at home and at Sunday school, I learned from memory, "Do unto others as you would have others do unto you." I learned that so young that I had to have it explained to me more than once; its meaning came on gradually. When a child reports some teasing or fights at play, right then is the opportune time for the parent to teach a lesson. "How would you feel?" Or "What could you have done?" Along with this I learned very early that God blesses peacemakers. I didn't understand it at the time either, but I came to understand what it meant later on, and by then it was engrained into my personality.

I have said earlier that even at 2 ½ years old, the child can feel shame. This is not on the adult level but is the beginning concept. This capacity indicates, therefore, that 2 1/2 years old is not too early to begin to teach these concepts. Just don't expect full comprehension at this age.

When I was 6 or 7 years old (in 1931, '32) in Oklahoma, we were in the dust bowl and in the throes of the "Great Depression." Since my dad was a good salesman, and good salesmen always have a job, albeit, he worked hard, long hours. But we were better off than many of the families around us. The standard greeting I heard at church or other places where adults gathered was, "Do you have work?" I didn't understand that very well at the time. But mother helped me understand it one day in this way. She was a volunteer to help feed poor children at school. She and some others made great pots of soup and served it at lunch. I ate separately and didn't understand why at first. I asked one day, "Why can't I eat soup with the others in the lunch room?" She said that I had breakfast and that many of those children did not have a hot meal all day except for the soup at noon. So all of it was for them. I was to eat at home or separately. I remember this vividly after 70 years because it made an emotional impact on me, and it was regarding food.

Such was not new to me. Before I started to school, I saw mother taking plates of food to people who knocked at the back door saying they were hungry. She explained to me what it meant to be hungry, that it was worse than just when a meal was late. She also said how those who had food ought to give to those who didn't have it. It may have been in a rudimentary way, but at 6 years old I got the message, because earlier I had been taught about my younger sister and brother having their needs. There were times to share and times to give in.

When the idea is repeated enough, "How would you feel (or did you feel) if you were in that position...?" The child will understand sooner than if you waited till you thought he was old enough. Start early!

TELLING THE TRUTH

Telling the truth is akin to fair play and can be learned in a similar way. Even though children don't understand the concept at an early age, they pick up a little at a time. Here is another situation where the parents must be alert to every opportunity to get the idea across. For example, a parent tells a small child, "I'll bring you something from the store." And then forgets to bring something. The child remembers and reminds the parent, "You told me you would bring me something." The parent agrees and says, "I told you the truth. I did intend to bring you something, but I got in a hurry and forgot. I'll make it up to you by such and such." The child can understand the parent's intent, even though the parent did not follow through.

Another example: Parent says to child, "Did you bring your tricycle off of the side walk?" And if the child says, "Yes," the parent can commend and praise the child for doing it and telling the truth about doing it. If the child says, "Yes," but did not bring the tricycle in, then the parent defines what telling the truth is and tells the child one must tell the truth. Talking to the other parent in front of the child about someone else's telling or not telling the truth enables the child to pick up on the lesson involved.

As soon as the child tells a story, when the parent knows it is a lie, the parent defines "truth" and how important it is to tell the truth. And about this time the child is learning how to put himself in another person's place; so the parent can give examples of how the child would be disappointed if the parent continually said one thing and did another. A lie is telling something other than the fact in order to deceive for personal gain.

It is important for the parent to understand the difference in a child's imagination and telling a lie. Your children at 3, 4, and 5 have vivid imaginations as a part of the maturing process. And TV and animated cartoons add to this. So the child may say he saw a bear on the sidewalk today. He should not be rebuked for "lying." The listener can merely say, "What happened?" or the like. So, distinguish between circumstances of imagination and lying. The most effective way to teach children about telling the truth is to set the right example. Too many parents will lie to someone while talking on the phone, and the child overhearing the conversation knows it is a lie. Parents often will have a child lie for them, on the phone or at the door, by saying something like this, "Tell him I'm not at home." "Tell her I have not returned yet." Under such circumstances the child is learning to deceive and is being taught it by the parent or other adult.

When the child has disobeyed and then is confronted about it by a question, here is the time the child is tempted to lie. When they tell the truth, they should be commended for telling the truth, even under difficult circumstances. Or, if they lie under such circumstances, they need to be taught and appropriate disciplinary action taken. Again, I emphasize that parents teach these difficult lessons in a spirit of love.

KINDNESS

A child is not very willing to share its toys with others at 2 1/2, but it's not too early to start encouraging this. Just don't expect perfection in this regard, yet. And the idea that "turn about is fair play" is probably one of the earliest lessons one can learn, because it comes close to the concept of fairness that we are born with.

Another very early memory I have is that I recall in my Sunday school experience we had little cards with pictures on them along with a verse we were to learn from memory. One of them was "Be ye kind." This is the positive side of sensitivity training. It follows close on the heels of not mistreating one's pets. "See how the cat purrs when you pet it? That's being kind." "See how the dog wags its tail when you come to pet it? That's being kind." "Is the dog happy when you feed it?" "Are you glad when I bring you candy?"

The concept of "identification" is not one the child can understand, but you can. When we put ourselves in another person's shoes, we identify with him/her. When we feel pained when our loved ones feel pain, we are identifying with them. This is the principle. Now, you can build on that principle when you are aware of the child's identifying with someone or something else. Look at the expression on the child's face. This will betray sympathetic identification. Then build on it.

For example, watch an older sibling's face when the baby drops its bottle and cries. Usually, you can see the child is "feeling with" the baby. Now observe out loud. "Jimmy, you can see how disappointed little sister is because she dropped her milk. She's still hungry and hurts. What can you do?" If Jimmy has not already given the bottle back, he will now...likely. When a younger sibling or visitor gets hurt or frustrated, ask the older one what she can do to make the other feel better. This is prompting the child to get the message that something can be done about helping other people. When the child has received such sympathy from you, the parent, it will understand more about passing it on to others.

Naturally, you need to be prepared for the older one to have a negative period at times, and "No" will be forthcoming from the child occasionally. Keep right on with the program. It'll bear fruit in due time.

I keep on repeating with all of the instructions and guidance you are giving your children, give them generously of your love.

FAIR PLAY

When children are at play, this is the best time to give them guidance with many principles of interpersonal contact. In fact, during play a child can learn most any principle of behavior. There are rules of the game that must be followed. Sometimes the group at play makes their own rules. At other times, they follow the "standard" rules they have learned from coaches or other leaders at school or in a sports program. There are rules of life, which must be followed, also. And this point must be made.

It doesn't take a child long to learn what "cheat" means. And s/he is quick to call this on someone who doesn't follow the rules exactly. To "play fair" is to enjoy the game, and the majority sees that one cheater is corrected or put out of the game.

I prefer the home yard or school yard informal games for smaller children. I think competitive sports are encroaching on younger children all the time, and they are not ready for that. Some school and sports programs have understood this, and the teams play, but no one keeps score; so, they get the fun of playing without overemphasis on competition and the touts of "We won. We're better than you are." It's a put down to small children who don't need it, and shouldn't have it. Too much competition at an early age encourages the "I win, you lose" concept too early in life. In the business world some far-sighted leaders and inspirational speakers are promoting a "win-win" concept in seminars all over the country. Cut-throat competition, upon which American industry was built, has been demonstrated to be undesirable. Although there is still a great deal of this philosophy left, the fact is there are enough material goods and business opportunities out there for all of us.

When kids organize their own games and choose up and play, even though they play to win, the next day when they choose up again, another group will be winners, and this passes the glory around. You win some; you lose some. As I said, this also prevents the parents and grandparents and others from getting so involved that the kids feel depressed when they don't win in front of family. Further, the competitive system promotes Monday morning quarterbacks at home, which, at times, can be depressing. Children have to learn to win graciously and lose graciously. This is life. And it is applied in the home when a child doesn't get its own way. It has to accept it. That's the way life is.

AN EXAMPLE

A 4-year-old in nursery school was very restless at nap time, and the teacher had to keep going back to him and asking him to be quiet. When finally allowed to get up, he picked up a long block from the shelves and held it aloft ready to strike the teacher. When he got near her he said, "I would like to hit you with this block," [impulse] then he lowered it a little and continued, "but know I shouldn't" [conscience]. He had learned this lesson well before he was ever 4 years old.

ETC.

Above, I have listed some basics. There are other traits than those I have listed that are necessary and vital to the grounding of the child. But by giving these examples, you know how to apply the principle to the peculiarities of your own situation.

CONCLUSION

Many psychologists and counselors these days are conducting "Sensitivity Groups," whereby, adults who did not learn the traits that I have described above, are presently learning these fundamental characteristics. There have been difficulties arise in college, or the work place, or somewhere else where people congregate. Slurs and harassments of various sorts make life miserable for those involved. Those who give these out and those who are the targets are having to learn compassion, kindness, and understanding belatedly. They would have been much better off to have learned these lessons at the age where they were most receptive to such lessons. And the larger our population becomes, the more important these principles are.

Among chickens, if one is injured or enfeebled, other chickens will start pecking on it at the point of injury and in due time peck the poor defenseless chicken to death. I have witnessed children act in a similar fashion. Of course, as an authority, I stopped the procedure and used the opportunity to teach. This happens often in many schools, and it is not discovered before it has done severe damage to kids who don't deserve such ostracism! The recipient of such action sometimes becomes the ticking bomb, ready to explode in some (usually anti-social) way. This is where a stable home life fortifies the child against such treatment. That child is a survivor.

POST SCRIPT

Steve Trujillo, of Newark, NJ solved a problem with a bully this way: "I was the victim of a bully in high school. At one point, I finally got up the courage to see a teacher, who told me to find the bully's weakness. I eventually learned that when he went to Great Adventures, he wouldn't go on any rides. He was afraid of heights. One day he took my lunch and told me, if I wanted it, I had to meet him outside and fight for it. I stood up and loudly said – so every one in the lunchroom could hear: "Meet me after school on the roof of the gym." More than 100 students came to watch. We waited 10 minutes before a teacher came. But the bully never showed up. And he never messed with me again."

Another boy solved a similar problem in a different way. Ron Megow of Houston said that, "The son of a friend of mine was in junior high school and was being taunted by a much bigger boy. He told his father, 'Dad, I just don't know what to do. This big kid at school wants me to fight him, and he says if I don't pick a time and place soon, he'll jump me.' His dad told him, 'Just tell the bully you'll fight him any time and any place, as soon as you get a letter signed by both of his parents saying they will not hold you responsible for any damages and injuries to their son.' The boy did what his dad said. After thinking about it for a few days, the bully decided he did not want to fight, and the two became buddies."

In Bluff City, Tennessee, in the Spring of 2004, two 13 year old boys were charged with aggravated assault after police said they carved a 10 inch cross and a swastika into a classmate's arm deep enough to leave a permanent scar. There was another victim of the same kind of assault at the same time in the bleachers of the football stadium during gym class. Police said they had never seen anything like this. This is another illustration of the kind of calloused, assaultive behavior that is taking place at younger ages.

QUESTIONS FOR MEDITATION AND/OR DISCUSSION

1) Have you counted the hours that your children look at TV each week? How do you feel about that time?

2) Have you noticed that some mothers compare the maturation level of their children with other children and are concerned about one being "behind" or "ahead" of another? Can you feel at ease about these comparisons now?

3) Do you remember any bullies in your schools as a child? How did they effect you or others?

4) Have you ever been on the receiving end of teasing? How did it make you feel?

5. What are some situations in your own current life experiences where you can teach your child to be aware of the suffering of others?

6) Have you ever taken a count on how many hours of meaningful time you spend per week with your child?

7) Ask your child, if he or she is in a school situation, if there are any children that are different from the others. Ask how they are treated. Encourage your child to treat them kindly.

CHAPTER 10

INSTILL PROPER GOALS, The Child's Seventh Right

Recently in Los Angeles we saw the musical, *Martin Guerre*, by the team that wrote *Les Miserables* and *Miss Saigon*. It raises all sorts of disturbing questions about identity. Based on an actual incident, the story is set in France in 1560. Two men, who were very good friends, fought together in war and saved each other's life at first. Martin's friend, Arnaud, thought Martin died in the battle, so he left and traveled. Eventually he arrived at the village of Artigat where Martin's wife, Bertrande, lived. Since Martin had been gone for 12 years, both the townspeople and Bertrande assumed that Arnaud was Martin. In spite of the fact that Arnaud did not claim to be Martin, Bertrande and the townspeople, looking for a hero, influenced him into the role. Three years later, Bertrande's uncle pressured her to break off with "Martin" for financial-political reasons and took his case to court. Then, during the trial where Catholic versus Protestant political forces entered the picture, the real Martin returned. He had survived his wounds.

Questions: "Can we ever know another person? Who are we 'really?' What do others see us as, or what do we think ourselves to be? Can we act ourselves into the role of another person successfully or even sincerely? By assuming another person's name, can one also assume his/her characteristics? Currently there are cautions and warnings pertaining to having one's "identity stolen." This is explained to mean that one can have his identity stolen by losing his credit card or having a bank deposit number appropriated. Of course, one's true identity is not a number or, for that matter, not even a name. Erroneously, people will hang their identity on their name or a credit card. Is that one's true identity? Others relate their identity by what their work is. Many men are now working in jobs traditionally held by women in such fields as child care, kindergarten teaching, nursing, and secretaries. Women are now taking positions previously held almost exclusively by men such as in the military, religious ministry, auto mechanics, road work, truck drivers, and other jobs of manual labor. Does this represent a confusion of identities?

IDENTITY

When a man and woman meet for the first time and start a courtship, they usually start with exchanging their names and then state what kind of work they do. But it will take a long time before they get to know each other in the sense of sharing their true identities.

The reason it takes so long is that one's true identity is so very complex that the various aspects of the person only emerge over a long period of time. Two people can go through a courtship; then get married and live together for years, and still not know each other very well.

A person's **identity** is not easily defined or explained.

One's identity makes up a body of feelings, which includes and results from, attitudes, opinions, judgments, beliefs, and conclusions from varied experiences. And they accumulate over the years. Obviously, the small child has not had enough time to accumulate a large body of such experiences, and his/her true identity continues to develop throughout childhood. There is such a thing as "family identity" by which we mean that there is a sense of feeling special about one's own family. A kind of family pride or an *esprit de corps* about the family unit is stimulated when family history reveals success in conquering obstacles. Sometimes that history has to do with solving problems or overcoming great difficulties or suffering. Such a history inspires a sense of family togetherness, which is strengthening and encouraging to the child, and contributes to its own developing identity and success in life.

DEVELOPING THE CHILD'S IDENTITY

The child from birth begins, ever so gradually, to develop into a separate individual in his own right. Technically, this is called the "Ego-Ideal" or the Self. This develops or grows over time when the child absorbs the parents' standards, as I have been discussing in the previous chapters. The child comes to behave more or less automatically in accordance with that previous training and conditioning.

For example, an infant is born with basic drives to satisfy and gratify itself. Then over time a set of standards to be used as guides are imposed and absorbed. They begin to control or modify the basic urges of childhood, and thus the conscience is formed. The conscience becomes the guiding force influencing behavior. At the same time, there are other values and standards of behavior and thinking patterns that accumulate in early childhood, along with the controls of the conscience. All of this together forms the "person" or "ego" or "self." In all of this, the child gradually ceases to operate only on the urges of the pleasure principle, but upon the principle of reality (or, one might say, "responsibility"). The child's parents are the primary guiding light, or force, of the child in developing all his actions and attitudes, including those with moral implications. And this person is one of a kind —different from all others.

WHO AM I?

In my professional career, I interviewed many people with severe problems who indicated sometime during an interview that they were uncertain who they were and doubted that anyone understood them. They could not make plans and keep them, etc. Frequently they had had many jobs and had several divorces and lived in confusion.

As one would expect, such a person is frequently more or less depressed and is usually erratic, unstable, and unreliable. Most often, with these people, something happened to them during the first six years of life, or they were deprived of some of these childhood needs.

Small, apparently insignificant acts and events, which put down that infant, gradually grew into larger more impressive acts, which suppressed the developing self. Very early, if a child is made to feel disappointed in itself a series of times, then it feels inadequate, anxious, defeated, and inferior. Such is the course, which happens "one drop at a time," until the self-esteem is crushed.

Low self-esteem causes some children to become fiercely competitive or severely alienated. The source of healthy self-esteem is that the small child feels lovable, capable, and accepted.

This is a very important part of child development because, to a degree, it determines what that person will do with his life as he becomes more mature. Figuring out what to do with one's life is a central part of identity formation for the adolescent, and it can be more natural and less formidable if the foundation has been laid in the early years.

PROPER GOALS

I like the metaphor that a counselor named Eric Middleton used regarding parental influence being likened to vitamins in the diet. *Vita* means "life." And vitamins literally give "life," but vitamin deficiency, as everyone knows, retards development and causes sickness. And currently, in the media are warnings about taking mega doses of vitamins, and the harm that can result. By analogy, parental influence in helping the child develop proper goals, can be deficient, or it can be over done. There is a broad optimal balance. While the beginning of this aspect of the child development is due in the pre-school years, this guidance continues well into adolescence. It is the start of such guidance that we are concerned with here.

In order to avoid too much detail I am classifying the goals for parental guidance during childhood into these areas:

→ **Goals for self -** in pride in clothes, toys, home, grades, self-acceptance, gender, achievement, child's feelings.

→**Goals for others** - including love, altruism, compassion, and consideration for the rights and property of others.

→**Goals for community** - support of groups, contribution to society, participation and cooperation with others.

GOALS FOR THE SELF

PROUD OF THE BABY

Jesus said that love of others must start with loving oneself (Matthew 22:39). The small child will be able to love others only if it is able to love itself, and it can only love itself if parents extend generous, sacrificial love to the child from the time it is born, even before birth. Now, accompanying that attitude, the parents are able to impress the child effectively with such ideas as being pleased with oneself. The parents show pride in the child all the way from infancy by the way the child is introduced to others as "one's pride and joy," "our new baby," etc. The child picks up on this very early. When the parents dress the child, even in infancy, and show pride by praising the appearance, the child is getting a rudimentary message of "who" she/he is.

The parents should talk to the baby constantly. When the baby learns to talk, look at him/her, listen, and respond in some way. Talk out loud about everything. You don't necessarily need a subject; it is a "thinking out loud." Singing gives a similar effect.

Use the baby's name constantly. Refer to the infant in the third person. "Stephanie is feeling happy today." "Does Abigail want some lunch?" "Does Ben want to play with his cousin Taylor today?" And any way you can encourage the small child to call out its own name is good: "Tell Mrs. Bost what your name is."

A TIDY ROOM

Even before the child is able to pick up things strewn about the room, the parents should take a "let's do it" attitude and encourage the child to help straighten the room. Experiments were done raising kittens from birth in a room with only black and white stripes all around the room. This confused them to such an extent that they could not maintain balance and effectively cope with their environment when they were removed. Even though there is a gap from cats to humans, there is a legitimate analogy. It is known that if children grow up in a stacked up, messy, conglomerated house, they don't understand what "clean up" means. Therefore, even small children need to have a relatively neat and tidy environment to develop pride in their surroundings.

What has been said previously on giving generous praise for the child applies here. Compliment the child's task when something is accomplished, be it ever so insignificant.

A SENSE OF FREEDOM

I want to be careful to be properly understood here. By making so many suggestions for parental care, there should be something said about giving the child a certain amount of freedom without control. Babies can be allowed to play with rattles, whether or not they throw them away. One year olds can be allowed to feed themselves, in spite of dropping or even throwing their food at times. Let the child have some time and freedom from being constrained, because this developing sense of freedom is necessary while still getting directions from parents and compliments along with the child's successes. Find the optimum balance between control on the one hand, and freedom on the other. All of this is building a sense of self.

Before ever going out to nursery school, or play school, and certainly before kindergarten, the child has the foundation for self-pride in appearance, caring for toys, pets, clothes, and following directions. Putting things away in bins or boxes can become routine and fun if the parent makes it fun. Do what it takes to make your child pleased with him-herself.

RESILIENCE

Dr. Peter Fonagy, Director of the Menninger Child & Family Center states very clearly that resilient, healthy children have the capacity to deal successfully with extreme stress. Certainly this is necessary in today's world, when there is so much in the air about the destructive effects of stress in our lives. A goal for parents must surely include resilience. The child who usually succumbs to stress in later years is one who is maltreated as a child. Even in childhood, before reaching adulthood, a child may suffer devastating consequences from stress, which activates pathways that control fear responses in the immature brain. An abused child may become a hypersensitive adult who will overreact to stress or trauma. This condition is a precursor to marital discord and work problems, as well as a miserable personal life.

Consider the positive side. Sue Shellenbarger has recently reported the results of several studies, which concluded that a sense of family history is linked to self-esteem and resiliency in kids. Stories of struggle and survival and of suffering and healing influence children to such an extent that they can expect to have fewer emotional problems, such as depression, than kids without this history. Building confidence in their own future, kids gain a sense of self in relation to other family members and to the past.

SEXUALITY EDUCATION

Sexuality is one of the most dynamic forces that humans have to reckon with. And most parents feel awkward or embarrassed about the subject with their children. It is also a matter of natural and intense curiosity in children. Why? Sexuality is a gift from God and should be treated with appropriate openness and respect. Because of its powerful potential in human relationships, it is vital that the child learn this from the beginning, and in a loving, wholesome, and truthful environment. Very few couples ever achieve their God-given sexual potential because physical, emotional, and spiritual maturity are a vital part of such an achievement. Specialists emphasize that the child should be spared reproaches, intimidations, threats, warnings, and punishments regarding physical manifestation of his/her sexuality. The example of the parents and the quickly perceived attitude of society are sufficient deterrents from unsociable behavior.

GENDER CONFUSION

Dr. Robert Stoller in a book entitled *Sex and Gender: On the Development of Masculinity and Femininity* reports on studies of case material at the U.C.L.A. Gender Research Clinic. One of the points made by Stoller is that a child's sense of maleness or femaleness develops within the first two or two and one-half years of life, and, one might say, settles in by four to five. There are three factors that influence this "core gender identity." They are:

1) A biologic force. Very early after conception the nervous system is organized to be female, but if there is sufficient androgen present, the organism is transformed into a male. Consequently, the female is born with the female reproductive system, and the male is born with the male system, each with its own balance of hormones.

2) The actual awareness visually of the child's own genitalia influences the thinking and total self-concept of that person. This visual awareness is further shaped as children play with and look at each other. (Review Chapter 8.)

3) Most important are the countless experiences the child has with his parents, through which the parents' assignment of sex is imprinted on the growing child. That is, parents treat little girls like traditional girls, and little boys are treated and talked to as boys have been traditionally. And, of course, such terms as "pretty girl," "good-looking boy," "growing to be like mommy," "big boy like daddy" are every day references in most homes.

There are times when something in the embryonic development goes awry. At a crucial time, for some reason, the hormonal balance is confused, and/or an abnormal size of the hypothalamus adversely influences the gender determinants in the fetus, and an infant is born with the body development dominating toward one gender, and the hormone balance influencing the other gender. Some of these infants may become homosexual or lesbian in their orientation, due to this anomaly.

Then there are those who, because of hormonal confusion, are born with elements of both male and female genitalia. These are called hermaphrodites. Cheryl Chase, Executive Director of the Intersex Society of North America, prefers the term, "intersex infants." She says intersexuality is more common than is generally thought. Ms Chase and others maintain that sex assignment doesn't depend on surgery. Yet, many of these persons desire sex change surgery.

Based on my own clinical experience, I believe there are several categories of persons without clear sexual identity. Those in these groups are the result of "environmental confusion." They do not have mature, natural feelings and attitudes toward themselves, or toward the opposite sex. Some individuals are confused about their sexual identity because they have been locked in at a pre-adolescent level in their sexual maturation. Others are confused because, for some reason, they have not seen clear cut male and female roles played out in their home environment in the pre-school years. It is unfortunate when a child is reared in a home where there are not two adults —one male, the other female – as parents or guardians. It is worse when there is abuse from one or the other of the guardians, or repression due to anti-sexual conditioning or extreme religious sexuality prejudice coming from home or religion.

There is a great need in the home to convey to the infant a **confidence in his or her own gender**.

PRIDE IN ONE'S OWN GENDER

Boys need to be glad they are boys. Girls need to be glad they are girls. And they need a mother and father in the home to illustrate the gender role. Furthermore, this theme must be repeated throughout these early years. Actively express to your child when the subject of "boys" and their activity comes up something like, "Aren't you glad you're a boy?" And to the little girl, "Isn't it good to be a girl?" Such statements put in the context of pleasure, fun, father-son and mother-daughter activity helps to build this part of the child's identity. In past generations many girls begrudged being girls because they were put upon, or saw their mother's put upon. This shouldn't be as prevalent as previously. As girls look to the future, the same thing can be told them about adulthood, viz., "You can be what you aspire to be."

Read stories that have male and/or female heroes to your children and help them to identify with such heroes. The Bible is a prime source, but not the only one. I think it is always best on the mysteries of life and death to bring God in on the answer or teaching. Stories from the Bible like Abraham and Sarah (Genesis 21:1-7) or Esther are good starting points. The Bible is a wonderful base for telling the story of life and the family. Also, a trip to the library or bookstore with your children will help you find sources.

Strengthening gender identity may be done indirectly, also. In a previous chapter on the child's curiosity, I referred to the natural curiosity about one's body and the body of the opposite sex. Acceptance of the child's curiosity and acceptance of his/her nudity is essential to developing this part of his/her identity. Some small boys will express such thoughts among themselves as, "I'm glad I'm not a girl because of. . ." And girls, talking among themselves, will say something like, "I'm glad I'm not one of those ol' boys because. . ." And they list their grievances about boys. These are healthy attitudes.

A certain amount of nudity by the parents around the very young children demonstrates this acceptance. Remember, the human body was created by God and was called, "Good." All the parts and functions of that body are miraculous in their functioning, and the church is likened to the body, (see Romans 12:5; 1 Corinthians 12:12ff; Ephesians 4:12ff). Indeed, the human body is described as a temple for the Spirit of God (1 Corinthians 6:19). When the parents let this view of the physical body control their attitude, they will automatically help the child develop his/her own identity. If parents are pleased with themselves and show confidence or pride in their own bodies, the children will also. There will be a sense of sanctity about the body, which will promote a wholesome attitude toward one's own selfhood. And those with this healthy, normal attitude will not be caught up in issues of homosexuality and same sex marriage.

To summarize, when an infant is born with male genitals, it needs a mother and father who recognize the good in this and accept it totally as a male by thought, words, toys, treatment, etc. The father is the needed role model, and the little boy learns to love and respect women by the relationship he has with his mother and the kind of relationship he sees between his father and mother. Similarly, when the infant is born with female genitalia, she needs rearing by a mother and father who demonstrate to her what males and females are like, and that they are loved for themselves. She sees her mother as a role model and needs her father as an example of what males are like. She loves both and grows to be like her mother in many ways. And the relationship with her father influences the kind of man she will eventually marry.

Re-read what I have said in Chapter 6 on satisfying the child's natural curiosity about the body. This will help here.

ACHIEVEMENT

Another aspect of developing identity is *achievement*. The meaning of *achievement* can only be taught in small parts in early childhood, but the foundation certainly can be laid. Parents can't expect much in the way of *achievement* from the infant, other than encouragement to sit up, crawl, and feed itself at appropriate ages, but the smiles and praise for these accomplishments get the idea across in a germinal way. Then toddlers are expected to talk and be toilet trained, while parents offer encouragement and praise. I have noted that some children are obviously pleased with themselves when they announce that they used the potty successfully *on their own*. I have observed that many children will turn and smile when they have pulled themselves up and walk while holding on to furniture around them or on to someone's hand. Obviously there is the pride of accomplishment.

When the parents create a home where there is *care, understanding, sympathy;* where the child *feels* wanted and secure; where there is joy and laughter, the goals for the self are automatically built in. Be available for your child to talk to you. Listen carefully and pick up on what his/her problems are and help the child solve them. Give assistance only as far as it is needed, then encourage the child to proceed on his own.

THE CHILD'S FEELINGS

Another fact of childhood, which some ignore, is that the child, even though small, is a human person with feelings about himself, others, and the world around, which will be a part of his/her life from now on. So, parents should be careful not to expect the same amount of control from a 2 or 3-year-old that they would from a school child. The little one should not be condemned for crying, or hitting, or whining, or kicking. Of course, seek to find out *why* he does these things and be sympathetic and understanding by using diversion or substitute tactics at the time. For example, a 2-year-old has been counting on going out to play, when suddenly, because of bad weather, he is prohibited. He stomps his feet and screams. Instead of arguing with him, be patient a minute; let his feelings be expressed; then go forward with some exciting activity for the time. A characteristic of childhood (and immaturity in an older person) is easy frustration and quick expression of anger.

When I refer to distracting a child or diverting him/her into another point of interest suddenly, I am not suggesting more trips to the zoo or outings to the park, which is all very nice, of course. But I emphasize that the child's immediate world around the home can be a captivating place with a variety of boxes or toys or looking at the changing scene out of the window; discovering another closet; a box of old toys that had been put away; coloring books or blank paper with crayons, even a talk on the phone to a friend or relative. Use your imagination. Children are surprisingly easy to entertain with the commonplace.

The kindergarten and school years are much easier for the child when the above principles have been instigated beforehand.

There is so much in the media, from a multiplicity of sources these days on our educational system, I am taking the space in the Appendix to tell how to make an "A" student.

A study by Harvard researchers a few years ago explored how parents could lay the best foundation for a child to achieve high grades in school. They concluded that by 18 months old the die was cast regarding the capacity of that child to be an "A" student. (See Appendix B for more detail on this.)

In spite of the weaknesses in the various school systems, you, the parent, can be the main influence on your child's grades. During the pre-school years you can lay the foundation for your child's success at school. I report from an authority on the subject, and his recommendations coincide exactly with the principles I have been writing about.

GOALS FOR OTHERS

AWARENESS

I've said that it takes around two years or more for a child to be consciously aware that other persons are different from himself. Jesse Stanton, education consultant in New York City, tells this story about how a 2 1/2 year old boy expressed his awareness of another child for the first time. The little boy placed three small wheelbarrows in a row against a wall and sat down in the middle one, and then left. Another little boy copied the same procedure and also sat down in the middle one. The first little boy looked at the reproduction of his arrangement across the room and then said slowly, showing by his facial expression how difficult this thought process was, "That's *Jimmy*, not me -- that's Jimmy, not *me.*"

There is another area of awareness of others that inevitably enters the picture. When children play together, someone's toy will get damaged or broken or lost. This is just the way it is with children. Sometimes there is even a strong disagreement over whom a certain toy belongs to. When these conflicting situations turn up, it requires parents who are virtual Solomons to make a decision as to what to do. If it is clear that your child lost or broke the toy belonging to another child, then your child must face this and learn to say, "I'm sorry." The two of you can share in a plan to replace it. Again, here is the opportunity to say, "How would you feel if Harry did that to your toy? What would you want Harry to do for you?" etc. An awareness of others' feelings can start at an early age. The need for this awareness was emphasized February 3, 2006, on the TV program, "20/20." A segment titled "What happened to manners in America?" reported that recent polls have shown an appalling decline and lack of manners in America today.

SHARING

Naturally, infants have no concept of what it means to have goals for others -- as we adults mean it. But children playing on the floor can receive the first lessons on this. Usually, mothers, daddies, or supervisors by nature will encourage a child to play with a guest or a sibling. Inevitably, two children will want the same toy at the same time and will have to be encouraged to "share" the toy while one is distracted. It's important that parents learn the art of distraction. While I knew of the procedure to be effective with children, my own impatience prevented me from carrying through as I should have when ours were little. I know it's difficult, but it spares the child many frustrating moments when a skilled parent can distract a child successfully from doing something that he/she should not. And it is when two or more children are playing together that distraction is so vitally important.

As the child gets beyond 2 years old, parents can do more reasoning with him/her as to why a sibling or visitor should have permission to play with the toys. "There are enough toys for everyone." "It's fair to share." "When you go to visit Cindy, you will want to play with her toys; so let her play with yours." etc. This is the place to emphasize how important it is to teach the child early that some gratifications have to be postponed. Simply, a parent can say, "You can get along without playing with that toy *until after Cindy leaves.* The parent can and should repeat often, "You can wait until so-and-so. Then do that." Or like, "We are going to eat our dinner now. You can play with that later." It is vitally important for life as one grows up that immediate gratification of desires is not always possible or best.

Some of you out there may be saying, "Scott hasn't been in our play room. I haven't seen an unselfish 2-year-old yet." Yes, no one is expecting even a 4-year-old to be a paragon of unselfishness. Don't expect a 2-or 3-year-old to share readily, except on rare occasions. But get started as soon as possible. It takes a while for the child to realize that these other children are not here to take care of "my needs."

VALUES

"Values" of the household are taught in small segments by such statements repeated over and over, "In our house we share." "Our house is kept neat." "Daddy and I love each other, and we love you too." "When visitors come to see us, we give something to them like refreshment, food, and courtesy." In other words, not only do the parents show an example of pride in the home and with others as an example, but also they talk about it to the child. "WE do this." "WE believe this." "WE share this way."

There is another aspect to values which is usually more obvious -- at least to older children. That is financial values. In spite of the fact that we are dealing with pre-school children, the first lessons can be learned by 4 years old. It doesn't take children long to become aware of money. They can't help but hear the subject discussed by their parents, and TV bombards them with its appeal to get this or that. They are frequently taken along shopping, and very early come to understand that groceries and clothes, yes, and candy and other supplies, are "bought." Very early in kindergarten they are introduced to spending, if they never were at an earlier age. There is lunch money, fees, supplies, and refreshments -- all bought with money. In fact, since finances are one of the key issues in the American home for survival, social standing, and spousal satisfaction, the child cannot avoid getting an early orientation toward money.

The child has lived with the fact that daddy, and perhaps mother, go out to "work at a job" in order to earn money to live on. The household has an income to use for clothing, groceries, recreation, cars, appliances, etc. Children should get an allowance as a share of this income, and to some degree it probably should start by 5 years old. Along with the allowance, the child must learn to save some for future needs, as well as proportion out what is available for day to day expenditures. Most of the time, when a child runs out of money, the parents should not rush to supply what is lacking, in spite of the temptation to do so. And along with the allowance, explain to the child what it is for. Children have to be told there are some things that cannot be afforded, even if there is money available for desired purchases. Money has to be "controlled," "budgeted," "saved." There are good reasons for this attitude. First, no child should have its every request granted for anything. The child should learn that early. This is a part of life, even when we live in the midst of plenty.

Second, the child needs to learn as early as possible that a decision needs to be made about spending on the basis of priority. For example, the child sees toys that a neighbor child has and wants one "like that." At the same time there is another request for a certain kind of clothing, say, a sport jacket. The child needs to be taught to determine which one he wants most, because he can't just rush out and purchase both. It can be simpler than that. The little girl is shopping in the grocery with mother. She sees candy that she wants and trinkets for her doll. Then there's a certain food like fruit or pies etc. that she asks for. Explanations that money has to be spread around to make purchases need to be given to the children as the opportunity arises. And the lesson of budgeting money and postponing desired gratification can be taught early in small doses.

EMPATHY

When a child is hurt, encourage another one to give sympathetic understanding by patting or hugging, showing concern, being patient and helpful. There are cases on record and shown on TV where a small 3 year old child can call 911 in an emergency. Practicing and make believe for emergencies around home can be good training for the child at several levels. This is the same principle. This awareness of other people and their desires, pains and needs can be taught very early in life in many small ways. I've mentioned this before, but it should be emphasized that here are the circumstances where the question should be repeated, "How would you feel if you got hurt that way and somebody helped you?" Or, "What would you like for George to do for you if you were hurt?"

CONSIDERATION

Young children can learn what "consideration for others" means. Inevitably, the child or someone else will have the TV or tape player turned too loud for others in the room or near by. Now is the chance to explain how one's actions can bother others. If the child does not get the point, the parent can take a loud tape player into the room where the child is watching TV. The child will learn how it feels.

CHARACTER TRAITS

Now, notice what has been included in the above suggestions. Along with pride in the self, there has been training in attitudes toward the environment and others. The child is learning the rudiments of *freedom, loyalty, responsibility, commitment,* all of which are a part of ego development.

In our artificial society, far removed from the agrarian circumstances of a few generations ago, children no longer feel they make a vital contribution to the family -- or to anything. This leaves a void in the ego. If a teenager is to have a feeling of usefulness, that concept needs to start in the pre-school years. Thus, the child needs to be taken into the home planning in every way possible. Even accompanying mother or father to the grocery, the child can share in some of the selections. In redecorating a room (especially the child's room) papering or painting, the small child can be asked about color or table arrangement or pictures that it prefers. Occasionally the child's request for eating out or a weekend outing can be respected. All of these little decisions add to the child's building up self worth and an attitude that will be expanded in due time to demonstrate goals for others.

GOALS FOR COMMUNITY

Goals for community involves an *awareness* of a wider world than the little circle of home and regular friends. Can such an attitude be started in the pre-school years? Yes, indeed, even though it seems remote at first. These days it is almost a forgone conclusion that the small child will be involved in groups where there are other children. If not with siblings, this may be in Sunday School, nursery school, child care, or simply cooperative baby sitting. In any and all of these settings, the idea is planted that there can be pride in the environment outside the home. Not only can the child be encouraged to help keep the place neat by helping the person in charge pick up after him/her, but the parent can also show concern by helping. Furthermore, the parent can talk to the child about what s/he can do to make the place more inviting or pleasant or better equipped. The parent can talk with the teacher to ascertain needs for equipment or decorations and then talk with the child and let the child help with shopping or selecting materials.

The small child can learn something about the plight of others in most of the world. Scenes are shown on TV of drought areas, starving children, and suffering humanity elsewhere. Most of the world has not been able to share in our good fortune. Pre-school children can be made aware that they can get involved with helping another city, race, or country to live a little better. Frequently there are disasters in our country and abroad where contributions are asked for. Let the child look at pictures and share in these opportunities, such as Christmas and Thanksgiving.

Not only are these situations an opportunity to assist with the basic needs of those deprived, but it is also a wonderful chance to expand the child's world so s/he may become aware of other countries, their life, and culture. By providing these opportunities and sharing information with the child about the circumstances involved, your young child learns valuable lessons and develops wholesome attitudes at an early age, which will stay with him/her for life.

As parents and children get in the habit of saving materials for recycling, it presents an opportunity to make the child aware of preserving our natural resources. At the same time, the child needs to learn about conserving our environment. Another way to get this point across is when the family cleans up after a picnic or camping outing. Reasons are given, and the small child can understand to a large degree. Similarly, when on outings into nature whether by traveling or camping, the point should be made to pick up and clean up after use. Also, the parents can call attention to how messy it looks when someone else has left their trash exposed. If careless people on the street throw trash into your yard, then is the time to show the child. Ask questions related to this like, "Does that look nice to you?" "Do you want to pick up trash that someone else carelessly threw into our yard?," etc. "This is the reason there are signs along the highway warning about littering the roadway. We wouldn't do that, would we?," etc. There are other ways to continue with this lesson, such as taking care of play materials and books at play-school. Thought provoking questions help the lessons to take root.

You see, when the parent takes the time to share these ideas with the child, that child develops an awareness of its own sense of well-being. And this sense of personal well-being contributes to its own stability and self-confidence. Moreover, the attitude toward others depends on the attitude toward the self. Altruistic people are the ones who have been taken care of. If they can't take care of themselves, then they will need to be cared for. Another built-in blessing with all of this is that *gratitude* is automatically taught along with these other lessons.

CONCLUSION

Question: *"Who* will your child be?" Your child will be the kind of person you have influenced him or her to be. This takes place one day at a time with the myriad of little incidents of interplay between you and your young child and others who gradually and briefly enter your circle. As the brain of your child develops faster than it ever will again, you're getting in there early with the kind of influence that really matters. These values and goals make up one's character. And when these traits are implanted in the early years, you won't be worrying about having an adolescent's lost soul at an age when its too late to alter the development of your child's ego. It's time consuming, yes. It also requires using your ingenuity, planning, and initiative. But it's worth it. And you will know it. I've been in hospital waiting rooms and in the corridors of courthouses with parents of teen-agers, who, in their tears, state plaintively, "I don't understand what happened. What have I done to cause this?" "Can we ever live this down?" "I can't believe this. How could s/he have done this?", etc. Although I have a pretty good idea of causes, in most cases, I don't voice my theories under those circumstances. We now are confronted with the present and the future that must be dealt with.

POST SCRIPT

I know a university professor and an adjunct who took a group of students on a "study abroad" program to Italy. This is the second time in a ten-year period that this couple have done this as a part of the university's study abroad education program. They report there was a radical difference in the group of students they took in 1990 and the group they took in 2000. The earlier group was cooperative, generally following the rules of procedure and expectations of a group of youth in a foreign environment.

The behavior of the group of 2000 was altogether different from the first group. The 19 year old students should have been better behaved than they were. This clearly reflects the early background training they received. While some of the students were from well-to-do families and thus may have been "spoiled rich kids," most of them were from middle or upper middle class families. But generally speaking, the decorum reflects very poorly upon their childhood conditioning, because their behavior indicates gross immaturity and poor childhood experiences in the home of origin. A give-away to the adolescent problem is the fact that their parents defended their actions. This was very likely what the parents had done throughout their childhood every time the children got into trouble. The leading professor summarizes their attitudes and behavior as follows:

- "If I don't understand or agree with a rule, then I don't have to abide by it."

- "If a rule is enforced, that means you don't care or aren't on the side of the students."

- "I'm 19 and deserve to be treated as an adult. However, if you think my behavior is crazy, remember I'm only 19, and this is what 19 year-olds do"

- "The difference between right and wrong? —whether you get caught."

- "I came over here to travel and party. The academic schedule should be arranged to accommodate my travel and clubbing schedule. This means I shouldn't be expected to read or have many requirements for the class."

• "Also, I can complain about any assignments given and sleep in class, because I've got to recover from the weekend or last night and be rested for tonight."

• "If I make a mess, someone else will clean it up."

• "*various, random acts of delinquency...*"could be anything from drinking a lot, not paying to ride public transportation, stealing things from street vendors, cheating, etc.

• "It is a status symbol to be able to consume large quantities of alcohol. 'If I drink so much that I don't remember what happened last night,' that is a real accomplishment. And if I engaged in bizarre, even destructive antics while drunk, my friends will find it funny. Also, I don't have to worry about any of my friends confronting me about my drinking."

• "Public profanity is perfectly acceptable, and if it offends you -- loosen up."

The preceding report is not an isolated situation. This is more nearly representative of a mass of today's adolescents than we like to admit. Witness to this is the fight and violence created by a group of youths in Decatur, IL, at McArthur High School in September, 1999. More than a mere fist fight, it was a brawl extending the length of the bleachers and spilling off the end. It caused some spectators to flee and others to duck and cover their children. The school expelled the students for two years in harmony with their school policy, which resulted in mass protests in objection to their punishment. Because of the protesters, the school district spent $100,000 defending itself--more than enough to hire two teachers for the year. Decatur's three high schools were closed for three days because of the fear of violence. Jesse Jackson, rushing to the defense of the fighters, described the riot as "something silly, like children do."

U.S. District Judge Michael McCuskey had a different opinion. In a ruling on the school disciplinary action, he said that "citizens and students of Decatur should be able to go to a high school football game and watch the contest on the field without worrying about a violent confrontation erupting in the stands." This should be true all over our nation. It used to be that way. Times are changing.

Decatur is not an isolated incident. On September 17, 1999, in Mount Healthy, OH, a riot broke out in a high school, which required the assistance of five police departments and ended with eight teens in handcuffs. As the fighters were being pulled apart and handcuffed by the police, another boy reached out and shoved Police Officer Schaefer to fight with him.

Elaine Leader, psychotherapist and executive director of Teen Line, Cedars Sinai Medical Center, from her rich experience states that "Teen stress can be deadly" through suicide and murder. She lists a series of living conditions that build up stress in adolescents over a period of time, and when parents' conflicts culminate in divorce, this frequently "sets them off" into depression, which is serious. She recommends that parents must "listen, listen, listen. Not tell them what to do, but listen, read between the lines..."

Clearly, the above examples vividly illustrate the behavior of *adolescents* (regardless of how old they are in years), who have been deprived of parental guidance and training in their early formative years. There is another factor, which I have not alluded to much yet, and that is the influence of religious training in the early years.

The Barna Research Group, Ventura, CA, observes that adolescent behavior by youth, similar to that described above, is explained in part by youth who have not had religious training. They state, "the younger the adult, the more likely the person is to be unchurched." When families went to Sunday School, children were taught basic Christian values and principles of civilized behavior (such as I have outlined in this book), along with a respect for authority. With the decline of discipline in the home and in the schools, as well as the decline in religious influence, we are suffering the consequences in every level of our society. Think about it. These are examples of the principle of cause and effect.

QUESTIONS FOR MEDITATION AND/OR DISCUSSION

1) Have your children, or the children of your friends, been in a group setting where bullying has taken place? How do you react to that?

2) What is your personal plan for helping your child develop a sense of healthy pride and self-confidence?

3) When you read a summary of the behavior of those college students, can you make some judgments on the causes of their behavior?

4) Have there been any incidents in your family history where someone has overcome great difficulty successfully? Have you shared this with you child?

5) In view of the foregoing material, what can you do to foster greater feeling of pride in your child?

6) At a time when we are nationally trying to improve our school systems, students are being sent to school from homes that have given them little or no preparation for cooperation with a teacher. These students subvert the classroom learning situation, and all suffer because of the few. What do you think could be done about this?

7) Have you considered how you can divert the attention of your child by using common supplies around the house, like boxes, wrapping paper, crayons, paper, tape, etc.?

CHAPTER 11

DEVELOPING SOCIAL SKILLS, The Child's Eighth Right

At a fundraising dinner for a school that serves learning-disabled children, the father of one of the school's students delivered a speech that would never be forgotten by all who attended. After extolling the school and its dedicated staff, he offered a question.

"Everything God does is done with perfection. Yet, my son, Shay, cannot learn things as other children do. He cannot understand things as other children do. Where is God's plan reflected in my son?"

The audience was stilled by the query. The father continued. "I believe," the father answered, "that when God brings a child like Shay into the world, an opportunity to realize the Divine Plan presents itself, and it comes in the way people treat that child." Then he told the following story:

Shay and his father had walked past a park where some boys Shay knew were playing baseball. Shay asked, "Do you think they will let me play?"

Shay's father knew that most boys would not want him on their team. But the father understood that if his son were allowed to play, it would give him a much-needed sense of belonging. Shay's father approached one of the boys on the field and asked if Shay could play. The boy looked around for guidance from his teammates.

Getting none, he took matters into his own hands and said, "We are losing by six runs, and the game is in the eighth inning. I guess he can be on our team, and we'll try to put him up to bat in the ninth inning."

In the bottom of the eighth inning, Shay's team scored a few runs, but was still behind by three. At the top of the ninth inning, Shay put on a glove and played in the outfield. Although no hits came his way, he was obviously ecstatic just to be on the field, grinning from ear to ear as his father waved to him from the stands. In the bottom of the ninth inning, Shay's team scored again.

Now, with two outs and the bases loaded, the potential winning run was on base. Shay was scheduled to be the next at bat. Would the team actually let Shay bat at this juncture and give away their chance to win the game?

Surprisingly, Shay was given the bat. Everyone knew that a hit was all but impossible because Shay didn't even know how to hold the bat properly, much less connect with the ball. However, as Shay stepped up to the plate, the pitcher moved a few steps to lob the ball in softly so Shay could at least be able to make contact. The first pitch came, and Shay swung clumsily and missed. The pitcher again took a few steps forward to toss the ball softly toward Shay. As the pitch came in, Shay swung at the ball and hit a slow ground ball to the pitcher. The pitcher picked up the soft grounder and could easily have thrown the ball to the first baseman. Shay would have been out, and that would have ended the game. Instead, the pitcher took the ball and threw it on a high arc to right field, far beyond reach of the first baseman.

Everyone started yelling, "Shay, run to first, run to first." Never in his life had Shay ever made it to first base. He scampered down the baseline, wide-eyed and startled. Everyone yelled, "Run to second, run to second!" By the time Shay was rounding first base, the right fielder had the ball. He could have thrown the ball to the second baseman for a tag. But the right fielder understood what the pitcher's intentions had been, so he threw the ball high and far over the third baseman's head. Shay ran toward second base as the runners ahead of him deliriously circled the bases towards home.

As Shay reached second base, the opposing shortstop ran to him, turned him in the direction of third base, and shouted, "Run to third!" As Shay rounded third, the boys from both teams were screaming, "Shay! Run home!" Shay ran home, stepped on home plate, and was cheered as the hero for hitting a "grand slam" and winning the game for his team.

"That day," said the father softly, with tears now rolling down his face, "the boys from both teams helped bring a piece of the Divine Plan into this world." (Author unknown, selected from the Internet)

The story above is a picture worth a thousand words of advice on training children for interpersonal relations. Obviously, the boys on these teams had had early backgrounds on compassion, fair play, and team work. Opposing ball teams now came together to cooperate toward one goal, which was bigger than any one person or any one team.

It wasn't just chance that several boys who were leaders communicated non-verbally, seeing the need to give a disadvantaged boy an opportunity to find some degree of fame in a bleak and lonely life.

"Too good to be true?" No. I have observed or supervised teams that were this considerate of the underdog. Contrast this behavior with the groups of boys about the same age who are going armed to school, and in many cases, shooting and killing fellow students, not to mention bullying and teasing. Other groups are engaged in gang wars. The early childhood background determines which type of group they will be in when they are adolescents.

BECOMING A SOCIAL BEING

Learning to relate successfully with other people is just as important in the child's development and growth as a well balanced diet and a loving relationship with the parents. And in interpersonal relationships of every kind, communication is the foundation of the relationship. In the work place, education, and certainly in the marital relationship, communication is essential. Business relationships require the same. In social relationships of couples with their friends, communication is the glue of friendship. Furthermore, in any of these situations or relationships, when there are inevitable differences, it takes skilled communication to resolve them.

Think for a moment on where one learns to communicate in the first place. It is in the home in the early years. The rudiments are in the relationships with the parents and siblings, if there are any.

Make no mistake about it, there is communication between parents and infant from birth – even before birth. The pregnant mother communicates adversely with the fetus by taking medicines or drugs that are known to harm its development. For example, boys born to mothers who were heavy smokers are eight times more prone to develop *conduct disorders*, than boys born to non-smoking mothers. Likewise, traumatic events, both psychological and physical, harm the developing infant. This is done by producing cortisol in the mother's body, which, in turn, inhibits social (as well as cognitive, and motor) development in the fetus.

Positively, parents, siblings, or others can communicate to the fetus by talking pleasingly, reading poetry, or playing calming, soothing music. Likewise, the pregnant mother requires a peaceful, loving environment for her well-being, as well as that of her infant. How does this "communication" take place? The neural circuitry (brain) is developing so rapidly and sensitively that the environmental conditions created by the mother have a great deal to do with what that infant will be like at birth, in addition to the genetic influence. Then, at birth, that infant has about 100 million brain cells (neurons). And each one can produce up to 15,000 connectors (synapses) to attach among these brain cells in order to form a complicated network. A strong, secure attachment between the family members and the developing infant, both immediately before and after birth, is essential to optimum development. Conversely, this sensitive brain can be harmed by environmental abuse, such as TV in the first years, to the extent that the infant is inhibited from forming healthy attachments to others.

What am I saying?

I'm talking about social development, and such development is founded on how mother and others close to her communicate to the infant before birth and soon after. Such communication is both verbal and non-verbal. An atmosphere of warm, soothing, loving relationships is essential.

Earlier it was said that, unfortunately, some parents post-pone efforts to "educate" the child, saying that should be left up to the kindergarten or school. Likewise, some parents feel that social skills should be left up to the time when the child is in kindergarten or school. That's too late. I'm emphasizing here that social skills are dependent on healthy, interpersonal relationships, and the aptitude for these relationships is conditioned starting before birth.

THE FOUNDATION FOR SOCIAL DEVELOPMENT (OR GROWTH STAGES)

Communication and relationship skills can involve a lifetime of development, but the first few years are the most critical in that training.

Starting at birth, the child does not distinguish itself as separate from its mother. This small world of its environment is ME. There is nothing, nor any one else. The mother is child; the child is mother. The breast is me. The bottle is child. On one occasion after another, if the child is holding a bottle of milk, and in its excitement of drinking, swallowing, and enjoying the warm flow of milk, it may become active and pull the bottle away. It does not understand what happened. It becomes flustered that something has happened to the milk.

When this same thing takes place when the infant is older, it becomes aware that "I" did that.

I'm going to be emphasizing encouraging your child to express itself and talk to you. But the earliest stage in communication is that *you* are talking to your child. Tell your child what you are going to do; talk about food, comfort, or plans – no matter how young the infant is. Sing and read to your child. Children's poetry and stories are good starters. Books from the library make a great impression. Bible story books are a must. Communication necessarily implies that two or more persons are exchanging words. With the newborn this exchange starts with your expressions until your child learns to respond with words. And remember, the more you talk to your child, the sooner the child will learn to talk, and the better its vocabulary will be.

ONE YEAR OLD

In the first year, if the infant does not have siblings, it needs to be put in the company of other infants or very small children. One of the earliest opportunities new parents have for introducing their baby gradually to other children is by going to church. Most churches have nurseries. Taking the baby once a week to the nursery is a good way of introducing the baby to a change in environment and the presence of other little ones. As the months go by, this experience is enlarged and expanded, giving the baby experiences with others as it becomes aware of strangers. This is a time to learn to share, to hear others, and, as it gets older, to assert itself in the earliest form of self expression to peers. You see that toddlers are physical and in the same period are social, and, thus, must be included with other small children. Humans have a "herd instinct."

TWO YEARS OLD

By age 2 this naturally self-centered child begins to be more aware when there is another child different from itself in the room. But at first, other children are just things like itself, to be investigated, but there is not an awareness that they are other people. For example, two infants are sitting on the floor together. One pushes the other. An anxious mother rushes to either scold or move them, imposing adult thinking into the scene. But to the infants, the awareness of the other is no different than if one had pushed a large balloon or ball. The companion for this moment is just another "thing."

THE FIRST LEVEL OF COMMUNICATION

In the room with other children, they are aware of each other's presence -- first by pushing one another or touching and experimenting with provoking each other. The first stage of communicating may be by one asking a question, like "What is that (train) there?" And another child of the same age will answer, "Cookies." There is no problem with this. They go right on with their play. Each has entered the exchange and is satisfied. . . on its own level.

I mention such a strange tidbit of interplay because the parent will judge this as being too odd to make sense. But at this age and level, this is all that matters. So, when parents hear questions from the small child, and they are acknowledged with *any* response, the child is happy. An interchange has taken place. This is early social contact. And statements or questions are for social contact, that's all. The conscientious parent gives a logical, sensible reply to a child's question, and the child either repeats the same question or maybe ignores the parent's response by some other means, and the adult is disappointed because the child does not acknowledge properly. The adult feels the child is not paying attention, or doesn't care, or is just trying to be aggravating. Not so. This is the first level of child communication, and it's quite *apropos*.

Even as young as 2 the child can act like a loser if it has been ignored or put down enough by the parent or care-giver. The child's attitude says, "I need to feel less than you," which is the attitude of one with an inferiority complex. Or, it may act out an attitude of "I am better than you," which is a superiority attitude. Your goal is to help the child to feel like, "I'm equal to you." This way both are winners.

By 5 these same children are able to play together, and to cooperate in stacking blocks or lego pieces. They laugh and cooperate until the impulse strikes one to knock them all down. At which time they laugh and start over again. This is social development. Awareness of someone else other than the self is taking place and the possibility that this other person can contribute to the fun and games of life, or to conflicts, has now become real.

THE GROWING AWARENESS OF OTHERS

As the world of persons opens up, and they become real to the child's presence, there comes an awareness that when a baby sister or baby brother is referred to, this means somebody else is around. The 2-year-old child does not grasp this like the 4-or 5-year- old child does. The attitude of the of the 2-year-old is, "so what?" The child of 3 or 4 may be excited until after the baby arrives. Then there may be a drastic change either of loving attachment or of "jealous" disdain. But the whole area of "baby" and pregnancy opens up curiosity. One child may be old enough to take delight in feeling of mother's tummy to feel a baby move inside. But the child has to be old enough to understand that just because an object is out of sight does not mean that it is gone. This difference is learned early.

INSTILLING SOCIAL GRACES

In essence, this is what childhood training is all about. Our culture has been built on certain principles or qualities of life. Such qualities have been laboriously developed over the ages of human experience. These qualities, based primarily on our Judeo-Christian heritage, are considered to be fundamental to our way of life and are passed on from one generation to the next. If these are not passed on from one generation to the next, then culture, as we know it, dies. These traits or qualities prominently include: **honesty, trustworthiness, courage, love of truth, dependability, self control, independence, loyalty, devotion to duty, unselfishness, respect for just authority, and concern for the rights of others.** All of these qualities are involved in interpersonal relationships—society, if you please.

Children are not born with these traits ingrained in their systems. They are learned from adults of the previous generation . . . most notably their parents. And it takes discipline to infuse these qualities, as standards of behavior, into our offspring. How is it best done? Well, it takes time; and parents who are not willing to spend time with their children will not instill these values.

EARLY SOCIAL CONDITIONING

The home is the center for learning how to get along with others. In growing up, the child is preparing to go out into the school world first, then the social and business world, while establishing his/her own family unit. Thus, s/he must learn how to get along with others, which requires that one must at times restrain impulses, postpone gratification of some desire, channel feelings into appropriate means of expression, and learn to love someone else. Parents must repeatedly demonstrate these traits in front of their children. The most effective way to teach these traits to children is by the guidance, explanations, and example of parents.

Over the years in a variety of situations, I have observed some parents who, in deference to visiting friends or neighbors, have neglected their own children. For example, a parent, in an effort to be polite, will say to one's own child, "Let Margie have your doll a while," when Margie is a visitor and grabs a favorite doll and tugs. Or if Margie breaks the doll, mother says, "Oh, that's all right; it doesn't matter." It may be a favorite doll or an only doll, and it does matter. Either parent should suggest that Margie wait and take her turn with the doll. Little children should not be coerced into meeting adult standards. In the outside world, children are expected to stand up for themselves and their own rights. They can also be expected to respect the rights of others and to help others, as well as accept disappointments. And parents should arbitrate in these situations.

PARENTAL GUIDANCE

These circumstances, so normal in the adult world, are strange to the small child. And s/he has no technique for dealing with these new circumstances. Parents must not only guide their children through various kinds of relationships from childhood on, as they learn to stand up for themselves, but also to share with others. Recognize it is better for small children to express themselves one way or another, than to be so withdrawn that they become the silent, isolated type who may become the recipient of bullying.

The answer here is for mothers (or fathers) who get together for their children to play, to talk about "rules for engagement" and agree on standards whereby their children can play together relatively peacefully, stand up for themselves, share, and resolve their differences by arbitration. Grown-up standards are usually too complicated for small children. They need their own set of standards of behavior, arbitrated by their parents. But such arbitration and interference should be delayed while children try to work out their differences on their own, when they are old enough. And frequently they do.

First, parents should not permit a child to be abused or overcome by another child. It's true that children may *appear* to be playing rough when in reality they are simply exploring and experimenting with each other normally. Under these circumstances no interference by an adult is needed, unless it gets out of hand. Children have to learn to be considerate of another's feelings as well as to give and take. A demonstration by an adult with a baby can show how to pat or rub another without hurting. Furthermore, the victim should not be forced to suffer in silence when being taken advantage of by another stronger, older child.

With older children, say 3- or 4-years-old, an adult should be patient and calmly, firmly insist that, according to the rules, they cannot be too aggressive.

Secondly, parental arbitration requires that a parent interpret a behavior for a child who does not understand the behavior of another. That is, when a child attempts to grab a toy away from another, an explanation such as, "Sarah just wants to be friendly with you," or the parent should say, "Sarah, you wait, and it will be your turn in just a minute." Then you find another toy and stimulate interest in it. *Explanation* and *diversion* are helpful procedures. If there are cries of protest, give words of solace and comfort, but stick to your guns.

Thirdly, one of the ground rules should be that no one child monopolize one toy most of the play time. Having several toys from which to choose helps to prevent this problem.

Fourthly, in case there is a much younger or a timid child in the group, protect this one from abuse by the other children. Help this one resist the more dominant child and have his turn for play. Timid or not, a visiting child should not be allowed to take over your playroom and deprive your own child of a new or favorite toy.

The playroom (or nursery room) is the first place where interpersonal relationships begin. And it is learned, not by lectures, but by guided play where the children take turns, share with others, learn to give and take, and control aggressiveness in company with others about their own age.

SOCIAL PROGRESS IN THE EARLY YEARS AT HOME

Parents must give a clear, immediate message that certain words or actions are unacceptable and won't be tolerated, so that, when the parents are away from the child, the child will be cooperative with a substitute parent. Don't overreact, but discourage the language or the act, rather than the child. When the child learns to speak correctly and properly, praise the speech or deed, rather than the child. I have already suggested giving the child a choice in selecting items for breakfast. But one should also give the child a choice occasionally about the disciplinary procedure. The parent can say, "You can apologize, or you can miss your program this afternoon. You decide what you will do." Again I stress that this prompts the child to respond with words expressing its feelings.

Since this is the period when the open, receptive mind of the child takes in the vocabulary and speech patterns of the parents, it is imperative that the parents watch their speech. Mother and father must remind each other when the wrong words are uttered in front of the infant, no matter how young it is. Not only must the vocabulary be guarded but also the tone of voice, arguments, disagreements, and outbursts must be controlled. Relatives who visit frequently must also be given these same cautions.

INCLUDE THE CHILD IN DECISIONS

It is always better to include the child in on the decision process as to what has been done wrong. This is best done by a series of questions. For example, the parent can ask calmly, "Why did you do that?" "Can you see the result of what you did?" "How can you improve on that the next time?" "What would you rather do?", etc. Evoke from the child -- even at an early age-- some understanding of the misbehavior or disobedient action. Questions of another sort may illicit a response from the child. When the child returns from an excursion, visit, trip to the zoo, or other exciting activity, keep asking the child what she did, what did he like the best, what were the refreshments, etc. At such a time the child is usually filled with emotion of the activity and, thus, is in a good position to practice communicating with you. An ideal time for this is with the family around the dinner table—a very important occasion.

It is important that parents encourage verbal responses from their child and this is done with most children by questions. After kindergarten or nursery school, pause with your child, with milk and cookie, and exchange conversation. Do not ask questions that may be answered only with one word like, "Yes," or "No." Ask specifics like, "What did you do in Ms Bate's class today?" "With whom did you eat lunch today?" "What did you and your friend Brooke play today?", etc. If you have trouble getting your child to talk, ask this one, "What did you not like about school today?"

Asking questions will do more than illicit a response from your child on the issue at hand, the child is coerced into thinking and communicating. An emotionally charged situation with you, the parent, will usually be an encouragement for the child to talk. This exchange necessarily strengthens the bond with you and your child. The child is learning to communicate, which is necessary, in order to build relationships and get along with others. In dealing with adolescent problems in the home, I constantly wished to myself that I could ask parents why they did not learn to communicate with their children during the early years. This would likely have prevented conflicts in the adolescent years. In treating hundreds of troubled marriages, I was deeply impressed that communication is a basic process, which the couple must learn early. All marriage counselors realize this. I'll explain.

In homes where there are older siblings, there can be a family meeting about once a month (or more often) where various issues of the family can and should be discussed. Smaller children can participate. Depending on the age, they may be observers or participants. Here they will observe the family exchanging ideas, which will prompt them to have some degree of participation. All of this is good experience in interacting with others in the family. Issues of the household may be discussed and will include daily routine about the house, leisure activities, vacation, purchases of furniture, remodeling, car, etc. The goal is family openness and discussion. Parents should encourage feelings and opinions to be expressed. Of course, in decisions the parents have the last word. Such meetings should be started early. Those families who wait till the children are teenagers have waited too long. In spite of all, some children just do not talk.

PLAYTIME AS SOCIAL TRAINING

Dr. Harry Harlow learned much about what to expect in human behavior in his work with rhesus monkeys. Experiments which could not be made with humans, could be made with monkeys. Some outstanding conclusions he and his staff made were later applied and verified in work with children. This prompted Harvard University psychologist Jerome Kagan to observe, "It's as important for a youngster to form healthy relationships with others his own age as it is for him to have a good relationship with his parents" in order to form social relations. A caution to parents is that an only child must be provided with playmates from early on. Otherwise, that child will be impaired to some degree in social relationships and in the sexual relationship in marriage

Three, 4- and 5-year-olds need playmates their own age. The neighborhood where the child lives may provide these companions. Or the child may be in a nursery school with such children. In other cases mothers who are friends in a neighborhood or the "koffee klatch" can turn into a group gathering with small children who learn to play together.

Children of this age group have valuable opportunities to exchange ideas for play together. First one and then another has ideas and suggestions for play, and this in turn prompts learning to give and take, sharing, cooperating, and leading. Adults should monitor as unobtrusively as possible. Nursery school teachers recognize that parents need to be playmates more than they can be. Through love, parents are motivated to take the time to give out "ooh's" and "aah's" when the child makes a joyous discovery of some kind.

In another setting a child may start to play some make-believe game, and the parent can supply imagination or materials which add greatly to the child's fun. The child may be playing "salesman" like daddy, and a parent supplies some scrap paper for orders or a paper bag for a brief case, or becomes the purchaser of the child's product. All of this is vitally important for the growing child. Children love boxes, packing materials, foam peanuts, etc. for their imagination. I have observed that refrigerator boxes are a favorite. The fun and interchange is rewarding for both parent and child.

Traditionally, as a part of the childhood period, children, including small children, have spent time during recess and after school playing unstructured games. They chose up sides, organized the activity, and discussed rules or adapted them to their circumstances. All of this required non-adult-supervised activity in which they learned the niceties of communication and getting along with each other. They were relaxed and enjoyed each other's company.

Bruno Bettelheim, who studied child development more than 70 years, maintained that such activity in childhood had many advantages for the child's development and well-being. He stated, ". . . Play is the child's most useful tool for preparing himself for the future and its tasks. . ." Bettelheim also said, "A hundred years ago the span of childhood was more than 10 or 11 years; now the years from about 5 or 6 to 13 years constitute childhood —at best some 8 years." To make matters worse, those 8 years are "encumbered" by adults, themselves pressured, who coerce the child into structured sports programs or into household chores along with doing more homework. This criticism is supported by the University of Michigan Institute for Social Research, represented by Sandra Hofferth.

Relaxed play after school has several advantages. Certainly, it enables children to communicate with their peers. It provides a change of routine, and the interaction in a relaxed atmosphere will help the child to make adjustments in order to get along with others, not to mention the health advantage. It will also relax the child from the strictures of school so that the child will rest better.

Overall, this undesirable condition of shortening play time and increasing stressful activities is shortening the period of "Childhood." A healthy, wholesome childhood is a stage of growth toward maturity and should not be curtailed. There are several reasons for this curtailment.

Bettelheim said, "Today's children are too often cheated out of their childhood because too many parents (and the media) worry them with adult problems. . . ."

EARLY FOUNDATIONS FOR MARRIAGE

Early pre-school communication practice with peers will help a later marital relationship. Adults who feel lonely are usually searching for intimacy, which they have never experienced. Some don't even know that's what they want. In the beginning Adam observed that all creatures had a companion but him – he realized he was alone. A companion was needed to complete himself. But having a companion necessitates the ability to communicate and share in order to have a true relationship. This preparation starts in the pre-school period of life. Small children can learn to share facts – what happened today. They need to learn to express their feelings – how they feel about those events. This is simple enough if parents are aware enough to prod such communication. This is the basis of human interaction.

SOCIAL RELATIONS AT SCHOOL

This is the place to say a few words about the child and kindergarten and school. By the time your child leaves home to start to nursery school, kindergarten, or childcare, the child needs to understand what it means to mind. When a child goes to a classroom not having received his fair share of love, attention, and discipline, he will not get off on the right foot in the group environment. He or she may be hungry for attention or may be from a permissive home, or from a home where s/he has been abused. In any of these situations, the child is carrying excess baggage with him/her. This usually affects his/her behavior at school in some way, such as being sassy, disruptive, impertinent, abusive of other children, using inappropriate language, being insolent, uncooperative, aloof, disobedient, selfish, etc. This is not a good way to start school. . . for anyone. At whatever age the child begins to spend time outside the home, that child must be prepared to be responsive to adult leadership and cooperative with peers, in order to make the adjustments so necessary for effective learning conditions to take place.

PARENTS MUST COOPERATE

As the child gets older, work at school automatically gives him/her the basis for continued encouragement to perform one's duties and do them on time. One of the problems in our education system, that all the government money in the world will not solve, is that for children to perform successfully at school, there must be cooperation and encouragement from the parents in that child's home. Teachers cannot be expected to be the only ones educating the child. When parents permit children (either by their absence or by their passivity) to park in front of the TV all afternoon and evening, the school assignments will not get done. It's that simple. And a subtle complication to this is that one of the biggest indirect disadvantages of children's spending so much time at the TV is that they are not relating to their associates by play and exchanges in their shared peer activity.

Furthermore, when the teachers cannot keep enough order in the class room to teach and demonstrate because parents have not taught the child to mind and get along with others, even the classroom time is wasted. Again, the parents must realize they are partners in the total education of the child. A child, well-disciplined in the art of inter-personal relations, is the one who will acquire the best education. Most schools these days appear to be very reasonable about their disciplinary procedures, and thus the average parent can afford to stand behind the school, just as one parent needs to support the spouse in being consistent in this guidance of the child's behavior. There will be exceptions. Some events are unjust and unfair, and the parents may need to support the child as opposed to the school disciplinary measures.

But investigate before going off half-cocked. The parents should know the teachers and the school well enough to know what stand to take on behavior problems at school, whether about homework or other behavior at school. Children sometimes go home after school and give an entirely different version of critical events at school rather than what actually took place. They have limited viewpoints.

Many a parent in time past, when schools used corporal punishment, has said to a child, "If you get the paddle at school, you can expect the same thing when you get home." This has worked for some. For others it has been unfair. It depends on the circumstance of the family unit and the school situation. Finding the middle ground on this kind of situation is what is important. But fortunately the "middle ground" is pretty broad.

SUFFICIENT REST IS NECESSARY

Some studies have determined that many children are not learning properly, or as expected at school because they are simply tired. It has been determined that adults and children, on average, require one more hour of sleep than they are getting. Parents can determine this by how hard it is to get the kids going in the mornings. A child that is sent to school being half asleep and without taking time for a wholesome breakfast, is not going to be a good student. There are multiple causes possible for such a condition.

It is obvious if the child stays out playing too long, or spends too much time in front of the TV, s/he won't get enough rest to be alert the next day. There are some kindergarten or first grade schools which require too much time for programmed activities after school is out. There has been no time for relaxed play after school, and thus the child cannot get prepared for the next day. Failing grades and/or failing deportment should be investigated to see if the student is simply getting enough recreation and rest for an otherwise demanding schedule at school. Such knowledge presupposes that the parent can control the situation; and the parent can control it at 12 or 14 years old if s/he has controlled it at 5 and 6 years old.

OTHER SOURCES FOR SOCIAL TRAINING

RELIGION

Another variable in the training of social relationships is the family religion.

Children who live in a Jewish neighborhood have a different routine from those in a Christian neighborhood. Even within the Christian neighborhoods there will be expectations by faithful Catholic families that are different from those that Protestant families have for their children. This will have to do with recreational activities, times that the children are expected in at night, the kind of behavior that is permitted between the sexes, and even where the children go to school. This is the reason I say repeatedly that parents must evaluate their peculiar circumstances, taking into account a number of factors, when determining the chores, school, and leisure activity, and other behavior of their children. These same principles apply when a family moves into a neighborhood with a different ethnic grouping. Parents, pay attention to what's going on, and you will be able to decide on the appropriate course of action.

CONSIDERATION OF OTHERS

Social skills are learned in this way with children. Behavior in the interpersonal relationships, which promotes smooth, pleasant relations, brings admiration and approval. When the child comes in from play, and by asking questions, the parent determines the child had a good time, then observes something like this, "When you get along well, you have a good time, don't you?" The child learns the significance of feeling "important" from such behavior. Virtuous behavior should be followed, then, by appropriate praise, and this, in turn, prompts the child to feel important and essential to a friendship. Capitalize on this. At a more mature level the child will appreciate receiving added privileges when s/he shows a sense of responsibility.

Another factor in "social skills" is that the child must learn to respect the rights of others. Children should learn early in life to be concerned for the outcast, the child that is "different" either physically or emotionally. Kids at school or on the playground can be cruel to those who are different from the group by teasing and ridicule. Very early a child can be taught to refrain from making fun or calling names to the child who is different.

One of my early memories is that mother told me that she had to wear glasses at an early age and at the turn of the last century her frames were large and black, and the kids at school made her feel terrible by calling her names. So she encouraged me to take up for children at school who were ridiculed by others and to be a friend to those who had no friends. I was glad to do this throughout school and had a deep feeling of compassion for my fellows and continue to ever since.

EXCEPTIONS TO THE RULE

CHRONIC AGGRESSIVE BEHAVIOR

Researchers in child development have given evidence that children who go to kindergarten frustrated, angry, and/or self-centered, cannot be directed toward cooperation in the learning process. Such research emphasizes that conflict and violence in the home is a prime cause of such pupil frustration.

SHYNESS AND HEREDITY

In their observations of monkeys (Harlow, and Stephen Suomi) and children (Kagan, J. Steven Reznick and Nancy Snidman), researchers detected that a certain percent of children appear to be born naturally shy. This is betrayed by hormone levels and response to stressful situations as early as 21 months old in about 10 to 15 percent of babies. Very timid children were more colicky, constipated, and irritated as infants than were other children. Many had allergies that continued into middle childhood. It is encouraging to know that both groups of researchers concluded that "Being born uptight need not be a social handicap."

In a report in *Psychology Today*, Kagan said there's nothing deterministic about the biological vulnerability of very shy children. "Nature gives the infant just a very small temperamental bias," he emphasizes. "The proper environmental context can change it profoundly. It takes more than simply a biological vulnerability to produce an inhibited child. You need a stressor plus the vulnerability." He continues to emphasize that very timid toddlers tend to stay shy for a time, but such children can improve with the help of their parents. Based on interviews with parents, Kagan believes that they helped their children overcome shyness **by bringing other children into the home and by encouraging the child to cope with stressful situations.** In those rare cases where parents observe that they have an infant who is retiring and shy, it does not necessarily mean that they have failed in a program, like outlined above, to train a child to be social. Second, in case a child is born to be shy, parents can diligently follow the course as presented above and expect the child to improve. They do need to be sensitive and recognize the shy baby soon

CONCLUSION

Our nation is gaining rapidly in population. We are living closer to more people than ever before, which presses us to communicate more clearly and effectively. We know that a high percent of people cannot communicate effectively. Just ask several people for directions on how to get to a place that they are familiar with. Then try to follow those directions. It's frustrating. Or talk to one marriage partner and then a spouse about an event they witnessed like a wedding, an accident, meeting a strange couple, or even an interchange they had among themselves. You will likely get two very different versions of the same incident. Lawyers experience this frustration all of the time. Two eye-witnesses to the same event may tell very different accounts of what happened. Most people do not communicate clearly. And the reason is that in the early pre-school years they were not taught.

So what? Well, interpersonal relationships are built on communication. Our ability to meet, get acquainted, and get along with others depends on communication, both verbal and non-verbal. Marital and business relationships are dependent on good clear communication, and that determines the success or failure of the relationship. Safety in air travel is dependent on clear communication. Carrying out a mission by the military has the same requirement.

But good communication is not the "be all and end all." Communication is the bridge between personalities. Developing traits that are conducive to getting along together, working together, showing consideration for the rights of others, truthfulness, being dependable, responsible, loyal, devoted to duty, etc. –all foster healthy social relationships. And such traits are communicated among people.

Progress and success in the adult world ultimately is the result of communication in enter-personal relationships. If "The hand that rocks the cradle rules the world," here is where it starts, viz., in guiding the baby through the first years into healthy inter-personal relationships.

One child who apparently had all the right encouragement at home returned from her first day at school with this expression of frustration, "I'm just wasting my time," she said to her mother. "I can't read. I can't write, and they won't let me talk!"

POST SCRIPT

"KEEP ON SINGING"

Like any good mother, when Karen found out that another baby was on the way, she did what she could to help her 3 year old son, Michael, prepare for a new sibling. They found out that the new baby was going to be a girl, and day after day, night after night, Michael sang to his sister in Mommy's tummy. He was building a bond of love with his little sister before he even met her.

The pregnancy progressed normally for Karen, an active member of the Panther Creel United Methodist Church of Morristown, Tennessee. In time, the labor pains came. Soon it was every five minutes…every three…every minute. But serious complications arose during delivery, and Karen found herself in hours of hard, relentless labor. Would a C-section be required?

Finally, after a long struggle Michael's little sister was born. But she was in very serious condition. With a siren howling in the night, the ambulance rushed the infant to the neonatal intensive care unit at St Mary's Hospital, Knoxville, Tennessee. The days inched by. And with every sad day the little girl got worse. The pediatric specialist regretfully had to tell the parents, "There is very little hope. Be prepared for the worst."

Karen and her husband contacted a local cemetery about a burial plot. They had fixed up a special room in their home for the new baby – but now they found themselves having to plan for a funeral. Michael, however, kept begging his parents to let him see his sister. "But I want to sing to her, Mommy!" he kept saying, insistently. Week Two in intensive care looked as if a funeral would come before the week was over.

Michael kept begging about singing to his sister, but as we know, children are never allowed in Intensive Care under any circumstances. Karen made up her mind, though. She would get Michael in there whether they liked it or not! If he didn't see his sister right then, he may never see her alive…

She dressed him in an oversized scrub suit and marched him into ICU. He looked like a walking laundry basket! But just as they headed past the Nurse Station, the Head Nurse recognized him as a child and bellowed, "Get that kid out of here now! No children are allowed!"

The "mother" rose up strong in Karen, and the usually mild-mannered lady glared steel-eyed right into the head nurse's face, her lips a firm line. "He is not leaving until he sings to his little sister!"

Karen walked Michael to his sister's bedside. He gazed at the tiny infant losing the battle to live. After a moment he began to quietly sing. In the pure hearted voice of a 3-year-old, Michael sang: "You are my sunshine, my only sunshine, you make me happy when skies are gray…"

Almost instantly, the baby girl seemed to respond. The pulse rate began to calm down and become steady. Karen caught her breath. "Keep on singing, Michael," encouraged Karen with tears in her eyes and a lump rising in her throat.

"You'll never know, dear, how much I love you. Please don't take my sunshine away." As Michael sang sweetly and softly to his sister, the baby's ragged, strained breathing became as smooth as a kitten's purr. "Keep on singing, sweetheart!" whispered his mother excitedly. She laughed and cried at the same time.

"…The other night, dear, as I lay sleeping, I dreamed I held you in my arms…"

The small body of Michael's little sister began to relax as rest— healing rest—seemed to sweep over her. Tears had now conquered the face of the once bossy head nurse. Karen absolutely glowed.

"'You are my sunshine, my only sunshine," pleaded Michael, "…Please don't take my sunshine away…"

The next day--the very next day--the little girl was well enough to not only be discharged from Neonatal Intensive Care, but she was also allowed to go home! *Woman's Day* Magazine called it 'The Miracle of a Brother's Song.' The medical staff even called it a miracle.

Karen called it a miracle of God's love.

I (JAS) say the song was a prayer, and God answered that little boy's prayer, motivated by love.

QUESTIONS FOR MEDITATION AND/OR DISCUSSION

1) Have there been any communication issues in your family (childhood or marriage)?

2) If you have a baby, have you noticed non-verbal ways the baby communicates with you? What does it say?

3) If there has been a pregnancy in your family, have you tried to communicate with the baby before birth?

4) Frequently, when a group of small children get together, there is one who is more boisterous or dominant. Also, usually there is one that is more passive, or reticent. How does the rest of the group react to these?

5) Have you tried sitting down on the same level with your child and asking questions to prompt him/her to talk? What happened?

6) Have you had your baby in a church nursery? What was your and the baby's experience?

7) What kind of experience was it when you and your child first went to kindergarten or child care?

CHAPTER 12

TO MATURE SPIRITUALLY, The Child's Ninth Right

Only be careful and watch yourselves closely so that you do not forget the things your eyes have seen or let them slip from your heart as long as you live. Teach them to your children and to their children after them.

These commandments which I give you today are to be upon your hearts. Impress them on your children. Talk about them when you sit at home and when you walk along the road, when you lie down, and when you get up. Tie them as symbols on your hands and bind them on your foreheads. Write them on the doorframes of your houses and on your gates. (Bible, Deuteronomy 4:9; 6: 6-9. NIV)

Children, obey your parents in the Lord, for this is right. 'Honor your father and mother' – which is the first commandment with a promise—'that it may go well with you, and that you may enjoy long life on the earth.' Fathers, do not exasperate your children; instead bring them up in the training and instruction of the Lord. (New Testament, Ephesians 6:1-4. NIV)

START SPIRITUAL TRAINING EARLY

Previously, I have referred to the fact that some parents erroneously think they will avoid personally educating their child till it is old enough to go to school. By the same token some parents believe they should let the child decide about its religious beliefs only after it is grown enough to make decisions. This false idea usually comes from a home where mom and dad do not agree on religion and usually have none in the home. Children must have religious concepts taught at the time when they are most receptive to them (in the first 5 years of life), then, when adults, they will be able to make decisions based on later information and more mature judgment.

PARENTS TEACH BY THE WAY THEY LIVE

The absence of religious activities in the home during early childhood usually will prejudice the children against religion in the long run. This void, like the absence of discipline or approval, is not easily or readily filled later in life.

Parents who start early to demonstrate a pleasant, positive attitude toward their religious beliefs, will give their children structure, which will enable them better to resist adverse peer influence. I'm thinking about the sixties revolution that emphasized the individual's freedom to disrespect law and authority. This merged into the seventies when violence, vandalism, bullying, cheating, drugs, and promiscuous sexual behavior gradually infiltrated into the school systems. Such behavior started with the upper grades and in the next decade filtered lower into the middle school age. Then in the next decade such behavior became ever more popular. These kids felt they had the right to this materialistic, hedonistic way of life and did not think they were doing anything wrong.

Parents, treat your children in the way you want them to behave. If you want the child to be truthful, tell the truth. If you want the child to be moral, behave morally right. Be fair in discipline. Expect respect. Teach by example. But there's more. Make observations, either to the child or in front of the child, to your spouse on the moral failures of public behavior in the news. Also, teach the children that they have the right to, and should, stand up for themselves and what is the right behavior. Those that have self-confidence can do this.

Parents who inculcate into the mind of the child the great truths of the Bible, are preparing the child to respect truth. And the search for truth is necessary for a full and successful life, as well as spiritual life eternally. When parents teach their children to obey God and His word, they are teaching principles of respect for authority, brotherly love, good citizenship, honesty, integrity, social responsibility, and altruism. The traits and characteristics of a strong moral character—typically taught in church and synagogue-- will stabilize the child for the vicissitudes of life in the adult world. Without these principles the child is left short-changed spiritually, morally, sociologically, and emotionally. In such a condition the child is left open to influence from the social and moral ills that are abhorrent to our people.

THE ORDER OF IMPORTANCE OF LIFE'S INSTINCTUAL DRIVES

We learn mostly about life's priorities from experience – some of which are painful. Based on a wide variety of experiences and psychotherapy, it has been determined that in the long run spiritual issues are the most important inner drives in our lives. Many prominent psychotherapists have listed what they think is the proper order of priority of life's instinctual forces. For instance, Freud thought that the sex instinct was the strongest driving force in life. This can be shown to be in error. In fact, if he were alive today, he probably would not take this position. Other theoreticians have suggested a different priority of appetites.

It can be demonstrated that the desire to **preserve the soul** is ultimately the strongest instinctual drive of humans. This is related to all matters pertaining to one's spiritual nature. It has to do with one's relationship to God. "God is love." This, then, would take in loving relationships, also, as being more important than other drives. This subject implies a belief that this earthly life with all its issues is but transitory, and the ultimate life is the life of the soul, strengthened by loving relationships, in union with God after death. This basic, intuitive need is found from the earliest human cultures to the latest.

Immediately after 9–11, the general population turned its focus to spiritual concerns. As Max Lucado observed, "Talk show hosts read scriptures; journalists printed prayers. Our focus shifted from fashion hemlines and box scores to orphans and widows and the future of the world...We were not as self-centered as we were..." When everything else in life becomes secondary, our thoughts turn to God and attendant spiritual matters. It has been succinctly stated in these familiar words: "There are no atheists in fox holes."

I cite this as brief evidence of how spiritual matters have the highest priority of the issues of life. People may live many years in a secular life, devoid of religious faith, in their drive for physical satisfactions. But in time of crisis, concern for one's loved ones and the instinctual need for spiritual security becomes manifest. It takes precedence over the desire for money, food, sex, or power, etc. And because of this, the child's early training, along with the foregoing childhood needs, as listed in this book, must include guidance to meet this most important need. I call it building *spiritual reserves.*

SPIRITUALITY IN THE HOME

We recognize that *the Lord God formed man from the dust of the earth and breathed into his nostrils the breath of life, and man became a living soul* (Genesis 2:7). Because humans have a soul at birth, it does not mean that they will develop spiritually without guidance and teaching. Just as the *capacity* for speech is inborn in every child, unless a child *hears* speech, it will not learn to talk. Real spiritual understanding is not taught merely by words, but rather it is shown most impressively by a *way of life*. Living according to spiritual standards is the most effective way to pass on our religious heritage. Religion must be a way of family life.

Families hear reports of how many are killed in violence around the world daily. The place of suffering in our world and the meaning of death are issues that can't be ignored. Since these issues are on TV daily, even small children have questions, whether they are asking directly or not. Parents must deal with the threat of death and the relationship with God early in accordance with the child's age and receptivity. Home is the place where this knowledge should start. And since we have a guide for death and the after life in the Bible, it is important that parents include the subject of spirituality in their early childhood training.

THE CHILD'S SENSE OF WONDER

The term "spirituality," like "religion," is a subject which involves God as the heavenly father, and this includes a sense of wonder. Children, having a natural sense of wonder, are therefore naturally capable of learning more complex subjects, such as the nature of God and ways of worshiping Him. My point here is that the **sense of wonder** is so natural to the small child it is the obvious foundation upon which to start spiritual training.

The center of the child's world is the home, which would include the mother, father, and perhaps siblings or other relatives. When devotion to God and to His Word, the Bible, permeates family living, children get the message. They pick up on the concept of the very important Bible standards of living very early. From the child's point of view, the parents are devoted to ideas and activities that are more important than life itself. And these ideas bring comfort, joy, reassurance, and security to their lives. The home is stabilized. Small children can feel this before they know anything about God.

Radiating from the home center would be teaching and guidance about God and the natural world of flora and fauna. All of these subjects lend themselves to the child's grasp because of its natural sense of wonder. As soon as a child learns to talk, s/he can learn the simple definition of God as "our heavenly father." The presumption in this is that, when the word "father" is used, the child has a concept of loving care, concern, respected authority, and admiration for the way daddy treats mother. I know this sounds like an "ideal," and it is. Hopefully, parents will work toward achieving this ideal for the sake of the child, as well as their own fulfillment. Significantly, when there is enough loving interrelationship in the home, a natural religious foundation is laid. Such homes provide a kind of microcosm for the spiritual growth of the child. (Review Chapter 2, "Feathering the Nest.") I have said, or implied, before that whatever is taught to the child from the loving atmosphere of the home, will be influential the rest of its life.

THE NATURE OF GOD

In spite of the fact that this sounds like a heavy subject for a small child, it is not. Even the idea of the "infinity of God" can be partially understood when the child is told that God, like the wind, is all around us but cannot be seen. (This is a legitimate comparison because of the linguistic relationship of technical terms for "life," "wind," "spirit," "soul" in the Bible.) The essence of the nature of God is "love." (1 John 4:8) The small child grasps only a limited concept of love as a receiver of love from the parents. But that's the start. (Review Chapter 4, Love, The Child's Second Need) The small child comes gradually to understand the sense of "fair play" and "right and wrong" as it gets older. Because we have a heavenly Father who loves us, an association with these traits is made early.

GOD'S LOVE

It is but a step from these early childhood experiences with these traits to an understanding that God loves us and provides for us. The child is captivated with nature very early in life, perhaps in its own yard as it walks barefoot in the grass. The flowers, the bees, and butterflies among them attract the child's sense of wonder – often expressed in the form of questions. A picture book about flowers, flowering trees, animals, fowls, and fish give the parent an opportunity to talk about our Heavenly Father, who put them here. The picture books can be followed by a trip to the zoo. Among these excursions please include one to the arboretum. This is sometimes neglected for the small child, but a percentage of these children have the nature of an artist that needs to be encouraged at an early age. All of this captivates the child's sense of wonder at how "wonderful" the works of God are.

When a child is taken to the church nursery or Sunday School, (or synagogue), here, among its peers, the focus is upon *God* and *relationships*. An early lesson I learned at the dawn of my memory is a little card from Sunday School with the memory verse, "Be ye kind one to another." I have spent my life learning more about the depth of the meaning of that simple verse.

PRAYER

Another fact about the nature of God that we teach at the earliest ages is that He listens to us. We talk to Him when we pray. There is nothing passive about prayer. It is active. Not only should the child be a part of family prayer, most often expressed when we give thanks at meals, but also the child should learn to pray at bedtime. Be careful what the implications are of the prayer that you teach them. For example, the phrase "If I should die before I wake..." is not necessary in any childhood prayer. Prayers should be about thanks, love, security, and protection. Books of childhood prayers are available at Bible bookstores.

While the only fear we are born with is perhaps of a sudden loud noise or of falling, many children pick up some other fears along the way from family, visitors, playmates and TV. Some children are afraid of the dark. Some are afraid of the boogey man. Some are afraid a kidnapper will come after them, etc. Here is where confidence in the protective nature of God should be instilled. This is done by a confident, reassuring attitude in a calm voice by the parent. And the parents, in prayers, ask for the protection of the child in all of its activities. Another verse in my early memory is "God cares for you."

There are many occasions for prayer in the family, and as these are expressed, the small child observes the family activity and learns from it. Before taking a trip, our family usually gathers in a circle, holding hands, and asks God's blessing and protection on us. Prayer at meals and at bedtime have always been habitual with us. Special prayers are offered up when one is sick or engaging in some unusual activity.

Some time ago my wife and I visited in the home of our daughter and son-in-law. After we said thanks for a meal, our 4 year old grandson suddenly blurted out this observation, "Daddy, Taylor (older brother) didn't shut his eyes when you prayed."

OTHER FAMILY OBSERVANCES

SPECIAL OCCASIONS

As in other significant procedures, habit and familiarity are essential to growth and development. This principle is embodied in religious traditions. Children love ritual and its attendant symbols. They love to know what is going to happen next. Sunday worship is one such act. In the Christian system Sunday, or the Lord's Day, is a day set aside for commemoration and remembrance. It doesn't take long for a small child to learn that there is something special about Sunday and the activities connected to it. Likewise, periods of Bible study or fellowship meetings intensify the importance of regular spiritual activity.

CHRISTMAS

There are yearly events which further impress small children. Christmas is probably the most popular occasion for children. In the home and at church there is talk about the birth of baby Jesus and its attendant events. This has a great appeal for children, not to mention the significance of giving and receiving gifts. Activity centering with the family at home and with the church family deepens spiritual impressions because of the emotion related to it. Such activity would include setting up a manger scene at home as well as at Sunday school. Reading the Bible story of Jesus' birth and the singing of appropriate carols are a part of Christmas. Furthermore, family gatherings with relatives and friends give weight to the significance of the occasion. Such events in the home make a life-long impression. It goes without saying that such occasions should be filled with happiness and joy, free of alcohol or family strife.

EASTER

Easter is another vital event on the church yearly calendar. While the rudiments of death and resurrection are only partly understood by small children, the deeper significance of sin and forgiveness is better understood by older children. There are some churches which sincerely believe that keeping

Easter and Christmas as religious holy days is not justified. They reason that the New Testament does not specifically refer to them, and no specific date is given for the birth of Christ. However, the Old Testament includes sufficient scripture on the Messiah's virgin birth and the suffering servant, along with the New Testament references to the fulfillment of such prophecy, that yearly commemoration is warranted. These two events impress the whole world with the two events of Christianity. And each generation needs to pass on the significance of these two world-changing events to succeeding generations.

The principles cited above, such as the joint family participation, special religious gatherings along with special music, and food, have been practiced throughout their history by Jews in the observance of their holy days, such as the keeping of Passover; and the whole society reaps the benefits.

FAMILY WORSHIP

It does not take a special annual event to encourage family participation in spiritual activity. There can be periods of family worship geared in length and content to the age of the children present. Throughout the year there should be occasions for one or both parents to read stories from Bible story books to their children. Children will usually have questions which give parents the opportunity to teach further on the subject at hand.

Family singing can supplement these story times. Tapes or CD's of Bible stories and religious music should be available for children to play at their discretion. Children's Sunday School songs are available for small children, and the world's great religious music is also recorded for the appreciation of older children. Usually children are ready for such music at a much younger age than parents suppose. Bible supplement books, appropriate to your child's age, should also be in your home library with the music. Such books would include maps and scenes depicting dress, animals, and customs of Bible times. All of this adds significance to the teaching you are giving your children.

"NOW ABIDE FAITH, HOPE . . ."

There are those who say that the real test of the depth of religious influence in one's life is one's response to a crisis. Each life will face the inevitable accident or sudden illness within the family. Those with a strong religious faith, and who have been practicing their relationship with God consistently, will respond with stability and confidence. It is easy to pray in an emergency when one is in the habit of praying. Of course, we hear in the media frequently about someone caught in a storm or trapped in a wrecked car and how their first thought is to pray. That's certainly appropriate, and, it is the evidence of the ultimate priority of God in our lives. But those on speaking terms with God find it easier and more natural to pray in faith in a crisis. I refer to this state frequently as "relying on spiritual reserves" in a crisis. Children will observe the family's reaction to such traumatic events and learn from them.

PARENTS SUPPORT THE CHURCH AND BIBLE TEACHING

The parents' attitude toward the church where they attend is also important. They should be in a congregation where they can support the teachers, leaders, and the preacher(s) without any criticism at home in the presence of children. Furthermore, criticism of the worship service or Bible study is uncalled for. If there is a legitimate problem among the church leaders, then the members, to the extent of their ability, should help solve the problem or attend elsewhere. It is important that the children see the joy of Christianity exemplified in the congregation where they attend.

Parents need to show respect for the authority of the Bible and what it teaches. This is our real hope for the future. The fact that the parents are attending a Bible class gives a message to the children about the importance of Bible study and knowledge. In teaching children, whether on the spur of the moment or in reading a Bible story, the parents need to emphasize the positive aspect of Christian living. That is, let commands emphasizing *what to do* predominate over injunctions of *what not to do*. And it goes without saying that the parents encourage the child to do Bible home work, memory work, and participate in Bible class projects. The child will be encouraged to communicate when parents keep up with the subject of Bible class lessons and ask the children questions about what they are studying.

RELATIONSHIPS WITH CHRISTIANS

Social occasions with fellow Christians are important. Parents should have the child's Bible class pupils in the home. And there are social occasions when parents have Christian guests in the home. The behavior of the guests reinforces what the parents have taught and demonstrated to the children concerning Christian behavior. For example, when children observe that a group of Christians can get together and have a good time with games, laughter, refreshments, and pleasant associations, it sets an example for them. Groups do not have to get drunk in order to enjoy each other's company.

It is also good to have the church minister's family and/or Bible teachers in the home occasionally. Children will observe the cordial relationship with Christian leaders and profit from this. Again, I emphasize that what the children observe in their parents' Christian behavior is the most impressive lesson they could have.

PARENTS STRENGTHEN THEIR OWN SPIRITUAL DEVELOPMENT.

In order for the parents to live up to their religious values automatically, they need a program of continuing religious education. This is achieved by taking religious publications, reading religious, devotional books, having occasional Bible studies in the home, attending regular Bible classes at church, attending special meetings or seminars, and availing themselves of other special or irregular meetings at church.

It is easier for parents to teach their children Christian behavior when they exemplify spiritual traits naturally. For example, the so-called "Christian virtues" should be practiced in the home to the extent possible. If one is interested in some quick lists, they are given in 2 Peter 1:5-7, Galatians 5:22, and Philippians 4:8. These lists are easy to memorize and essentially encourage the same traits such as, *love, joy, peace, patience, kindness, goodness, faithfulness, gentleness, and self-control.*

THE GODLY COUPLE STRENGTHENS THEIR MARRIAGE

Evidence is accumulating, proving that a great deal of damage is done to most children when their parents split up. Christians are not immune to the stresses of daily life and how these stresses somehow influence the marital relationship. There are so many causes for this that I can't begin to list them here. But I do emphasize that no couple should presume that just because they are Christians and believe that divorce is wrong, they are exempt from marital strife. There are many Christian couples who are divorced in spirit, though they are still living in the same house.

I emphasize that an "ounce of prevention is worth a pound of cure" in this respect. Periodically couples should avail themselves of counselors who help them inventory their relationship. Many churches and synagogues provide these opportunities and are prepared to assist if the couple is beginning to feel a strain in the marriage. I liken tensions in the marriage to cancer. Most cancers do not have to be fatal, but rather are curable when they are diagnosed in time and treated appropriately. So it is with marital dissension. When a couple realizes they have a problem, they must seek professional help immediately. Too many couples, like cancer patients, deny the existence of the disease until it is too late to treat and cure it. Early diagnosis means easier and more successful treatment.

I have seen many, many couples seeking divorce, rationalizing that it is better to divorce than to exhibit dissension in front of the children. In most cases this is not true! Where alcohol or drugs are involved along with abuse, yes, separation is to be preferred. But the average divorce based on "incompatibility" or "irreconcilable differences" is not justified, in my opinion, especially when children are involved.

First, the couple should seek help as soon as they realize they have a persistent problem. Secondly, as in the case of cancer, they usually need to resign themselves to prolonged treatment, because when the conflict is serious, it takes time to readjust their personalities and bring back to the home the harmony that they had in the beginning. And for the benefit of the children, this is essential. No matter what the arrangement after separation, the children will suffer. The child's rights have a higher priority than the parents rights!

Since even the deepest love can die, it is imperative that parents work at keeping their loving relationship growing through the years. It's worth the effort. . .for themselves and their children. It is also true that many couples who think their love is dead may have it renewed with the proper treatment.

"YE FATHERS. . ."

Paul, in Ephesians 6:4, gets our attention with these words and gives advice that I alluded to earlier in Chapter 4. It is necessary to say something regarding a father's responsibility in the area of spiritual training. The reason for this is that so many men leave this area up to their wives, feeling that it is "a woman's work" because the children are so small. I wish to correct this misapprehension.

It is this verse that gives a challenging contrast to fathers. After Paul prohibits fathers from provoking their children to wrath, he commands them to rear their children in the nurture and admonition of the Lord. This is very clear.

Ephesians 6:4 gives a special admonition to fathers through guidance and education to lead the child into a personal relationship with Christ and His way of life. Such teaching prepares the child for life and for heaven after death. After all, this is the ultimate goal that parents have for their children.

The father needs to recognize that he not only must participate, but he should also take the lead in showing the children the way of the Lord. He reinforces the values that mother teaches them. Of all the subjects that the children are to be taught in the first five years of life, religion is the most important. And the children need to be taught the truth of the Bible. In accordance with the importance of setting the proper example, he will take the family to Sunday School and church or synagogue.

Within the home the children need to see daddy, along with mother, lead in prayer in front of, and with, the children. They need to see him as one who tells the truth; who uses appropriate language (rather than cursing). They need to observe that when he gets angry or loses his temper, he apologizes to all who hear. Then they observe as he improves his self-control. The father is expected to be a tower of strength and a guiding example for all of the household.

George F. Will, in the *Washington Post*, insightfully said, "Biologically, adults produce children. Spiritually, children produce adults. Most of us do not grow up until we have helped children do so. Thus, do the generations form a braided cord." This calls to mind what the prophet Malachi said, *He will turn the hearts of fathers to their children and the hearts of children to their fathers.* (Old Testament, Malachi 4:5)

"THE GREATEST OF THESE IS LOVE"

The origin of love is in the very nature of God, *for God is love* (1 John 4:8).

From the beginning God exemplified his love by His creative activity. The marvels, beauties, and physical laws of the natural world give evidence of His thoughtful concern from the beginning; "design" if you please. During the Old Testament period God demonstrated His love to Israel, providing a patient, Fatherly love for His children, in spite of the fact that the children did not always behave as He wanted. But He always took them by the hand and led them back.

Christians believe that God's love was made obvious to us by sending His son --the promised Messiah (1 John 4:9). By His life of service dedicated to the lower classes, outcasts, and misfits, he demonstrated God's love and concern. This is the kind of love our heavenly Father commands us to pass on to others. The commandment from the beginning (1 John 3:11) is the same as the "new commandment," that we must share (John 13:34) namely, that we "love one another." Therefore, *we love because He first loved us* (1 John 4:19).

When parents feel love toward each other and show this to their children, the children learn how to love one another and share this with others. Since God is love, this is the essence of spirituality.

CHILDREN LEARN TO LOVE

Children learn love when the spiritual pattern is followed. Within the family, children learn to love by receiving love from their parents. Then, as children mature, they are able to return love to their parents, and, hopefully, to siblings. We assume the parents show themselves to be lovable. In learning to love, it's easy to love those who are most like ourselves – and we should. The family relationships should foster and encourage love within the family circle.

Next, the circle begins to widen as the family loves those beyond the family circle. This includes friends, acquaintances, and fellow Christians. As the ability to love matures, one is encouraged to love those who may be strangers and who are different from ourselves. They are more difficult to love – but we must learn this. And we learn it by practice. That is, spiritual love (*agape*) does not have to be an emotional attachment, as with friends or family, but is the **will to do good**; one seeks what is best for the other person. The objects of this love are groups of people who are unlovable for one reason or another.

In Jesus' time they were the outcasts, deformed, maimed, lower levels in society, and different races. Parents must show interracial respect and brotherly love for those of a different race. When they do, their children will be fortified to resist unreasonable prejudice, which they could pick up at school or on the playground.

Finally, those most difficult to show love to are our enemies. Those whom we dislike, for whatever reason, we are commanded to love. I like this quotation,

Love is an act of endless forgiveness. Admittedly, loving one's enemy is difficult and cannot always be done readily. Note that this "love" is defined as "the will to do him good." This is not the natural love that one has for one's family. This is the highest spiritual experience, because we are most like God and Jesus when we practice this kind of love. This kind of love is more of a "decision" than it is a natural "emotion." We have to learn to do this. It comes with experience. And this learning starts in the home.

Now you can see more clearly why I say this ability to love has its foundation in the love that mom and dad have between themselves and then show to their children. Such a foundation in the pre-school years prepares the children so they will want to become Christians when they are old enough to make the decision and take the initiative on their own.

Children learn to make such choices by their parents guiding them to make choices early in the pre-school years. During family time get everyone's point of view in making group decisions. Explain how and why certain decisions are made. This may be done by the simplest decisions like going to the store, watching TV, or major decisions like vacationing, or moving or redecorating. And when parents make decisions about right and wrong issues, they explain the bases of such a decision.

A SOCIAL EXAMPLE

Byron Johnson, a criminologist and director of the Center for Research on Religion and Urban Civil Society (CRRUCS), is a social scientist concerned with evaluating the effect that "faith based programs" have on children and youth. Johnson has observed religious institutions, and how effective any of them are, in helping to solve big-city problems, saying, "We're looking to see if these organizations are effective or not."

Johnson has "found that religious commitment and church attendance offer 'protective factors' to 'high-risk' inner-city youths." He further observed that religious youths are more healthy —they are less likely to fight, drink and drive, or carry weapons; and more likely to exercise and eat right. "His report suggests that religious faith —'*inner change*' —enhances rehabilitation." (Emphasis mine – JAS)

He observed evidence of this when 2000 former drug abusers and their families reunited at "God's Mountain" recently. This is the name of a Teen

Challenge treatment center in Rehrersburg, PA. It is called "the mountain" by those who kicked their drug habit with the help of a program based in Bible study and Christian faith. Johnson went "to conduct focus groups and to interview the men whose lives had been turned around by what happened to them on the mountain.," reports Jon Hurdle in the *Penn Arts & Sciences Journal*, fall, 2003. Johnson reported that more than half of the 125 inmates interviewed said, "**I am not who I used to be.**" And this was the result of the two-year rehabilitation program.

A preliminary evaluation of the program found that inmates who complete a two-year rehabilitation program immersed in Bible study and Christian worship have a better chance of staying out of jail, once released, than members of the general prison population. Johnson observed that we have a very limited view of faith based organizations, which are trying to combat serious social problems. And he calls it inexcusable that unbiased, scrupulous, empirical, and statistical methods have not been utilized up till now to evaluate such faith based programs.

The subjects of this report are youth who were reared devoid of Christian training, and because of some form of delinquency, were incarcerated. The purpose of the training was to rehabilitate them by "inner change," rather than by traditional behavior modification procedures. Bible study and Christian faith involved character development to the extent that the individuals recognized that, "I am not who I used to be." Granted, this program comes late in the lives of these young men, but it shows what is needed when parents fail to give spiritual guidance in the home during early childhood. The purpose of an organization like this is to change the behavior of the delinquent by improving the inadequate character. And apparently they are successful in doing so to a great extent.

I cite this report because it is another avenue that gives support to the value of spiritual training with youth. When I maintain that Biblical based faith can change the social world in which we live, here is evidence. And yet, it is not just "spiritual" training but the total training of youth during their formative, most impressionable years that will prevent their being caught up with juvenile delinquency. If, as new parents, you feel that you just do not have the time to spend with your child(ren) as I have described in the previous chapters, please consider the plight of parents who spend much more time, energy, and money on juveniles *after* they have gone astray. You will save time and emotional energy in the long run by making the effort to follow the directions I have previously given for the first years of life.

Rearing children in today's world is a big job and requires time, planning, devotion, and self-sacrifice. Give plenty of time early, and you will most likely be spared the emotional and physical pain that results from children going astray during adolescence. It takes time and money to pay a lawyer, leave work and go to court, get out of bed in the middle of the night and go to the hospital, make arrangements for drug rehabilitation in a hospital, etc.

Religion and its attendant spiritual truths are the backbone of our nation. And our nation's greatness will endure as long as the individuals who make up our citizenry have developed and matured spiritually. .

May the Lord make your love increase and overflow for each other and for everyone else, just as ours does for you. – 1 Thessalonians 3:12.

CONCLUSION

There are many indications in our country today that we are becoming more secularized and materialistic. And whether we recognize it or not, we are being influenced adversely by the rest of the world, also. It thus behooves us to give guidance to the coming generation to forestall further deterioration. We can start simply with the children in our own homes, and the spiritual guidance of these children is of primary importance. In the annual study by Columbia University's National Center on Addiction and Substance Abuse, it was observed that students attending smaller schools or religious schools are less likely to abuse drugs and alcohol. It may sound a little threadbare to say that the hope of the future is in our children, but it is a fact. And people who care are the ones who will take the responsibility of guiding the next generation.

POST SCRIPT

When Minister Joe Wright was asked to open the new session of the Kansas Senate with prayer, everyone was expecting the usual generalities, but this is what they heard:

"Heavenly Father, we come before you today to ask your forgiveness and to seek your direction and guidance. We know Your Word says, 'Woe to those who call evil good.' But that is exactly what we have done. We have lost our spiritual equilibrium and reversed our values. We confess that: We have ridiculed the absolute truth of Your Word and called it Pluralism. We have exploited the poor and called it the lottery. We have rewarded laziness and called it welfare. We have killed our unborn and called it choice. We have shot abortionists and called it justifiable. We have neglected to discipline our children and called it building self-esteem. We have abused power and called it politics. We have coveted our neighbor's possessions and called it ambition. We have polluted the air with profanity and pornography and called it freedom of expression. We have ridiculed the time-honored values of our forefathers and called it enlightenment. Search us, Oh, God, and know our hearts today; cleanse us from every sin and set us free.

Guide and bless these men and women who have been sent to direct us to the center of Your will and to openly ask these things in the name of Your Son, the living Savior, Jesus Christ.

Amen!"

The response was immediate. A number of legislators walked out during the prayer in protest. In 6 short weeks, however, Central Christian Church, where Wright is pastor, logged more than 5,000 phone calls with only 47 of those calls responding negatively. The church is now receiving international requests from India, Africa, and Korea for copies of this prayer.

Commentator Paul Harvey aired this prayer on his radio program, "The Rest of the Story," and received a larger response to this program than any other he has ever aired.

With the Lord's help, may this prayer sweep over our nation and wholeheartedly become our desire so that we again can be called "one nation under God."

QUESTIONS FOR MEDITATION AND/OR DISCUSSION

1) In your home have you been practicing teaching and guiding your children in religious matters?

2) If you have, what influenced you to do this? If you have not, what has hindered you from such a program?

3) Have you noticed various ways in which your children show (or have shown) a sense of wonder or awe at the natural world around them?

4) Considering that you attend a service of public worship, is there a program for children there?

5) What ways do you demonstrate before your children your devotion to God?

6) How do your children respond to your efforts to teach and guide them in religious matters?

7) In your home, as parents, do you have a definite program for strengthening your marital relationship? If not, what can you do to start such a program?

CHAPTER 13

LIVING ABUNDANTLY

WHAT DO YOU WANT FOR YOUR CHILD?

Train up a child in the way he should go, and even when he is old he will not depart from it. (Proverbs 22:6). There are parents who doubt this statement when their child is in trouble and they seek to understand "What happened?" Most parents aim to "train up" their child with a strong and noble character. Some succeed and some fail. And some get part of the way.

Some years ago a judge in Nashville told of a 12 year old boy who was brought before him for repeated theft. Upon talking with the boy the judge found out he went to Sunday School and could recite the Ten Commandments and the Beatitudes from memory. This boy could list some rules, but he could not apply them to his daily living. His moral standards or ethical rules were in one compartment of his mind, and his behavior urges were uncoordinated in a separate compartment

There is confusion in some circles in understanding that "strong character" and "external behavior" are not necessarily the same thing. This event from the ministry of Jesus illustrates aptly what I mean.

> 23 *"Woe to you, teachers of the law and Pharisees, you hypocrites! You give a tenth of your spices--mint, dill and cummin. But you have neglected the more important matters of the law--justice, mercy, and faithfulness. You should have practiced the latter, without neglecting the former. 24 You blind guides! You strain out a gnat but swallow a camel.*

> 25 *"Woe to you, teachers of the law and Pharisees, you hypocrites! You clean the outside of the cup and dish, but inside they are full of greed and self-indulgence.*

26 Blind Pharisee! First clean the inside of the cup and dish, and then the outside also will be clean.

27 "Woe to you, teachers of the law and Pharisees, you hypocrites! You are like whitewashed tombs, which look beautiful on the outside but on the inside are full of dead men's bones and everything unclean. 28 In the same way, on the outside you appear to people as righteous, but on the inside you are full of hypocrisy and wickedness. Matt 23:23-27 NIV

Jesus made the point that while the religious leaders appeared to be very righteous to the people because they paid great attention to minute details of their religious ritual, they, in fact, did not have a sincere devotion to traits of character that were much more important.

CHARACTER AND RULES

In the foregoing chapters you have observed that I have not paid a great deal of attention to the teaching of *rules of behavior,* like customs of politeness. It's good to teach children to say, "please," "thank you", etc. It is important to tell them how to be courteous and have good manners. But I have emphasized how you, as parents, can instill in your children, during their earliest years, *traits of character.* You are instilling *traits* rather than emphasizing a list of rules of behavior. Distinguish between a person of "weak character" and a person of "strong character." A person of strong character is one who has integrated into the self those "characteristics" such as "confidence" because s/he has been **accepted**; who has respect for and serves others, because s/he has been **loved**; who can make her/himself behave according to the standards of maturity, because s/he has been **disciplined** in the early formative years. That person who is looked upon as a "born leader" is most likely an oldest child who was **approved** of repeatedly in early childhood. The leading educators and scientists will most likely be those whose **curiosity** was stimulated and whose questions were answered in the early years.

The person who has a trained **conscience** will have a healthy respect for the rights of others and himself. The politician who demonstrates a sincere desire to "serve" the community and contributes toward the "general welfare," is one who has absorbed in early childhood an understanding of what "**goals**" are about. When **social skills** become second nature to a person, s/he will be a leader who contributes toward making the world a better place. The persons most admired for the unselfish contributions they have made for the well-being of their fellows, and for helping set the moral standards for the community, will be mature persons who have strong **spiritual** values.

THE DOMINANT ROLE OF PARENTS

Of course, parents aren't going to specialize in just one of the "child rights," but will, as opportunity provides, do what they can to influence their children in most or all of these important **characteristics**. This is what building character is all about. And the strong or integrated character is one who has something of all of these traits.

Now you can understand why I say the dominant role of parents is not to focus on a list of rules, only to neglect or to ignore these "weightier matters of the law." Parenthood for too many people is to focus on the outside rules, such as "please," "thank you," "open the door for others," "make good grades," "look nice," "come in early," "who are you playing with?" "be nice," "don't fight," "don't swear," etc. These childhood rules are fine, but will come more as a consequence to character training than to be the primary focus of parents' training their children. Even worse than a list of rules is the household where the child is coerced into certain iron clad patterns of behavior, i.e. a rigid environment which suppresses the child's freedom.

LOGIC TIGHT COMPARTMENTS

Strong character is not necessarily recognized by external behavior; it is not described by giving a list of a person's habits. The person of noble purpose with integrated character will be one who has the internal fortitude to "follow through" consistently and persistently on what is right. That's what Jesus was talking about.

I know of a professor in a world famous university seminary who taught classes on very liberal theology that denied the divinity of Jesus. But on Sundays he went out to a small rural church and preached. He was asked how he could go out and preach as he did after teaching the theology which was so liberal. His reply was, "I keep my theology in one drawer and my preaching in another drawer."

This well illustrates a concept which many psychologists call "logic tight compartments." The human mind is perfectly capable of separating certain secular issues of life from their religious belief system. Many people think of their religious/moral/ethical beliefs separate from the issues of daily living. For example, an upstanding man may attend church on Sundays and serve on committees, but will justify shady business practices by saying, "That's just business." We have seen in the news serious examples of separated compartments when church leaders abscond with the collection or abuse children. Typically, these people are immature and do not have an integrated personality. Lately we have also seen men, prominent in the community and business world, practice serious dishonesty and theft from investors and employees.

Another example: I know of two families with children who were required to attend the same Sunday School and church regularly. In one family, as soon as the children grew up and left home, they stopped going to church at all. In the other family the children grew up and left home, but continued to be loyal and faithful to the church. On the surface the children were taught to develop the same habits.

In the first home the parents' attitude may have been negative, or critical of the church or its leaders or of some of its programs. The parents went because they felt they had to, and for them Christianity was a chore; their heart was not in it. The children felt it. And they could have picked up on it by observing little inconsistencies in their parents, like telling "little white lies" about things they had done or places where they had gone, etc. In the second home the parents loved the people in the church and took pleasure in all of its functions. They volunteered their time and talents. For them church was their life.

THE INTEGRATED PERSONALITY

When character traits become built into a person's psyche, that person will have a realization of the self. That person will not be asking, "Who am I?" S/he will have a self-awareness, self-esteem, or self-realization. **Self-discipline** is also a characteristic of the integrated personality. All of these character traits, of course, will result in appropriate behavior. And when love permeates that person's character, there is a great inner strength and the potential to help others, even at one's own expense. That is a primary trait of the "Heroic Personality." This is true unselfishness. And this brings to the surface another outstanding trait, that of **self-control**. But the foundation to all of these "self" traits is **love**. Adults with these traits will most likely make a wise selection of a mate and succeed with a happy marriage. However, if parents rear a child with little or no love, that child will have a void within, like the proverbial "black hole." If the parents mistreat a child, the child will likely develop hate, and character and relationships cannot be built on hatred.

This is the reason "love" is so dominant a force in parent--child relationships and from there to all other relationships. Paul said, "... *the greatest of these is love.*" (1 Cor. 13:13)

Another self evident Christian truth is stated by Paul thus:

7 Do not be deceived: God cannot be mocked. A man reaps what he sows. The one who sows to please his sinful nature, from that nature will reap destruction; the one who sows to please the Spirit, from the Spirit will reap eternal life. Let us not become weary in doing good, for at the proper time we will reap a harvest if we do not give up. Gal. 6:7-9 (NIV).

I'm taking the liberty to rephrase this in terms I have been talking about. You'll see the point:

"One cannot make a mockery of God. A person reaps what he sows. The one who lives a self-centered life will reap destruction. One who lives a spiritual life in love will reap eternal life. Don't get tired of living the heroic life. Eventually we will reap a harvest if we do not give up."

Have you noticed Jesus did not focus dominantly on outward rules of "do's" and "don't's"? His spiritual teaching centered on building inner character.

This should encourage every parent to be persistent. Is it worth it? It certainly is. These seeds planted in childhood will surely bear fruit in adulthood. Have you thought about this: the parent who devotedly rears children by giving, sacrificing, suffering discomforts, and self-denial is by this way of life demonstrating all of these traits in love to the child by example? And we know that children learn best by example. Of course, it is possible to overdo this to the extent that a parent becomes fatigued and loses good health or becomes haggard, or even burned out; God forbid! Total self-sacrifice by the parent is an extreme and not called for.

A SENSE OF HUMOR

I agree with Milnes that "The sense of humour is the just balance of all the faculties of man..." A sense of humor softens the barbs of life, and the inevitable hardships are made more bearable for all concerned when we can laugh at ourselves and the awkward positions we get ourselves into. This trait can be encouraged from the earliest relationship with your little one, especially by your example. Smile a lot. Laugh and kid. Look for the lighter side of your daily routine. Never laugh *at* your child, but laugh *with* him/her all you can. You can even make light of some of the daily tragedies of the household, if you get in the habit; and you can train yourself to do so. When you're prone to get upset over something trivial, "Laugh and the world laughs with you..."

THE VALUE OF COMMUNICATION

I haven't said enough about family communication, but it is a foregone conclusion that the "Rights" I have been talking about have to be communicated to the children in one way or another. "Companionship" with the children is the key to success with the entire "Rights" program.

At every age there needs to be a close enough relationship with your child to share, to talk, and to express yourselves openly and frankly, according to the age of the child.

START EARLY

The parents who talk to their baby starting before birth gain an advantage. It is known that the baby in the uterus, in the last two months, hears and mechanically differentiates sounds like music and voices. Parents who can talk soothingly and pleasantly and sing to the unborn infant are laying a foundation impression. Then, after the child is born, those voices are familiar. You already have the child's attention. Communication continues without words as the mother nurses the child, rocks it, and cuddles it. And, unless you do something to alienate the child, you can keep its attention while you read, sing, teach, and guide it as it grows older. Then, because you can communicate, you will be able successfully to meet the child's deserved needs.

There are some children who, after they learn to talk, are more prone to respond and converse than others. Here are some suggestions to encourage two-way conversation:

First, where possible create an environment and climate which is conducive to conversation. Of course, it depends on the age of the child as to what these conditions will be, but the child should be comfortable and able to relax. Perhaps in the child's own bed or room is the best.

Second, establish a reputation for being a good listener. Make yourself open and receptive by your posture, facial expressions, and tone of voice so the child feels no threat. Good listeners don't interrupt. If your child suddenly wants to talk when you absolutely can't turn loose of what your doing, get down on the child's level and give an explanation as to why you can't listen right now, but you do want to hear what s/he wants to talk about, and set another time as soon as possible.

Third, there are times when a shared activity is a good setting for talking with your child. This should be something the child likes to do. For the older child it may be a game, or eating, or a physical activity like strolling, fishing or bike riding.

Fourth, it's good to ask your child sometimes what s/he wants to talk about. Don't ever put the child down for some particular subject. Remember, adult standards are not the basis for your judgment of the subject.

Fifth, if your child is "the silent, non-communicative type," then you will need to prime the pump by asking questions that require an answer more than simply "Yes" or "No."

Sixth, verify and acknowledge the child's feelings, rather than denying them as some are prone to do.

Seventh, show interest in what the child does whether at school, church, or play. This can be done by bringing up that subject or by asking questions as the child talks about it. This attitude enables the child to feel free to bring up the subject (or a related one) again at another time.

THE SILENT CHILD

I have talked with many parents who say they have a child who just won't talk. And I believe there is a genetic factor here affecting the "silent child." It requires great ingenuity to provoke such a child to communicate. But give time and thought to it. Accept it as a challenge for your skills and be persistent. In bringing up subjects or asking questions, ask so that the question cannot be answered by just one word. Pick a time when your child is emotional —either on a high about winning a contest, or angry at a teacher, for example.

Make an observation, "You seem to be excited today. Tell me about it. Etc." Or "You appear to be upset. Did something happen when you were playing with Jimmy today?" If it appears that the child is not going to talk about it, it may be that s/he is too emotional at the time. Then say something like, "I can understand you're upset. We'll talk about something else now and then after dinner we can talk about what upset you." Here you have recognized the child's feelings, but set a time when the subject will come up again. Perhaps the child will be ready at that time.

Basically, most children want to talk, and, if you started early enough with them, as they get older they will continue to talk. Even if your child persists in being silent, you, the parent, talk. Keep words flowing between you. Take pains to provide a conducive atmosphere. It has been my experience in working with school age children, that if there has been conflict among them, they are ready to talk and explain their side of the event.

CAUTION

Most any good thing can be over done. It has been observed by no less an authority than Dr. John Rosemond, that extreme attention to the child after the toddler period can result in the child's ongoing expectation that the parent's job is to pay constant attention to him/her. In other words, the child becomes too self-centered. After that age the key word is **supervision,** rather than attention. Of course, it's a question of degree appropriate to the child's age and individual development.

LIFE AS ADVENTURE

EXCITEMENT IN ADVENTURE

"Adventure" is an exciting word, and one reason is that "excitement" is an integral part of adventure. It has to do with the newness of discovery, an escape from the routine and ordinary into a new environment, and/or a new activity which is different from the immediate past. All humans enjoy adventure. Of course, what is adventure to one may not be adventure to another, just as what is new to one person is not necessarily new to another.

A honeymoon has all the ingredients of adventure, like new activity, a new level of relationship, a trip to a new environment, leaving the past behind, etc. A vacation is similar. A change in jobs or job locations has these elements of an adventure. Travel is adventurous. In fact Paul Tournier makes a good case for the fact that the need or desire for adventure is an instinct in all humans. He says, "...the instinct of adventure is one of the most obvious explanations for the characteristic behavior of man, one of the great driving forces behind his actions, as important as the instinct of self-preservation..." I would like to go one step further to say that one's entire life can be, or even should be, a series of adventures.

RISK AS AN ELEMENT IN ADVENTURE

It must be added here, that a part of much adventure is the element of risk. Many adventures involve a hazard or peril with uncertain outcome. Many daring sports appeal to people because of this factor. And this is the very element that appeals to the participants. Skiers, rock climbers, rafters, stunt pilots, slalom runners, and similar activities appeal to some persons because of the risk with uncertain outcome. And the body responds with a variety of hormones and enzymes which give the person a high. But one does not have to be an active sports enthusiast to enjoy this kind of high. Some people in the commercial and financial world seek their fortune in daring enterprises. There is speculation involving a series of unforeseen twists and turns, which could bring on a serious catastrophe or a great victory. But adventure may be experienced with uncertainty instead of risk.

BIRTH AS ADVENTURE

At the time the sperm unites with the egg, the dynamic of a great adventure begins. The union of these two invisible cells will result in a human that metaphysically is in the image of God. Furthermore, because of DNA this embryo is different from every other embryo ever conceived. At this point there are a multiplicity of avenues open and possible for this solitary organism to pursue in starting this great adventure. Who knows what the determining factors are that will cause this microscopic bit of humanity to "choose" from among the potential mysteries that will open up the pathway that it will follow from now through eternity? The cells multiply and, by predetermined factors deep within them, will become body parts. Similarly the spiritual and psychological determinants will interplay with the environment and become individual traits that make up the psyche. Truly this is the great adventure of living.

In the last two or three months before birth, the maturation process of the fetus is going in high gear, as the baby is preparing for a journey. The brain is developing very rapidly, which in turn involves the glands and the body maturity. If there are adverse influences from the mother such as alcohol, nicotine, harmful drugs, or other harmful stuff ingested by the mother, the baby reacts and suffers harm – sometimes irreparable harm. And, if the mother suffers trauma physically or emotionally, this also interferes with the baby's preparation for birth. If the baby is unusually large or the mother is unusually small for that baby, the baby suffers because of over crowded conditions.

If the mother is healthy and is emotionally happy; if there is a calm, pleasant environment with music, singing, and talking to the baby, it is well prepared for the adventure of birth.

Yes, birth itself is an adventure. There is the dramatic change from the embryonic environment to the outside world. It is at that moment that the embryo becomes a total human being *And the Lord God formed man from the dust of the earth and breathed into his nostrils the breath of life, and man became a living soul* (Genesis 2:7). This dramatic ejection propels the newborn into the beginning of this great adventure. Hopefully, that outside world is ready and waiting to welcome that newcomer into warm, loving, arms, which have a familiar voice that goes with them. If there is a prolonged birth with trauma, the adventure turns into an unpleasant or even painful crisis, and, unfortunately at times, death.

Amazingly, this same process of birth is an adventure for the mother, also. It is an unusual, new experience with an uncertain procedure or outcome for her. . .and for the father, who should be present, giving support in his own way.

A SERIES OF ADVENTURES

The new born's first several years are composed of one adventure after another. Hopefully, each adventure has a satisfactory, if not pleasant, conclusion as it segues into the next one. The mother nurtures and comforts the crying infant. The father holds the baby with strong arms and speaks gently. A sibling may read to and play with the infant. Each episode is an adventure in the new world as the baby learns about a variety of tastes, pleasant and unpleasant sounds, odors, comforting or rough arms that hold it, new voices, new faces, and changes in the environment.

Brain cells are multiplying rapidly and turned on, as all of these various experiences fill the baby's first days, months, and years. And these experiences have an impact on the architecture of the baby's brain: traumatic experiences for harm, and pleasant ones for fulfillment. The totality of experiences and relationships are shaping the child's future and are forming the foundation as to whom that bubbling newborn will become. Not only this, but also the first experiences set the foundation for the next experiences and the next, and so on.

It's an adventure for the newborn to experience the mother's breast again and again. Repeated encounters with parents and/or siblings are adventures. The infant discovers its hands, feet, and surroundings. Each encounter with a mobile is adventure. The sounds, odors, activities, relationships are all new to this neophyte, and, thus, every day brings on more adventures. Furthermore, as the child grows, there still is a world of adventures awaiting it. This includes new relationships, and constantly new and expanding activities and skills. Learning to ride a tricycle is new and risky, but the child persists and learns to ride, which brings on a reinforcement of self-confidence. This cycle persists throughout childhood. In the world of music, dance, sports, friendships, travel, and, hopefully, even education, each new successful skill mastered brings the challenge of adventure followed by a growth in confidence. The growing child is a microcosm of these experiences.

You can see why any criticism, discouragement, or even a look askance could interrupt the joy and satisfaction of the adventure of living for the developing child. Such discouragements in the younger ages must be kept at a minimum. These ascending experiences and feelings, drop by drop, are forming character. And character will be the foundation for the academics of an older age. When these developmental experiences and relationships proceed positively, the child's point of view of life is permanently formed for good.

Brain imaging technologies have made it possible to watch as the child matures in these first months and years. With the facilitating environment, the brain turns on impressively. It actively lights up like a Christmas tree loaded with lights. If the environment is harsh and negative, the brain is inactive and does not bubble over with rapidly multiplying cells, like it should.

What am I saying? These first months of adventure are predetermining what the first few years will be like. And the first few years are predetermining what childhood and adolescence and adulthood will be like. As the parents and care-givers relate to the child with acceptance, love, discipline, approval, etc., the adventure of living is ensconced, and the personality is beautifully formed.

THE FATHER'S HOME EXPERIENCE

The word "mother" has been used -- perhaps overly so – in the preceding chapters discussing the early years and the significance of home impressions during that formative period. Much of what has been said regarding mothers applies also to dads. But there is more to this. If father has not spent all day repeatedly with an infant or young child, he needs to have this experience once in a while. He needs to have some first hand, hands on experience with the baby. What about his job, profession? What about wife's job or profession?

If mother does not have an outside job during the child's earliest years, then the father needs to understand what she is doing and provide all kinds of emotional and physical support. He needs to relieve her of some of the burdens and responsibilities of the child and the house routine at times. He needs to give constant encouragement and praise for her devotion. He should take the initiative in providing some occasional outside help. He needs to back her up with time with the child, with consistency with discipline, with help in feeding, cleaning, reading, teaching, and guiding in all the ways mentioned in the preceding pages.

I have heard men rely on the excuse that when they come home from their hard days work (its always a "hard" day), they have the "right" to take it easy, relax, and ignore the rest of the family. To my way of thinking, based on my years of experience in family and marriage counseling, I have heard this to the point of nausea. There are very few jobs that I have heard described, which I recall at the moment, that were as hard as a wife/mother's home job with small pre-school children at home. One is that of an Air Traffic Control officer who worked a double shift; and another is that of the physician/surgeon who started before day-light and pushed hard with the sick for the next 16 or 24 hours. There are other positions that would fall into this category of the exception, but they are rare. My point is this, that the work of the wife/mother with small children at home has practically no relief. She doesn't go home to a change in scenery and to different people from whom she "works with" daily. It's the same day and night with no relief, unless dad stretches a point and gives her some, which, from the standpoint of the children, he is duty bound to do.

But there is another point. If parents take rearing their children as secondary in importance, then they should have considered that before they got pregnant.

I know a man with 4 daughters who refused to take advancements in his position at work because he did not feel he could leave so much responsibility of the children with his wife. His advancement would require more time and responsibility at his job. And, just as important, he felt his need to be at home so he could be a proper influence on his daughters, participate as a coach in week-end sports, and take them on school trips. When the youngest one is in college, he will be ready for advancement. I can hear some men out there saying, "By that time he will have waited too late for advancement in the average company." And that appears to be coming to pass. But he and his wife will have peace of mind about their children because of the maturity that has been built into their lives. (These children are my granddaughters)

MY BLESSING

When all is said and done, you parents have taken on the most difficult and challenging job of humanity. And perhaps this job is more difficult now than ever before, what with our modern, complicated way of life. When you do your best, the flexibilities of nature and the help of God will give you success and satisfaction. Children don't change instantly, either to become bad or good. Be at peace with your spouse and work together, and you will succeed. I have had a lot to say in the foregoing pages in an effort to be thorough and complete. But it really is not complicated or difficult when you take the whole procedure of rearing a day at a time and take this material a chapter at a time. Not only will your child mature, but you parents will grow greatly during this process, also.

You are striving for happiness and a sense of freedom for your children in order that a basis is achieved on which inevitably they will build a heroic existence. Any one who lives a heroic and productive existence may not always find it easy, but the compensation for this is to feel satisfaction and gratification helping others. A difficult lesson for children to learn is that a heroic existence generally means helping someone else who is less fortunate. Isn't that what you also are doing as parents? This may often require taking risks, and such risks can be uncomfortable or even tragic. But this is what true "heroism" is all about. Children need heroes for their own example. The story of the Good Samaritan is a hero story (New Testament, Luke 10:25 - 37).

CONCLUSION

I haven't given a list of specific and detailed rules or suggestions for each of the child needs to be used at each particular age. For this size book that would be prohibitive. But I have given more of a "philosophy" for parents of small children. Developing your own point of view of yourself and your goals for your children will enable you to make the right decisions for your own peculiar circumstances. Your background and your own individual personality will stand you in good stead. With this philosophy of child rearing you will develop your own confidence and this is better than looking up a rule in a book for what you should do now in a particular situation.

When you have done your best, you will feel satisfaction and will be guilt free, no matter what. And the rewards are great. Your children will "rise up and call you blessed." (Proverb 31:28).

POST SCRIPT: LIVING HEROICALLY

An excellent example of the integrated personality of a youth took place in the 1965 Wimbledon Tennis Finals, as was reported by Leonard Griffith*. After a player's second service, the linesman called out, "Fault!" Certain that his ball had been fairly within the line, the player protested to the umpire who upheld the linesman's decision. His opponent, however, was also certain that the serve had been a fair one so, when the ball came over the net again, he stood aside and did not return it, thereby conceding a point. This generous gesture might have cost him the game but it was the kind of gesture that enhances the sport of tennis." (*"This is Living," p. 120)

What percent of young people would have made such a sacrifice based on a principle of "right" and "wrong?" It is saying the obvious to say here was a young man with "integrated character." Being right was more important than winning one game of tennis because he did not stand up for truth. He had obviously been trained in the way he should go. He was "living abundantly."

QUESTIONS FOR MEDITATION AND/OR DISCUSSION

1) Pause, put down the book and reflect back on what you have read. What one point comes to your mind first? Why?

2) Are there many subjects that have come up in your mind that you feel you need more information on? Identify those subjects. Go back and read again the material on that subject.

3) When you remember your own childhood, what were the gaps in your own parental relationships?

4) Can you understand why your parents may have been weak on this or other subjects?

5) Now pick out the areas of your life where your parents had their strengths. How did you benefit?

6) Has your spouse ever complained that you don't communicate clearly? If so, is it justified? Why?

7) If you have a small child, have you caught on to what I mean by the child's "adventures?" If not, how can you make more experiences into "adventures?"

THE MEANING OF LIFE

I'm not sure who the author is of this quotation, but it is certainly apropos here.

"Life is not a journey to the grave with the intention of arriving safely in a pretty and well preserved body, but rather to skid in broadside, thoroughly used up, totally worn out, and loudly proclaiming: '**WOW – What a Ride!**'"

APPENDIX A

THE BIBLE AND CORPORAL PUNISHMENT

BIBLICAL REFERENCES AND BACKGROUND

I emphasize that the word "discipline" means to "teach." In early Biblical times the concept of "beat" and "teach" became merged in this way:

In the Old Testament the word *lamadh* literally means "to beat" but very early came to mean TEACH. It may have meant "to beat with a rod," "to chastise," and may have originally referred to the striking and goading of beasts by which they were curbed and trained. By a noble evolution the term came to describe the process of disciplining and training men in war, religion, and life (Isa 2:3; Hos 10:11; Mic 4:2). As teaching is both a condition and an accompaniment of disciplining, the word often means simply "to teach," "to inform" (2 Chron 17:7; Ps 71:17; Prov 5:13). The glory of teaching was its harmony with the will of God, its source in God's authority, and its purpose to secure spiritual obedience (Deut 4:5,14; 31:12-13). [Cf. ISBE]

THE O.T. ON SPANKING

What is the Biblical position on spanking? It depends on one's view of the authority and place of the Old Testament in an overall view of life, as to whether certain Biblical statements will influence a parent to spank or not. For example, certain passages from the Old Testament are glibly quoted by those who believe in corporal punishment (2 Sam. 7:14; Proverbs 13:24; 23:13f; 29:15). These passages have nothing to do with us today *and should not be used to justify "spanking"* for the following reasons:

First, consider the **cultural context**

Note that the social-cultural setting of pre-Christian times was severe.

The general context of these verses is for a period of time in which the nation of Israel had to have men toughened for battle by mid-adolescence. Years ago many a father was advised in our country to put his son in the Army in order to "make a man out of him." This simply meant that the boy was undisciplined, did not respect authority, and perhaps was uncontrolled, or was too weak to make it as an adult in the work-a-day world. The strict disciplinary methods of the military training or conditioning would teach him to be on time, to carry out orders, and to be tough enough that he could take the discomforts, and even the pains inherent in military life. Even today Special Forces of the military, Navy Seals, Marines and other special units go through periods of severe endurance training in order to "be prepared."

In Israel during the period of the Kingdom (1000 B.C. on) they constantly fought for their survival. This meant having a pool of men who could be conscripted into the army on a moments notice. Therefore, fathers had to make men of their sons during childhood so that they would be well-disciplined as adults, either for the rigors of military life or for the harsh conditions of daily survival in a severe environment. Their lives were short and it was necessary to be able to "take it like a man" for the heads of households as well as for the soldiers. It was a question of survival.

Historian, Arthur Hermon, commenting on Scotland's formation of a "citizen's militia" in the mid-eighteenth century said, *When liberty is threatened, can anyone expect young men raised in a cushy commercial environment to risk their lives on the battlefield against tough and hardened warriors?...they need something that taught them self-sacrifice, discipline, and loyalty.*

This same author, in another context, refers to small nations struggling for survival under the conditions of a harsh environment or a harsh, pressing enemy, and said they must be guided by the authority of those whom they trust—"the elders of the tribe" or *a warrior nobility. The laws are strict and the punishments harsh.*

The culture of both Israel and her neighbors had been, and continued to be, patriarchal, authoritarian, nomadic, and agrarian. As such, the nature of their lives as civilians was harsh. Their physical environment was mountainous, arid, desert. Their customs and standards had to be rather rigid. The civilization of that time was much more primitive than ours. Jewish literature indicates that children were not worth an adult male's attention. Women, children, and slaves were inferior and did not merit an adult citizen spending time with them away from his responsibilities of work or governing. Roman literature before Christ reflects the same view.

The laws of Near Eastern culture in the Second and First Millennia B.C. prescribed severe physical punishment for infractions as compared with our (Christianized) standards. This was true of Israel, and it was worse with their neighbors (Assyrians, Syrians, Babylonians, Moabites, and others). Even though the laws of Israel's neighbors required severe penalties, there is some doubt by scholars as to what extent the judges actually required punishment to the letter of the law. That is, the letter of the law might require stoning, decapitation, physical mutilation (such as castration, cutting off the nose or ears or hand, branding and the like), or being thrown into the river for judgment.

It is thought by some scholars that these penalties were cited as threats to scare people into obedience and were not carried out with every infraction. (Again, this more civilized view may be influenced by a view in retrospect from Christianity). Such an outlook filtered down to the patriarch in the home. Physical severity was a way of thinking by the entire culture, not just the Jews of the Old Testament.

In Roman times babies were exposed to infanticide. They were associated with animals, women, slaves, and tyrants, those who symbolized behavior contrary to the adult, male citizen. The Qumron community considered children as full members of the community only when they were twenty years old. Some of those legalities found their way into the laws of Mohammed, and in some Moslem countries they still prevail.

In Palestine in New Testament times much of this flavor of the Patriarchal system still prevailed. A careful study of the society in which the apostles circulated betrays this. The social strata considered the treatment of children on a par with women, outcasts, servants, Samaritans, tax collectors, and Gentiles.

A careful study of Luke indicates that the apostles, like others in their social context, viewed children as lower class and not worth the Master's time. They rebuked those presenting children to Jesus for a blessing. (Luke 18:15f; Mark 10:13f; Matthew 19:13f). Jesus rebuked the apostles and insisted that children not be hindered. Then Jesus used these circumstances to teach another lesson on accepting those from the lower strata of society to be among His followers. A condition to accepting Him as the Messiah and receiving the Kingdom was made dependent upon their accepting little children.

Second, consider the **Old Testament text**

The word "rod" was often used as a figure for control and not necessarily always to be considered literal in its application. There are basically two Hebrew words used in the Old Testament which are usually translated "rod" 79 times. There is a range of meanings for these words. For example, one is used for *branch, tribe, rod for correction, scepter for ruling, lance for throwing, or stick for walking.* Another word is used as *branch, a stick for punishing, a stick for writing, fighting, ruling, or walking.* Both are used in a literal as well as figurative sense. "Rod" is used in most of the examples in a figurative sense as a symbol of authority and frequently used of God's anger. The point is, that out of 79 times it is used, 4 are in a context of discipline of a child.

Under these circumstances there is a great deal of doubt as to what instrument was used, how it was used, or if it was used at all, other than a kind of threat, in the above quoted passages (2 Samuel and Proverbs).

Even so, those passages, whatever they may mean as examples or commands, **never applied to us in the Christian age.** The commands practical for that period of time on corporal punishment, 1000 years before Christ, do not necessarily apply to our lives today any more than the proverbs on "remove not the ancient land marks" (22:28; 23:10) or cheating by using false weights on the balances for doing commerce (20:10, 23; 11:1 etc.). The book of Proverbs generally presupposes a desert culture with small towns or villages and a way of life different from our own. They understood references to a "hedge of thorns," to "thorns crackling under a pot," to "working a yoke of oxen," to "taking up the arrow and the spear," whereas we do not. The book further reveals a different view of the position of women than we see today.

But even those aforementioned proverbs (on discipling a child) are modified by other verses. For example, Proverbs 17:9 states that a rebuke to a smart person is more effective than 100 stripes to a fool. "A wise son listens to his father's instruction" (13:1). "Whoso loveth correction loveth knowledge" (12:1), etc. Other examples: Proverbs 22:6, "Train up a child in the way he should go, and when he is old he will not depart from it." (This instruction is good for every generation.) Proverbs 23:15 - 24 encourages parents to take pride in their children and children to live to make their parents proud. Proverbs 15:32 generally applies to our time in stating one that can tolerate discipline loves his soul. "A wise son makes his father glad" (10:1). These and other references in the Old Testament (e.g. Deut. 6:4-9) imply a close family unit. And there is much more in the book of Proverbs that would be good guidance for us today.

In spite of the above references in the Old Testament to using the rod, the nation of Israel passed laws against spanking in January, 2000, joining nine countries in Europe who outlaw corporal punishment.

Third, consider the **Christian teaching on the home**

1) Jesus' teaching changed society's attitude toward children

Mark 9:33-37. In teaching humility to the apostles Jesus took a child and said, *Whoever receives one such child in my name receives me; and whoever receives me, receives not me but him who sent me.* (RSV)

Mark 10:13. *And they were bringing children to him that he might touch them. And the disciples rebuked them,*

14 But when Jesus saw it, he was indignant, and said to them, "Let the children come to me, do not hinder them; for to such belongs the kingdom of God. Truly I say to you, whoever does not receive the kingdom of God like (receiving) a child shall not enter it." And he took them in his arms and blessed them, laying his hands upon them. (Compare also, Luke 18:6.)

Jesus' attitude toward children (like his attitude toward all of the oppressed) met with resistance from his apostles. The apostles, like the rest of society, had a hard time readjusting to the fact that Jesus came to change society's attitude toward the outcasts. (Luke 9: 22-62; 10:1-11;18:1-17, etc.)

These passages exemplify an attitude toward children, which is vital for every parent or guardian, and that is tender love, compassion, and concern for the well-being of the child. For one who "receives" and treats a little child compassionately is seen as doing this toward Christ.

In the Sermon on the Mount, Jesus exemplifies "Fatherhood" by several statements.

Matt 6:25-27.

26 Look at the birds of the air, that they do not sow, neither do they reap, nor gather into barns, and yet your heavenly Father feeds them. Are you not worth much more than they?

28 And why are you anxious about clothing? Observe how the lilies of the field

grow; they do not toil nor do they spin, 29 yet I say to you that even Solomon in all his glory did not clothe himself like one of these. 30 But if God so arrays the grass of the field, which is alive today and tomorrow is thrown into the furnace, will He not much more do so for you, O men of little faith? -

Matthew 6:26, 28-30 .

31 Do not be anxious then, saying, 'What shall we eat?' or 'What shall we drink?' or 'With what shall we clothe ourselves?' 32 For all these things the Gentiles eagerly seek; for your heavenly Father knows that you need all these things. 33 But seek first His kingdom and His righteousness; and all these things shall be added to you. 34 Therefore, do not be anxious for tomorrow; for tomorrow will care for itself. Each day has enough trouble of its own. - Matt 6:31-7:1.

9 Or what man is there among you, when his son shall ask him for a loaf, will give him a stone? 10 Or if he shall ask for a fish, he will not give him a snake, will he? 11 If you then, being evil, know how to give good gifts to your children, how much more shall your Father who is in heaven give what is good to those who ask Him! (Matt 7:9-12) (NAS)

One of the most severe warnings of Christianity is given to those who mistreat a defenseless child (Matthew 18:1-6). V.6: *But whoso shall cause one of these little ones that believe on me to stumble, it is profitable for him that a great millstone should be hanged about his neck, and (that) he should be sunk in the depth of the sea.* (ASV)

In fact, the child's attitude is exalted as an example of what a Christian's attitude should be.

The above verses speak for themselves in demonstrating a totally different attitude in the father-child relationship than one finds in Proverbs 13:24; 23:13, etc. God is an example of a patient, understanding, loving father. Obviously, this is the lesson for us today.

2) Other New Testament references

There are other passages in the New Testament on the treatment of children and their relationship to parents and to God: Ephesians 6:4; Colossians 3:20,21. These passages indicate a relationship wherein the children are obedient, and the parents teach in a loving, accepting atmosphere, and include a caution against provoking a child to wrath (Ephesians 6:4).

Colossians 3 and 4 is a section on interpersonal relationship at a variety of levels including husbands, wives, masters, servants, children, and parents.

Children (3:20; Ephesians 6:1-3) are encouraged to obey their parents in the Lord. And fathers again are commanded not to provoke their children to the point they will become discouraged (Colossians 3:21,22). There are many other passages in the New Testament of a more general nature pertaining to love, acceptance, mutual respect, patience, etc. All of these traits start, or should start, in the home. And the home is where life and a way of living commences by guidance from the previous generation as it is passed on to their children.

Hebrews 12:11 summarizes most of the principles I have cited above:

No discipline seems pleasant at the time, but painful. Later on, however, it produces a harvest of righteousness and peace for those who have been trained by it. (NIV)

SUMMARY

Thus, if you're looking to the Old Testament for justification, or a command, for spanking, forget it. The Bible nowhere commands you to spank your child.

The New Testament indicates an altogether different atmosphere than is apparently indicated in the passages in Proverbs. Just because a particular standard of behavior of a father toward his son was practiced in Israel in 1000 or 800 B.C., it does not indicate that it is either proper or advisable in Christianized countries today. Israel at that time was not as highly developed as they are now. They lived in the midst of ethnic neighbors that were barbarian with some of their practices. A view of Arabs that we see on television daily gives us some indication of the types of people who were Israel's neighbors. And this is the 21st Century.

It is known from studies in our day that parents who are overly punitive produce rebellious children. The positive side of discipline encourages parents to nurture the child while admonishing and/or disciplining the child. This is an excellent summary of sound parental guidance.

If the Bible is to be used as a guide for discipline, the Christian standard of the New Testament is an excellent source of authority. The teaching of the New Testament regarding child treatment gives us generalized principles but does not specify or give examples of such details as whether or not to spank. The guidelines and peculiar circumstances on this issue are cited in Chapter 4. "To spank or not to spank?" It all depends. .

THE PLACE OF CORPORAL PUNISHMENT

There are some children who, because of their nature, probably benefit from spanking. Since character is not inherited, but is achieved, parents must consider what it takes to achieve that in their own children. It is unfortunate that a proverbial saying like, "Spare the rod and spoil the child," has become such an integral part of our modern culture. It is most certainly applied too widely and is not justified. Parents must face the fact that the "rod" has little to do ultimately with the resultant behavior of the child.

Suppose a particular set of parents, who have not spent enough time with their child(ren) to create a bond of love resulting in willing, obedient behavior, become exasperated at the children's lack of obedience. In anger and desperation those parents take to spanking the child. Suppose in *fear* the child produces "good behavior" outwardly, but inwardly resents or, even worse, hates the parents. What has been accomplished by way of character building? In adulthood those children are likely to have emotional problems to some degree or another. This is usually the case with children who grow up hating their parents.

Outward, ethical behavior can be produced out of fear of the consequences, but this is not behavior of character. It is *controlled* behavior by fear.

"Now," you may say, "you have cited an extreme case where perhaps the parents administered too much or too severe corporal punishment, which resulted in the child's hatred of the parents." Yes, you're getting the point. The key to the above case is the word, "love."

For the rebellious or obstinate child, it may be that the parent must resort to occasional corporal punishment. Where there has been a bond of love since birth, the parent may successfully use some corporal punishment. The child is fully aware of the love of the parent and that the parent is spanking him/her out of love. The child understands that proper behavior is in its own best interest. This creates a different context for corporal punishment. Character is still being built, but the foundation is *love*. This is where that saying, "This hurts me worse than it does you," is true, but only in a situation like this. **Physical "punishment" should never be applied to a child, except by someone who loves the child and whom the child loves.** In fact, some rare parents may even stimulate greater love between parent and child by corporal punishment. It depends on how the total situation is handled.

A swat on the rear of a three year old may be necessary to startle him back to reality from a temper tantrum. But there is the reassurance of love somewhere in the context. For the older child, if a spanking is necessary (under extreme circumstances), again an explanation and reassurance of why the parent must take this action in order to have respect and obedience (by the child) is a part of the discipline. This takes extra time, but it is worth it.

Now come back to the context of Jesus' teaching of adult-child relationships. What is in the child's best interest in the long run? It is the salvation of that child as a result of loving adult guidance. In some cases this includes spanking; in most cases, hopefully,without spanking.

THE DANGER

It is known by specialists in human behavior that brutal treatment can breed brutal behavior. It has been demonstrated over and over again that harsh and brutal treatment to small children simply encourages brutal treatment by them to others. Violent behavior is most often the result of a central nervous system dysfunction caused by extreme corporal punishment in childhood.

CONCLUSION

As you make a decision on the methods of guidance you use for your children, consider these issues in summary. If a child (boy) hates his parents -- no matter how they have tried to control him --he will not develop character whatever methods they use. On the other hand, if his parents have fostered a loving relationship, it is unlikely they will have to rely on corporal punishment. However, if the nature of the child is such that parents feel constrained to use more than verbal constraints (some form of "corporal punishment"), then if they do it in love, they will most likely be successful in channeling the child's behavior into proper obedience. And the child will respect and "honor" the parents who continue to show love, even in the disciplinary action.

PASSIVE TYPE PERSONALITIES

The issue of whether to use corporal punishment is not so simple as a parent's making a decision whether to or not. The unknown and variable factors that must be taken into account involves the personalities of both the parents and the children. Parents who have weak or passive personalities and who do not exercise control over their children during the first 3 years, may have rowdy, raucous, disobedient, and uncontrollable children by the time they are 3, 4, or 5 years old. The children may be problems at kindergarten or school, or in other places where there are other children (visitors, Sunday School, etc.). For the children to respect authority (which they must do when in a group setting), drastic measures will have to be taken in order to modify their misbehavior quickly. Professional help will usually be required under such circumstances.

Parents who have weak or passive personalities and who do not use corporal discipline, on the other hand, may have children who are well behaved, obedient, and who respect adult authority. The personalities of the children, the environment, and other factors may contribute to a harmonious household.

STRONGER, LEADERSHIP TYPE PERSONALITIES

Parents who are more natural type leaders are more apt to have control over the children from the beginning, hopefully, without the use of corporal discipline. The use of a strong voice and a firm facial expression is all that is needed to maintain respect of the children.

Another scenario is that parents with this type of personality may become too dominant over the children and the children may feel over-controlled. This may promote rebelliousness and callous behavior, which is not desirable.

Hopefully, by the time the child is 3 years old, the parents, whatever kind of personality they have, will have shown sufficient love, attention, guidance, and control that no corrective measures are necessary to maintain a harmonious and respectful household as the child prepares to become more social.

POST SCRIPT

In addition to the case of little Ja'eisha Scott cited previously in in Chapter 6, here are other examples of what the child care agencies and schools are having to put up with. In 2004 a kindergartner in St. Louis was handcuffed for disruptive behavior. In April (2005) a 7-year-old in Bethlehem, W. Va. was cuffed for similar acts.

Columnist, Leonard Pitts, Jr., reported that parents in Kansas harassed a teacher for flunking kids who cheated on a project. A mother in Chicago dismissed her daughter's part in a mob assault as something that just "got out of hand." A mother in New Orleans blamed the school —a school with security guards and metal detectors—after her son and another boy shot each other.

In these and many similar cases, the parents blamed the school and refused to accept responsibility for a disruptive child. It is most likely that in the younger years all of these children were neglected in some form from being disciplined in a proper manner. When the children are not taught in the younger years, they can get out of hand and produce this kind of disruptive and antagonistic behavior.

Now note the kind of home I think these children should have had. I don't know the author of this, because it is taken from "spam" but it is sound philosophy.

MEAN MOMS

Some day when my children are old enough to understand the logic that motivates a parent, I will tell them, as my Mom told me:

I loved you enough to ask where you were going, with whom, and what time you would be home.

I loved you enough to be silent, and let you discover that your new best friend was a creep.

I loved you enough to make you go pay for the bubble gum you had taken and tell the clerk, "I stole this yesterday and want to pay for it."

I loved you enough to stand over you for two hours while you cleaned your room, a job that should have taken 15 minutes.

I loved you enough to let you see anger, disappointment, and tears in my eyes. Children must learn that their parents aren't perfect.

I loved you enough to let you assume the responsibility for your actions, even when the penalties were so harsh they almost broke my heart.

But most of all, I loved you enough...to say 'NO' when I knew you would hate me for it.

Those were the most difficult battles of all. I'm glad I won them, because in the end you won, too.

And someday when your children are old enough to understand the logic that motivates parents, you will tell them.

APPENDIX B
THE MAKING OF AN "A" STUDENT

THE MAKING OF AN "A" STUDENT

Psychologists have been rather pushed into spending much of their research time on the "abnormal" or deviants from our system. It has been only recently that the "concept of the normal" has had its fair share of investigation. One such example is the Harvard Pre-School Project of Dr. Burton White. He was determined to find out what goes into optimal child rearing. He studied 400 children who were 3, 4, and 5 years old. He set out to determine what enabled children to cope in a superior fashion with any situation, day in and day out. Take note, please: He found that most qualities which distinguish an outstanding 6-year-old began to appear around 1 year old. By 3 years old these characteristics were strongly evident.

White observed that in the period of 10 to 36 months old, children develop many attributes, which will either bless them or curse them throughout life. So he went to the homes where children were considered superior because they were making primarily "A's" in school. He investigated the homes where children, who were otherwise normal, were developing poorly in school. He found there were markedly different environments for the children, and that the age period of 10 to 18 months was crucial.

EIGHT AND NINE MONTHS OLD CHILDREN

White's study began with the 8 and 9 months old children. In the homes of the most successful pupils, he found that the mothers went out of their way to bolster the child's language capacity. They talked a lot to the child under all conditions where the two were together, while dressing, bathing, playing, eating, etc. These were face-to-face conversations.

When the child began to crawl, the mothers of the better pupils allowed a tolerable level of infant-induced clutter. The occasional mishaps were, for the most part, ignored. The children were encouraged to explore by having a variety of toys and materials. Incidentally, it doesn't take expensive store-bought toys to fill this bill. Empty boxes, pillows, wood blocks, old rags, or old pots and pans all provide the avenue of exploration and fun that the small child utilizes. Mothers of the "A" children rarely confined them to the play-pen for more than a brief period of time. With this "freedom" there were some slight safety risks, but these mothers shied away from over-protecting the child. In the home they kept dangerous and valuable objects put away and out of reach.

By contrast the mothers of the "C" children left the children more to the TV. Some of the mothers in this class hovered over their children to the extreme when they weren't confined. Everything interesting or appealing to the child was considered "off limits," which, of course, brought on a chorus of "No's" and "Don't's" from the parents. Children from these homes had more in between meal snacks, which seemed an artificial way of expressing love. It was perhaps the only way the parents knew to express love. Such snacks were used to pacify the child instead of accepting the challenge to interest or stimulate the child.

FIFTEEN TO TWENTY-ONE MONTHS OLD

After one year the child reveals a growing sense of individuality and a blossoming personality. This age child tends naturally toward "negativism" with the testing of boundaries.

Parents of "A" children had skills to help children overcome "No's" and develop a basically positive attitude. These parents did not impose their own will needlessly on the children. They sought to distract the attention from something potentially harmful to another subject or activity for the child. The mothers of these children demonstrated things to them or made suggestions in keeping with their interests. Children were allowed and encouraged to instigate playtime activities. These mothers prohibited some activities and did so consistently and firmly.

A common mistake of the ineffective mothers was the failure to set limits for their children. Well-meaning parents who do this seem "afraid to thwart" their children. Instead, they deprive them. Children at this age are quick to test their parents, but are also quick to accept firm decisions. If firm decisions are not forthcoming, the child is uncertain and insecure regarding its behavior. Some of the ineffective mothers were inconsistent in this area.

Failure to help the child overcome negativism and uncooperativeness at this age leads to quarrelsome and frustrating situations for both. Furthermore, the situation hampers social growth and skills.

TWO YEARS OLD AND BEYOND

During the second year the child seems to be learning a great deal about his mother and her reactions. Although he has become more separated from his mother, there is still a strong attachment to her. And because of this the mother's reactions largely shape the infant's view of himself and his basic orientation toward people in general.

- Successful mothers were highly interested in their children and their activities.

- These mothers were happy to have their children play near them -- despite interruptions.

- They stopped to help their children.

- They expressed approval in their accomplishments.

- If the child's request was truly inconvenient they would tell the child to wait. She, too, had rights.

The following is an example of a report by one of the observers in this study. He first observes the successful mother and then reports on her child.

"She is easily available to him and is often heard answering his questions or explaining something to him."

Regarding her son he wrote: "The most striking features of his behavior are his social maturity, his remarkable poise for a two-year-old, and his outstanding use of expressive language, including clear articulation and easy handling of compound and complex sentences."

Another example of a report pertaining to an "A" girl-- As above, he reports on the mother's activity and attitude and then gives an observation on the daughter:

"The home is firmly run by a talented mother who expects her children to act with maturity." The atmosphere was warm and loving but not particularly child centered. About the daughter he said, "She is remarkably calm and dignified for a two-year-old, but she has the capacity for enthusiastic responsiveness as well.

"She is best described as a child who really desires to perform well and tries to model her behavior on adult models, despite the fact that she appears not to be unduly pampered or catered to by her mother."

White's study confirmed what others have found (see Chapter 5) that children tend to live up to expectations, whether they are good and wholesome or bad and unrealistic. The following is a case worker's report from the home of a "C" male student. (Please note that in a previous chapter I alluded to the fact that parents need to be sensitive to the number of children they can have and provide for. There are some parents who have enough love for two children and some enough for three or more. There are also some parents who get in over their heads and have more children than they can deal with properly and successfully.):

"He is the youngest of 6 children in a family that seems generally overwhelmed by the daily problems of living... He is rarely encouraged to do anything and is often severely threatened for something he has done. Most of his mother's interactions with him are disciplinary in nature, although there is little consistency or follow-through in her approach. Even friendly exchanges are worded aggressively as, 'Hey, bad boy, get over here' (said with a smile)."

"His approach to the testing situation is marked by general unresponsiveness and lack of enthusiasm. He ignores all directions addressed to him. He has a remarkable ability to 'tune out' requests. He uses one word requests when he wants something. . . His mother has a lot to do, has many children, and is not a very contented woman. She tended to be harsh with this child when he was nearby, and she tried to keep him away from her as much as possible. . . Watching this child was a fairly depressing experience."

CONCLUDING OBSERVATIONS ABOUT THESE MOTHERS

Mothers should take a self-inventory and determine that the rearing of the children in their care can be an immensely rewarding experience with some personal adjustments. Naturally, some will say, "You just don't know what all I have to do. This is too much pressure on me." I am in sympathy with this. I have heard it many times from strung- out parents. However, this is a